十年

TEN YEARS

zhuang hui's photography

庄辉摄影作品

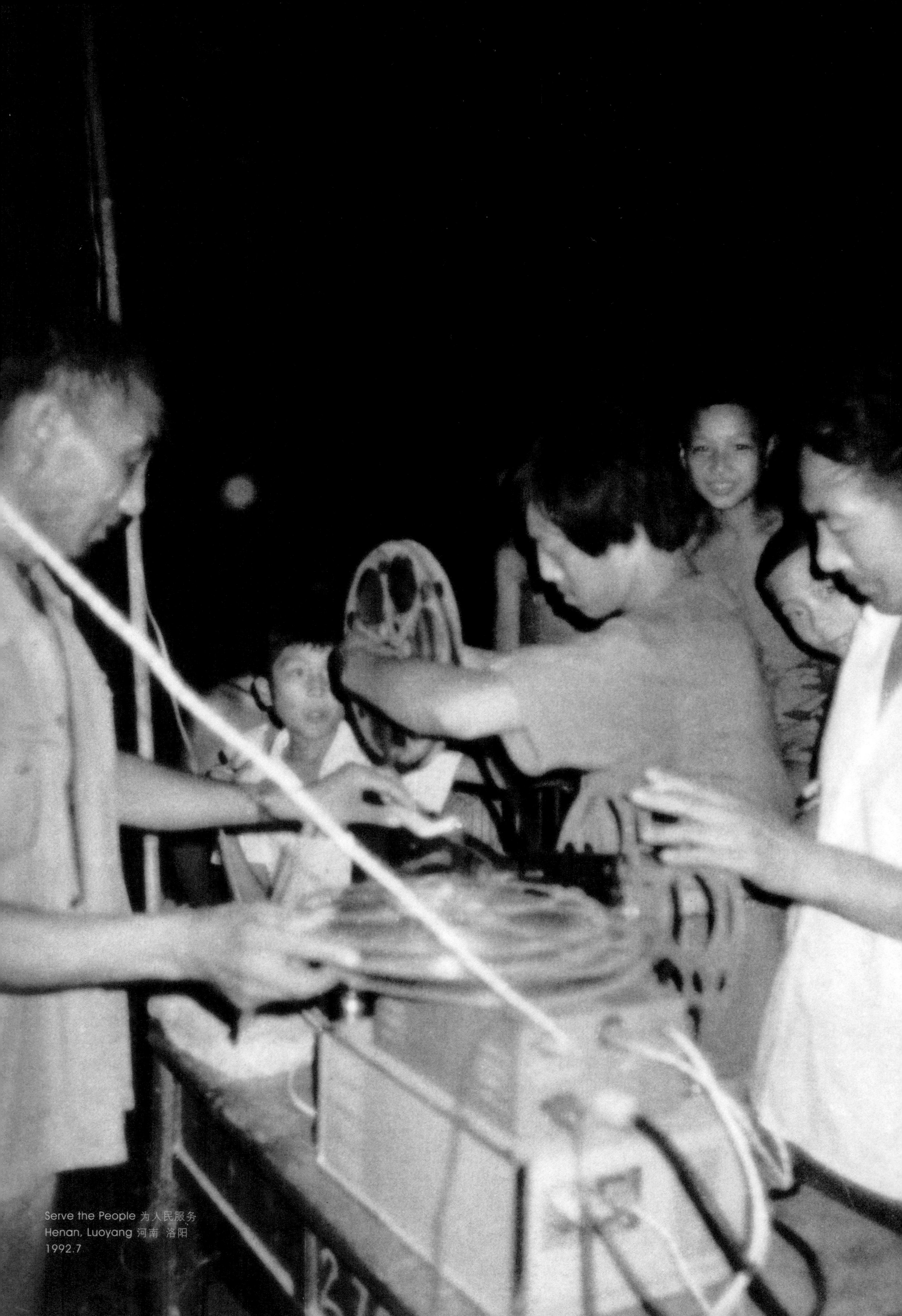
Serve the People 为人民服务
Henan, Luoyang 河南 洛阳
1992.7

Zhuang Hui: Embracing The Ordinary

Meg Maggio Director, Courtyard Gallery

Beijing-based artist Zhuang Hui is well known for his photography and performance-based work. However, his new 100 color photo series, "Ten Years," may be best understood by examining his latest sculpture installation. Last spring in Beijing, Zhuang Hui exhibited a life-size installation piece entitled "Chashan County, June 25."[1] Zhuang's surprise choice of a non-photo based medium, coupled with its provocative subject matter, created a healthy buzz here among exhibition goers.

The site-specific work, installed in the corner of a cavernous, newly opened experimental artists' space, consisted of an enormous patch of rich vegetation miraculously replanted indoors as antidote to the interior's minimalist concrete warehouse-like design. However, upon closer examination - and only after visitors reached out to touch the plants - it quickly became evident that all "green garden" items were in fact artificial. Replete with grass, weeds, flowers, trees, and a myriad assortment of other plant life, visitors could enter the wholly man-made natural setting and stroll along its footpath. The better to admire its authentic look and feel, even down to the made-in-China blades of knee-high grass lining Zhuang's indoor nature preserve.

For Zhuang, the choice of artificial plants and flowers was an instinctual one, and wasn't meant to parody China's latest manufacturing prowess in recreating greenery from man-made products. Instead, the plants stood in homage to youthful decorations and the ubiquitous profusion of fake plastic flowers in Chinese households of bygone eras. Unlike today's more sophisticated urban dwellers, Zhuang's aesthetic doesn't shun plastic reminders of less affluent days. Au contraire: He has always embraced them.

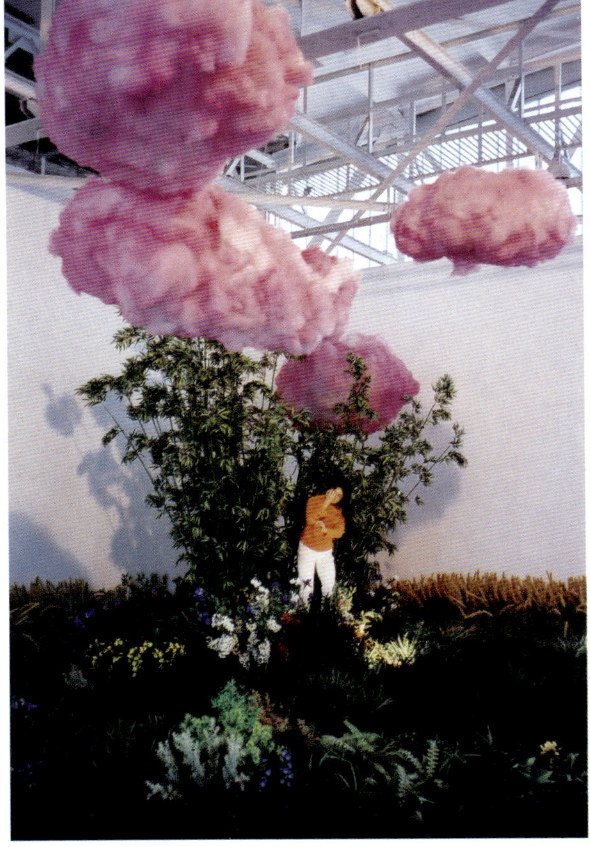

Chashan County, June 25
Sculpture Installation
2001-2002

The figure of a lone girl stood in the center of the idyllic garden installation. She was made of amazingly life-like plastic silicone materials. With one hand she clutched her eyes as blood ran through her fingers. The text accompanying the installation was inspired by an article Zhuang read in "Shenzhen Weekend," a popular tabloid newspaper, which reported the following: "Ms Wang Hanyun, a 20-year old itinerant factory worker in Chashan County, Dongguan City, Guangdong Province, was abducted not far from her factory gate and later found wandering alone in a vacant lot behind the factory. Local police reported that Ms Wang was spotted shuffling haplessly in the lot clutching her eyes, now only blood-filled sockets. The eyes of Ms Wang, believed to be the victim of a gang of human organ smugglers, were surgically removed with a swiftness and precision which could only be attributed to persons with medical expertise and training."

Fluffy pink cotton clouds hovered over Zhuang's vacant lot installation in eerie contrast to the image of the girl without eyes below.

The installation paid stunning tribute to all that China's emerging tabloid press now promises to deliver: slightly menacing, yet tantalizingly macabre tales of the everyday. The sensational new pictorials are currently enjoying robust sales as each tries to outdo the other with increasingly lurid tales of the everyday. Despite the graphic photos, grisly texts and on-the-scene reporters, can we believe them? Has life in the South really become this sordid and dangerous? Have things spun this out of control in China's factory-filled Southern towns, where poor girls are said to work for subsistence wages to support families back home? The spooky part was that while the story seemed factually beyond the pale, emotionally, Zhuang Hui's larger-than-life rendition left us with an uneasy and somewhat irrational feeling of, "Why not?" The rush for profit in China had long ago extended to traffic in human organs, and today all tales of crime and corruption in "New China" are widely perceived to contain at least some grains of truth.

Like any good tabloid reporter, Zhuang Hui first outlined a well-known scenario both reassuringly affable and believable to his viewers. However, once we, his willing audience, were drawn into his narrative and began warming up to the familiar, Zhuang then hit us hard with the terrible "news" from Dongguan, leaving us reeling in shock and disbelief at the possible truth of the installation against all odds and rationality.

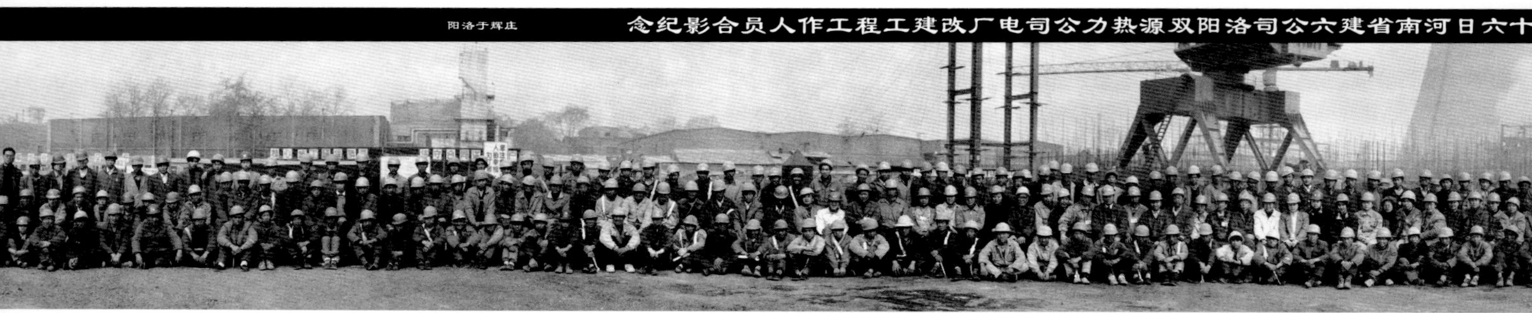

The Staff of Shuangyuan Energy Source Company, Luoyang City, Henan, March 26, 1997
Photograph
Luoyang, Henan
101 x 735 cm
1997

The veracity of the account - which Zhuang takes as fact despite this writer's skepticism - is no longer important. What matters is the way the installation works as sheer sensation. We, here in relatively law-abiding northern China, will never forget the girl without eyes wandering alone in the vacant lot, her plight graphically mirroring the mood of desperate poverty said to permeate China's factory towns.

The tone of Zhuang's latest photo work "Ten Years" is much the same: comprising raw, unvarnished windows on to seemingly ordinary events. Defying the inherent sensationalism of color photography, the subjects of his latest color images are deliberately innocuous. His presentation is almost excessively bland and straightforward. However, like the girl found wandering in the vacant lot, we may be missing something at first glance.

"Ten Years" is in fact the product of Zhuang's meticulous editing of a huge body of prints compiled over the last decade of shooting throughout China and abroad. The result is the 100 carefully chosen color images which are the subject of this exhibition. There are no titles provided, nor references to places or things. Instead, the works hang together in simple presentation sans narrative or explanatory text. "The images," Zhuang explains, "are what they are." One can't help drawing comparisons to the photo work of Wolfgang Tillmans had he grown up under a Chinese communist/socialist regime.

In "Ten Years," Zhuang's artistic focus remains steadfastly on the everyday, even the touristic, and especially on the banal and commonplace in the people and places he encounters. Subjects are chosen seemingly at random and typically from the same socio-economic roots as the girl from Chashan County: village shopkeepers, barbers, field workers, farm girls, waitresses, and old girlfriends. Settings are sometimes cloyingly scenic; mountain streams, bridges, dams, steel plants, farmers at harvest, factory grounds, smiling minority women, waitresses, shopkeepers, subway rides, hometown shots of friends and neighbors - namely, the interior and exterior lives of ordinary people, places, and utilitarian things, which together comprise the very quotidian - and dare I say, proletarian - heart of Zhuang Hui's oeuvre.

The visual strength of the photos is of course found in their banality. Nostalgia, for Zhuang, is firmly rooted in the unembellished now. The artist's photographic memory of youthful moments creates a visual link to history, and a contemporary historical framework is born. The result is deliberately old-fashioned and vernacular, and harkens back to the happy imagery of populist magazines like "The People's Pictorial" and "China Reconstructs" as well as local neigh-borhood photo salon shoots.

The difference is that Zhuang's images are now emblazoned with the terrific bounty of today's more technically advanced color film. The brightness of the prints, coupled with their seemingly casual observations, are what give them their contemporary feel. Inspiration is clearly

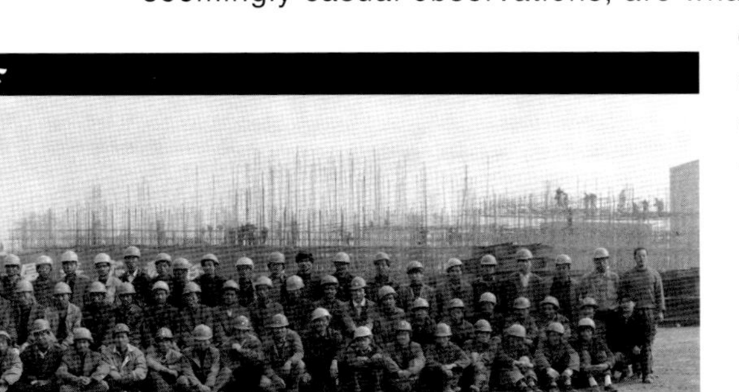

drawn from plastic framed, brilliantly colored shots of waterfalls and palm tree-lined beaches which adorn the walls of newly constructed highway restaurants stretching from one end of New China to the other. Today, China is rapidly making up for the austere color-blindness of its revolutionary years with a wild fiesta of billboards, neon signs, outdoor lighting, and other eclectic Las Vegas-inspired decorating techniques. Zhuang Hui's photos borrow something from this contemporary palette.

It is reassuring - and even revelatory - to know that in the many years Zhuang worked shooting his panoramic black and white group portraits of workers at various danweis (state work units) across China,[2] he was also shooting the local environs in vibrant hues of color. These color "souvenir" images are at the heart of "Ten Years."

Like Zhuang's installation piece of last year and much of his earlier work, "Ten Years" takes a deceptively simple and forthright approach, affecting a posture of artistic nonchalance. However, such nonchalance is never directed at his subjects. His enormous affection for and identification with his subjects is finally, and perhaps inadvertently, what gives the photos their artistic strength. Zhuang's anti-art style may well be the best approach to finding one's own identity within the act of observing and photographing others.

[1] *"Chashan County, June 25," sculpture installation, exhibited in the group exhibition, "Run, Jump, Crawl, Walk" curated by Zhang Li, April 28-May 22, 2002, at East Modern Art Centre, Beijing.*

[2] *See for example, "February 26, 1997. Henan Province. Provincial Construction Company No. 6. Renovation Of The Electrical Power Plant Shanyuan in Luoyang. Souvenir Picture of the Workforce. Zhuang Hui in Henan."*

庄 辉 ： 在 平 淡 与 惊 奇 之 间

马芝安　四合苑画廊　执行总监

庄辉生活、工作在北京，他的作品以摄影为主。但是，要想更好地了解庄辉最新的100幅摄影作品《十年》，我们不妨从他的最新的一件装置作品《6 月 25 日 · 茶山镇》^注开始。他出乎人们意料地放弃了以照片作为媒介，利用现成品做成与实物等大的装置，为我们展现了一个非常生动的空间。

　　　　这是一件依据现场环境制作的作品。作者选用塑料的花、草、竹子等植物，结合雕塑做成的场景，为观众还原了一个真实事件发生的瞬间。

6 月 25 日 · 茶山镇

2000 年 6 月 25 日中午，在广东省东莞市茶山镇打工的 20 岁女工汪汉运去给家人打电话。刚走出厂门不远，就遇到了两个骑摩托车的年轻人，汪认识其中一位姓陈的四川人，陈看到她便走上前来说："想跟你谈点事..."遭到拒绝后，陈恼羞成怒，突然上前用手紧紧地卡住了汪的喉咙，之后她失去了知觉。当她清醒过来，怎么也睁不开眼睛，只感觉眼窝处又痛又麻。她以为天黑了，本能的用手去掰眼皮，摸到的却是缕缕血丝。经过医生抢救，她才知道自己的两只眼球，被贩卖人体器官的组织挖走了。

　　　　那些用蓬松棉制成的粉红色的云朵，虚假地漂浮在作品的上空，和其它物品一样，都试图严肃的以假乱真，美丽得让人心痛。这件作品所产生的效果是令人震惊的，它使我们联想起媒体为了营销而一贯采取的卑鄙做假手段。人们不禁会问："难道这件事情真的发生了吗？"是的。如果你真正深入现在中国社会的底层，疑问便会烟消云散。

　　　　这个看似美丽却平淡的现场，给观众制造了一个突如其来的事件，丝毫没有顾及我们的接受能力。我想人们将不会忘记那个被剜去眼睛的可怜的打工妹的形象。庄辉最近的摄影作品《十年》也大致相仿，向我们打开了一扇粗糙而简朴的窗户。他借用彩色图像本身具备的日常性，力求表达上的单纯、直白，轻易将观众引向图像本身。

　　　　这100幅照片，是作者在十年中用傻瓜相机拍摄的几百卷胶片中挑选出来的，被简单地悬挂在展厅，没有任何多余的解释。庄辉在这里表述了他一贯的观点——图片既是图片的力量。我们不禁会产生联想，假如艺术家 Wolfgang Tillmans 生活在今日社会主义的中国，他们的作品是否会在同一条道路上。

　　　　在《十年》这组作品中，庄辉一直将自己的镜头聚焦在日常的生活当中，你现在看到的照片才是庄辉自己眼睛看到的世界；自己动手按下的快门；135 负片的原始效果；跑了大半个中国记录的真实。有车祸发生的现场，有农田里健康的妇女，有他的外国朋友和钟意的宾馆服务员的合影，瀑布等各种各样普通百姓生活的场景。这些看似平凡的画面，我敢说就是中国无产阶级跳动的心脏。图像的力度就在于它的平凡。对于庄辉来说，怀旧的情绪一直深深根植在他

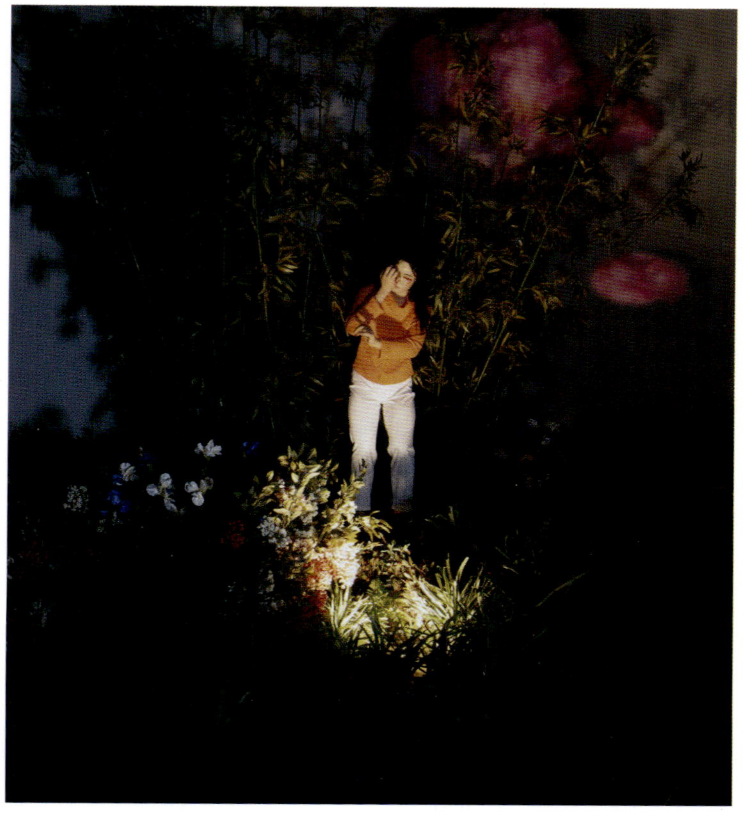

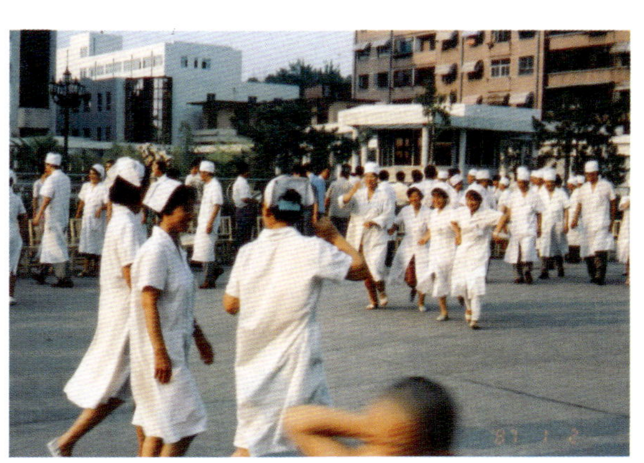

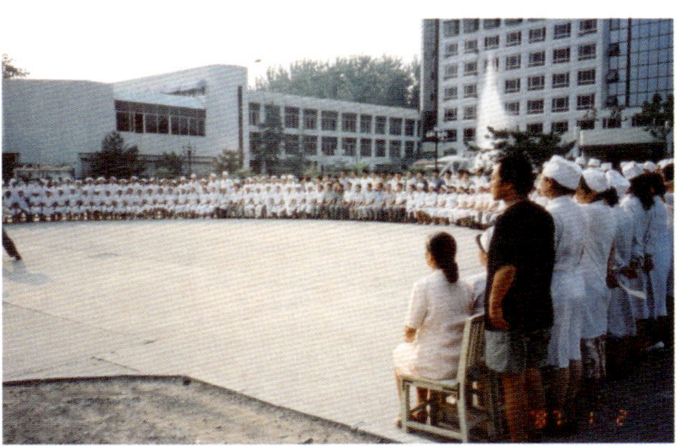

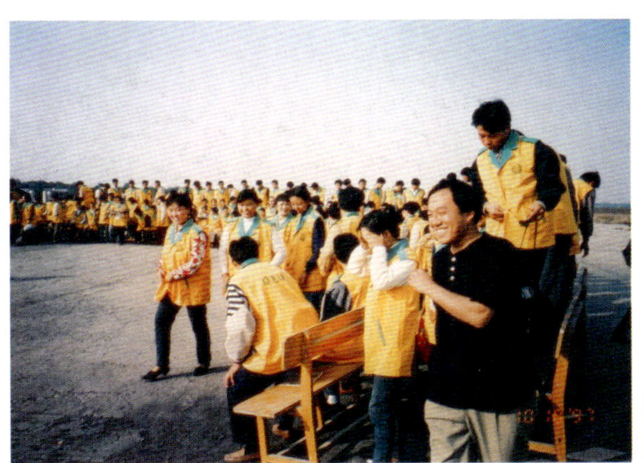

的内心深处。艺术家采用摄影方式将这些瞬间的记忆连接成为一个可视的历史，使我们回想起流行于六、七十年代的《人民画报》上那些劳动者们快乐的面孔（虽然那时的彩色照片很单调）。如今，中国到处是纵横交错的公路，小饭馆里大都装饰着色彩亮丽的图片。中国正在弥补它毫无色彩和生机的革命年代的简陋情怀，取而代之的是以疯狂多样的卡拉OK、霓虹灯和稀奇古怪的城市景象。庄辉的照片就是从这块当代社会的调色板中借用了一些常规而异样的因素。

令人高兴的是，庄辉在过去许多年中，拍摄黑白"合影"照片的同时，也为我们留下了这些色彩艳丽的"纪念照"。

与庄辉以往的工作一样，《十年》的摄影作品以其朴素、直白的表达方式，为自身寻找了一条艺术工作的方向。

注作品《6月25日·茶山镇》参加2002年4月在北京远洋艺术中心由张离策划的"跑、跳、爬、走"展览。

Zhuang Hui and His "Ten Years"

Zhang Li   Independent Curator and Critic

Zhuang Hui was born in 1963. When he was young he received an orthodox socialist education. Children grew up in those years under the heady influence of idealism and romantic heroism. His father was a photographer in a small town. As the offspring of an ordinary worker, Zhuang Hui's memories of the Cultural Revolution are full of passion and vitality. This left Zhuang Hui with many memories of the bright sunshine of his youth of that time. However, those happy memories were cut short by the death of his parents, which resulted in his all too early experience of hardship and a vagrant life. The boy, not yet adult, once slipped onto a passing train and did not return home for several months. He even made several suicide attempts. The hardships he endured at an age when protection and care were most needed molded Zhuang Hui's character of resoluteness and rebellion. At the age of 15 he graduated from middle school, entered a factory and embarked on one of the most arduous and tiring of professions. He was once injured in a work-related accident. These accumulated experiences in his early years shaped his attitude toward life, and would greatly influence the artistic road he would follow in the ensuing years.

This rough road of life has remained with Zhuang Hui. These early experiences have lowered his requirements for daily living and material success. He enjoyed painting early on as a child. After joining the factory, he painted and read while working there. After enduring an inferno-like work environment where he was required to undertake heavy and dangerous tasks, he would later use his book-learned ideals and those feelings gained during this confined and solitary period of his life in his artwork. Art became the primary need of his life. In the midst of great spiritual and material difficulty, Zhuang Hui still retained a strong desire to express brightness. In his early oil paintings he sought to depict a bright and healthy mood in the landscapes he painted. However, this was very different from the heavy tone popular among the academic artists in fine art circles of Henan province. In despair, and as a result of the lack of cultural studies courses, Zhuang Hui lost interest in attending university. Nevertheless, the social environment had already begun to improve from that of the Cultural Revolution. In the process of societal transformation, more opportunities for individual pursuits were becoming available. Looking back at the development of contemporary art in China, people will find that the development of artists outside the art academy system has effectively brought vitality and diversity to the current composition and healthy development of the modern arts.

All contemporary artists who were active in the 1990s were influenced by the modern art movement in China in the 1980s or participated directly in it. The oppressive atmosphere after 1989 stimulated the sensitive nerves of the artists, and their works began to express more of their own personal moods and feelings. No longer learning and copying from Western fine arts as was the case in the 1980s, the contemporary art scene in China in the 1990s was well known for its independence of outlook. One very important reason for this was that artists were more deeply attuned to the attributes of man as individual and his place and personal existence within society. As an artist from the non-academic world, Zhuang Hui started his creative activities in the early 1990s. Combining his experience struggling at the lower rungs of the social ladder with his status as an artist, Zhuang Hui gradually reduced his artistic explorations into his own personal psychology and social reality and adopted a wider perspective which would enrich and deepen the valuable realist spirit and tradition in contemporary Chinese arts.

In July 1992, Zhuang Hui staged his performance piece *"Serve the People"* in the rural township of Foguang near Luoyang in Henan Province. The performance included Zhuang's distribution of towels at a local limekiln, using a brush to write the slogan of *"Serve the People"* on the 200 meter-long dam and showing films in the town square. In October that year, Zhuang Hui made a red, extra large-sized slogan *"Serve the People"* in the East Is Red Square in Luoyang. Between 1995 and 1996 he implemented a work called *"One and Thirty,"* which was a mosaic of two-person group photos showing himself and each of a total of thirty workers, farmers, children and artists. Beginning in 1996, Zhuang Hui began creating his large-scale group photo works. He used a panoramic 360-degree camera and each time organized as many as several hundreds of workers, farmers, doctors and nurses, soldiers, and students into group photo shoots. What was different about this photo from ordinary group photos was that the artist's own image appeared at the right side of each picture. In 1998, Zhuang Hui adopted a technique of non-stop surreptitious shooting with an automatic camera to produce his work *"Public Bathroom."* Between 2001 and 2002, based on an incident widely reported near Shenzhen in which a working girl was maimed, Zhuang Hui completed the installation work *"Chashan County, June 25."* This series of very influential works, all done in the short history of contemporary Chinese art, represent Zhuang Hui's body of work and the result of his non-stop artistic exploration. In particular, the group photo work has become one of the iconic works of the "new photography" phenomenon in Chinese contemporary art.

However, Zhuang Hui has never been satisfied with perfecting his artistic technique by relying solely on one medium or form. He has always attempted to explore and experiment with all kinds of different languages of artistic expression, making tremendous commitments in terms of time, energy and funds. For Zhuang, art is always the door to fresh vitality and the carrier of spiritual force.

As to the underlying connection among his works in the various periods of his artistic career, Zhuang Hui remarked:

From " Serve the People" in 1992 to "Group Photo," " Public Bathroom," and the most recent installation work, "Chashan County, June 25," there is an underlying connection. My works are concerned with the life and current status of ordinary people. I am not an intellectual. Firstly, I am a laborer at the bottom of the social structure, and share common feelings and tastes with all people. Today, this lowest, disadvantaged group has been deserted by society for their lack of sufficient aspiration. Their fate amidst rapid social change, their feelings, and their cultural needs are something not many people bother to care about. However, they constitute the cornerstone of our social hierarchy. From birth through primary school, high school and college, many people have never truly experienced the life of the populace at the bottom. In the past, the slogan of

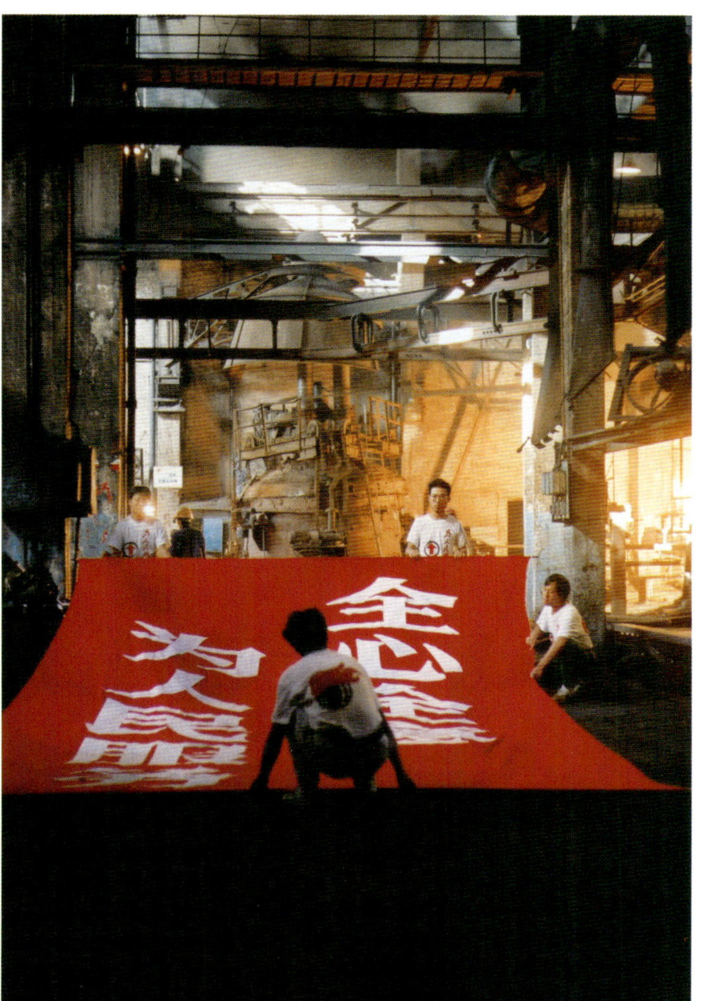

Serve the People
Automobile factory
Luoyang, Henan
1992.10

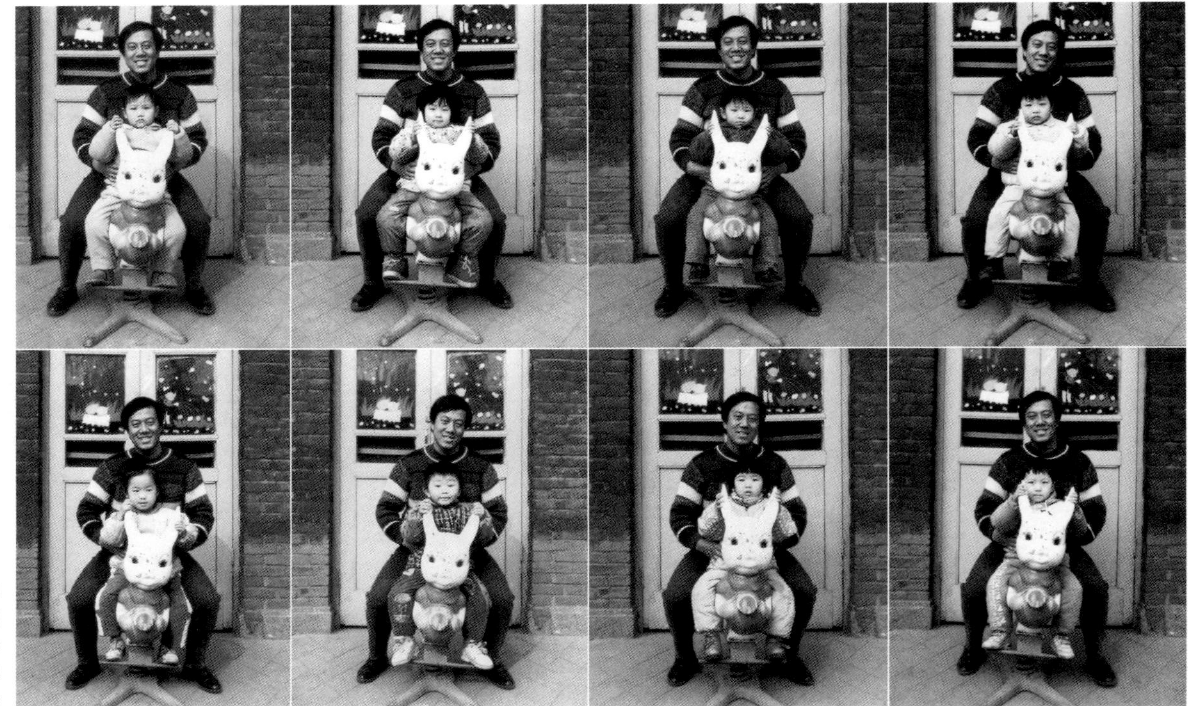

One and Thirty Children
(detail)
Photograph
50 x 60 cm
1995-1996

"Serve the People" also represented a way for people to raise themselves higher and then look down. I hope I can show, through artistic forms and expression of feeling, that I share a great deal with them. I need this. I like to walk while traveling. Whenever I go to a new place, I choose a road to walk for a while, jostle onto long-distance buses just as the local people do, and live on earth beds for two RMB yuan a night. This connection to street life and feelings is like a transfusion of fresh blood for me. Losing this would be like a baby being prematurely weaned from its mother's breast; it would be very difficult for me to grow as an artist without this nourishment. Sometimes, I will also encounter setbacks and come up with certain ideas to create strange works. These are times of personal crisis and obstacles. Then, I stop and allow myself to make less works for a year or so and give myself more time to reflect on the underlying themes and principles in my work.

While he was producing works which would become well known in the Chinese contemporary art scene, Zhuang Hui was also taking and sorting through photos during the ten-year period approximately from 1992 to 2002 and has recently turned these into his latest photo work project "Ten Years." This exercise represents the specificity and perfection of his attitude to artwork. Looking through the photos as though they were selected from one's own personal photo album, we can identify landscapes and scenic spots imbued with colors of the 1960s and 1970s, of ordinary people from different social strata. There are also very casual daily snapshots of artists, personal friends, and even prostitutes. These images have been stripped of the "artistry" we have come to expect from typical photo-based art works. Instead, on the basis of straightforward observation, these images were selected and set aside with the author's signature. Sometimes impressionistic feelings arise in the process of reprinting, which highlight the essence of what interests the artist. Throughout the hardships of his career, Zhuang Hui's life principles, easygoing character, and over-riding confidence have infused his work with an implicit simplicity and naturalness, displaying a mature mastery with no vestiges of affectation. He aims for "increasing intuitive, increasingly personal" works in his artistic production. What is important in understanding these works is the atmosphere of the images. Like Zhuang Hui's other "formal" creations, they express a certain density of life. On this, Zhuang Hui himself said:

In fact, entirely objective records do not exist. The act of photographing is the same.
Meaning is always formed amidst one's mood and comprehension. This is exactly what we finally
gain from photos. Photography touches upon and intervenes in our own existence. Every viewing
changes us. Photography as an artistic tool is thus very attractive to artists. Zhuang Hui repro-
duces his feelings toward life, and the photos he selects are simple, colorful and popular, with a
sense of after-rain freshness. Speaking on this point, he explained:

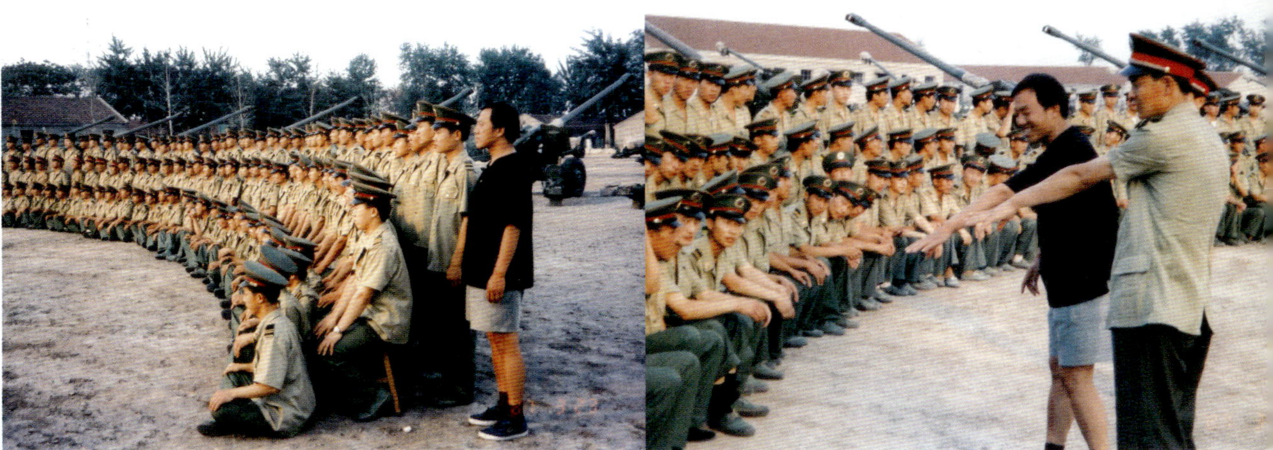

Group Portrait Site
Handan, Hebei
1997

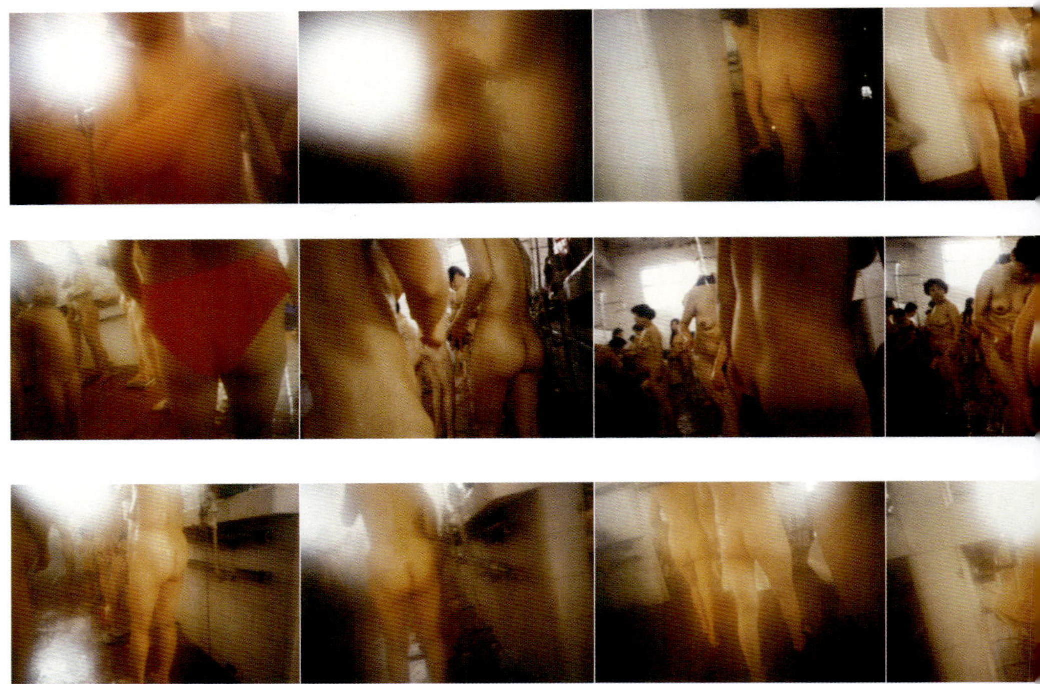

Zhuang Hui has made the subject matter of his work reflect the vivid interests
and needs of his life. Art activities concurrently lend support and meaning to life. His approach is
the result of the accumulation of time and continuous sampling, choice, and crystallization. The
emergence of this latest body of work "Ten Years" is proof of the valuable spirit of a mature artist
in exploring and questioning the ultimate challenges of artistic creation. The rare qualities of an
artist are dissatisfaction with one's current success, continuous initiation of fresh starts, perpetual
return to the original motives of artistic creation, and the pursuit of the true necessities of one's life

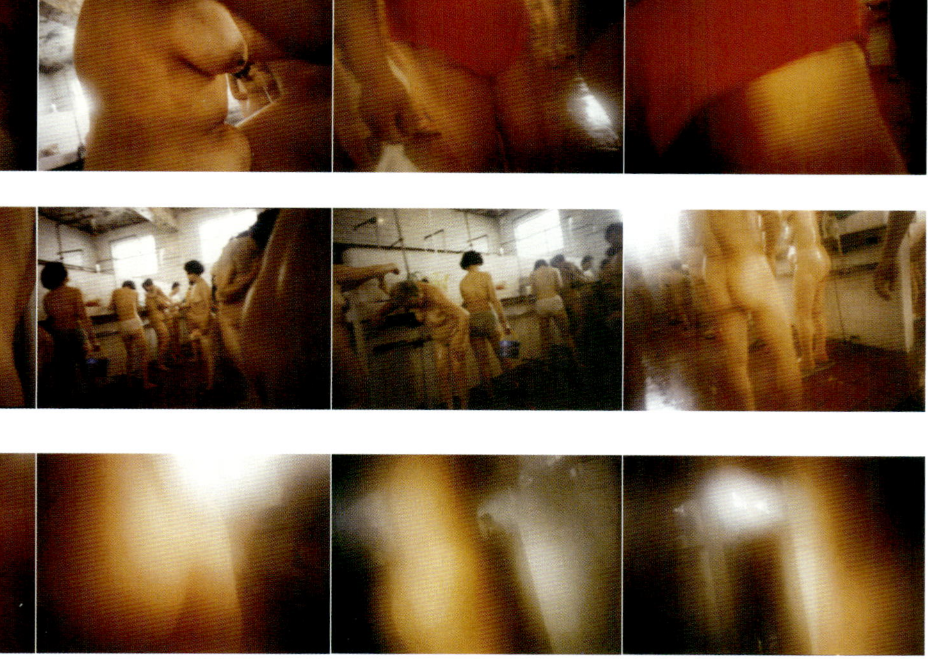

and artistic creation. Artists who can clearly hold on to the initial emotional impact of an art object or artistic creation will not be held down by the fleeting clouds on the surface of society, nor will they be fettered by art world movements and fashionable trends.

Zhuang Hui's attitude toward and practice of artistic creation presents a serious challenge to our traditional understanding of contemporary art. Within certain well-established parameters, we have already gone too far in our pursuit of art for art's sake, and oftentimes have become too "artistic" for the sake of an artwork's completion. When this happens, we have lost the independence and free will of the subject. Art is above all an individual practice and a reflection of an artistic tendency in human nature, something we should feel fortunate about. However, if the need for art exceeds the other needs of mankind, then artistic creation will, by necessity, be no more than affectation and falsehood. The essential sense of life lies in man's independent humanity. Zhuang Hui's works can inspire us to understand the essence of life, refuse the deception and enslavement of elitist power, resist the allure of material things, and maintain our own integrity and health in a materialistic and susceptible environment.

If it is said that these photos are only meaningful to the author himself, then we may have misunderstood the context from which the works were created. Against a backdrop of modern art sliding down towards alienation, the exhibition of this body of Zhuang Hui's works should be seen as an ice-breaking move.

庄 辉 和 他 的 "十 年"

张离　独立策展人　批评家

庄辉出生于1963年，少年时代受到正统的社会主义教育，那时的孩子生长的环境伴随着理想主义和浪漫英雄主义的影响。他的父亲是一个小镇上的照相师傅。作为一个普通劳动者的后代，文化革命带来的是激情和活力，这对年幼的庄辉来说是充满阳光的一面。但由于父母的去世，使他过早地经历了困苦和流浪漂泊。少年早熟的他扒火车沿铁路线流浪，几个月不回家，甚至有几次试图自杀的经历。在需要保护和关爱的年龄经历苦难，形成了庄辉秉性刚强和富有反叛精神的性格。他在15岁中学毕业进工厂，开始从事工业生产中最苦最累的体力劳动，曾经在事故中受伤。早年的经历造就了他的人生态度，极大地影响了他后来的艺术道路。

生活道路的坎坷一直伴随着庄辉，使他对生活和物质上的要求越来越低。他从小喜爱绘画，到工厂工作后，一边工作一边画画、读书。在忍受地狱般的工作环境和繁重而危险的劳作后，他将自己作为有限生命个体而产生的理想和情感转换到艺术当中。艺术已经成为他的生命需要。在精神和物质上最艰难的时候，庄辉反而有强烈的表达光明的欲望。他在早期的油画风景中追求明快、健康的情绪，这与当时河南美术界学院派中流行的深重色调十分不同；加上对文化课程的荒疏，庄辉在失望中失去了对上大学的兴趣。然而当时的社会环境已经不同于文革时期，在社会转型的过程中，在一定程度上产生了允许个人发展的空间。回顾中国当代艺术的发展，人们会发现，学院体系之外的艺术家的成长，为当代艺术的多元构成和健康发展带来了活力。

活跃在九十年代的当代艺术家都受到80年代的中国现代美术运动的影响，或者身处其中。1989年之后产生的沉闷气氛刺激了艺术家们敏感的神经，他们将与个人自身密切相关的感受和情绪表达在作品中。不同于八十年代对西方艺术的模仿和借鉴，90年代的中国当代艺术以它独立的面貌而被世界所认识，这当中很重要的一点在于艺术家们更深入地认识了作为个体的人的属性，以及个体的生存状态与整个社会的连接。庄辉作为一个非学院出身的艺术家的创作活动出现在90年代初期。以他在底层的生存经历结合他作为艺术家的身份，庄辉的艺术尝试和探索逐渐向个体心理和社会现实切入，以更开放的角度使中国当代艺术中可贵的现实主义精神得到丰富和深化。

1992年7月，庄辉在河南洛阳附近的农村——佛光乡实施了作品"为人民服务"，内容是在石灰窑场分发毛巾；在200米长的水库大坝刷写"为人民服务"标语；在乡公所广场放电影；10月，庄辉在洛阳东方红广场地面制作了红色巨幅标语"为人民服务"。1995年至1996年，庄辉实施了作品"一个和三十个"，是他自己分别与三十个工人、农民、儿童、艺术家的双人合影。1996年开始，庄辉制作了规模很大的群众合影作品，他利用旋转式全景相机，每次组织多达几百人的工人、农民、医生护士、解放军战士、学生等按照传统方式进行集体合影。与普通合影照片不同的是，艺术家本人的形象出现在每幅画面的右端。1998年，庄辉采用自动相机连拍的方式制作了作品"公共浴室"。2001至2002年，庄辉根据发生在深圳的一个残害打工妹的社会事件制作了装置作品"6月25日茶山镇"。这一系列在中国当代艺术不很长的历史中很有分量的作品是庄辉在不同时期不懈地进行艺术探索的结果。特别是集体合影的作品，是中国当代艺术中"新摄影"现象的标志性的作品之一。但是庄辉从不满足于一种趋于完善的方法和形式，他一直在探索和尝试各种不同的表现语言，在时间、精力、经费上大量投入。艺术对他来说永远是新鲜活力的出口以及精神力量的载体。关于庄辉各个时期的作品的内在联系，他在访谈中说：

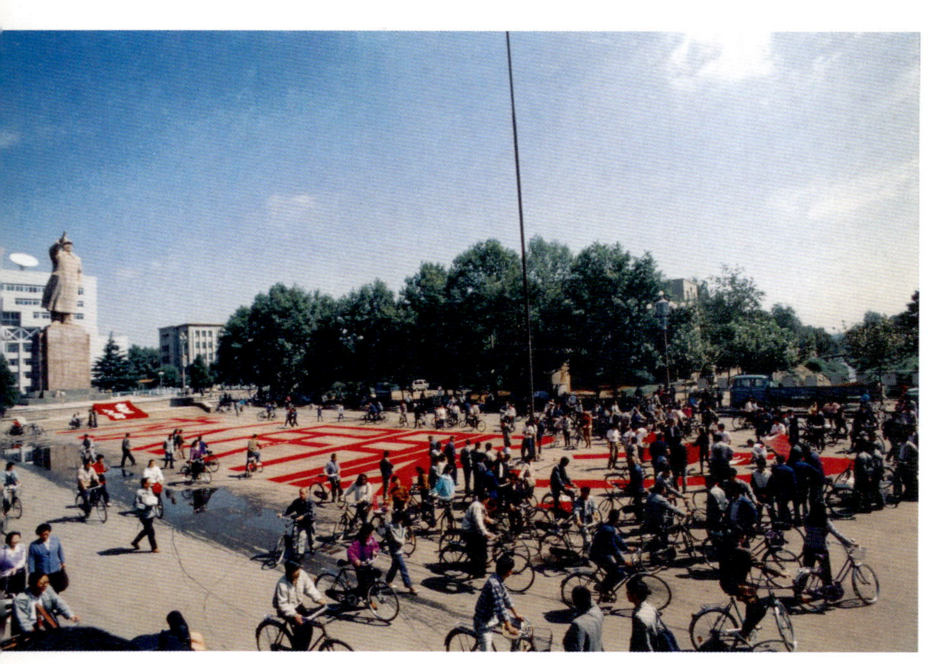

为人民服务
东方红广场
河南 洛阳
1992.10

从1992年的"为人民服务"到"合影"、"公共浴室"，以及不久前的作品"茶山镇"，它们都有着内在的联系。我的作品关注普通人的生活和现状。我不是一个知识分子，首先，

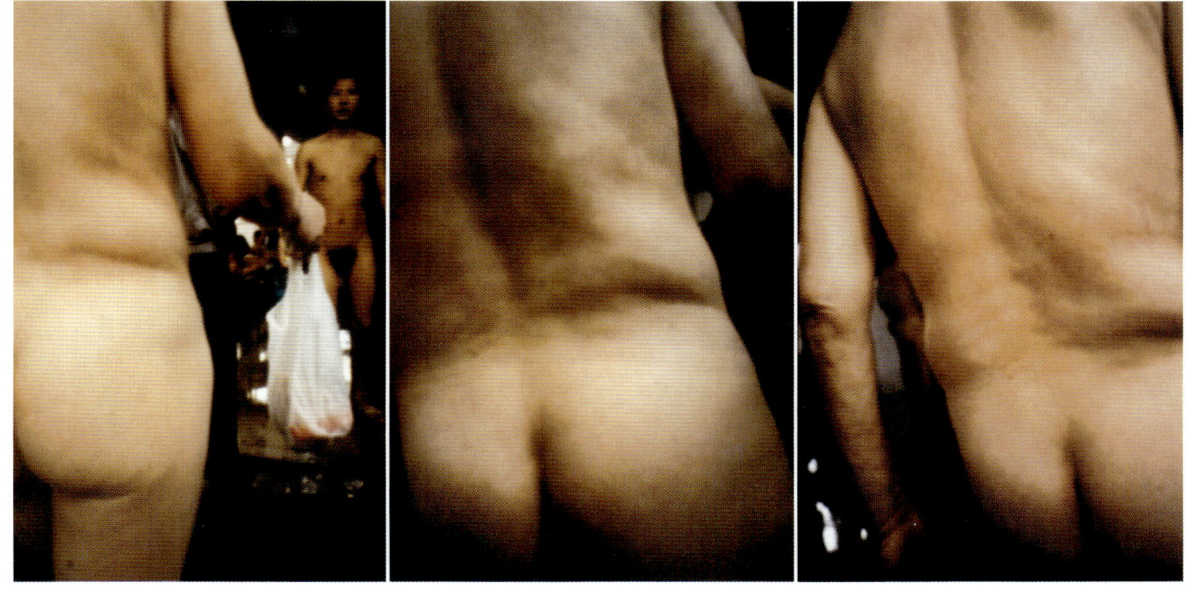

公共浴室 · 男（局部）
照片
100 × 150 cm
1998

我也是一个底层的劳动者，和大家一样在情感和审美上有着共同的需要。在今天，这个底层的、弱势的群体因为没有太多流行时髦的由头而被社会遗弃。他们在社会变革中的命运，他们的情感，他们的文化需求，没有太多的人去研究和关心。但他们真正是我们这个社会结构的基石。很多人从出生、小学、中学、大学一直没有真正亲身经历过底层百姓的生活。过去"为人民服务"的口号也是把自己抬高了往下看。我希望自己从艺术的形式和情感的表达上和他们是共通的，我需要这个。我旅行的时候喜欢走路，到一个地方以后选择一段路来走，和当地人一样挤长途汽车，到两块钱一晚的土炕上去住。这种生活和情感上的联系，就像我的供血机器一样，如果断了这个，就像断了奶，艺术很难再往前走。有时我也会出一些岔子，冒出一些想法和点子，作些奇奇怪怪的作品，那是抛锚的时间，所以我会让自己在一年中少做一些作品，多考虑一些问题。

   庄辉在做这些合乎一般的当代艺术概念的作品的同时，将1992至2002十年生活中的照片整理出来做成作品，这是对他从事艺术工作的态度的明确和完善。观看这些貌似纪念影集中的一张张照片，我们可以识别出带有六、七十年代色彩的风景和名胜古迹，各地不同身份的普通人；还有很随意性的生活快照，涉及艺术家，私人朋友，甚至风尘女子。这些影像脱去了作为摄影艺术作品一般意义上应该具有的"艺术性"，而是在客观纪录的基础上，在后期制作中还原作者对影像最初的，有时带有主观性的印象和感觉。构图上有的进行剪切，以突出作者感兴趣的主体。以庄辉的坎坷经历，他的人生历炼，以及从容和自信的性格和气度，很自然地将作品的形式感把握得质朴而洒脱，显得信手拈来而毫不造作。他将"越来越感性，越来越像自己"作为理想的状态。理解这些作品重要的是感受影像的气氛，它们同庄辉其他的"正式"创作一样，表达了一种生活中的重量感。庄辉自己说道：

当时拍摄和现在挑选都是凭感觉，没有什么"主题"。每次回老家和出去玩，我都带一个傻瓜相机，哪怕是借的。见到朋友，有的刚认识，说合个影吧。不是为了别的，就觉得是一个纪念。这成为我的习惯，对以后产生合影那样的作品有一些影响。这不是表达什么主题，包括我的装置作品，我都是看了这个故事，突然对它有一种切肤之痛，凭着这种感受来做我的工作。这十年的照片更是这样。比如在路边，转过一个山头，就看到一个地方，气势磅礴的，我会忽然发现这个地方很刺激我，就什么也没管，赶紧拿相机把它拍下来。我们最开始画画的时候，学习要强调事物的第一感觉，这些照片就是我在所有这些日常活动中的第一感受，比较感性的东西，没有题材的选择，只是在冲洗时将颜色和构图找回到最初的印象。

   实际上从来都没有完全客观的纪录，摄影也是这样，意义总是产生在情绪和感悟之中，这正是我们从照片中真正得到的东西，它触及和干涉了我们的自身存在，每一次的观看实际上都使我们发生了改变，摄影因此而被艺术家们所喜爱。庄辉将他生活中的情感状态复制出来，所选择的照片朴实、艳丽、通俗，有一种雨后的清新感。他在谈到这一点时说：

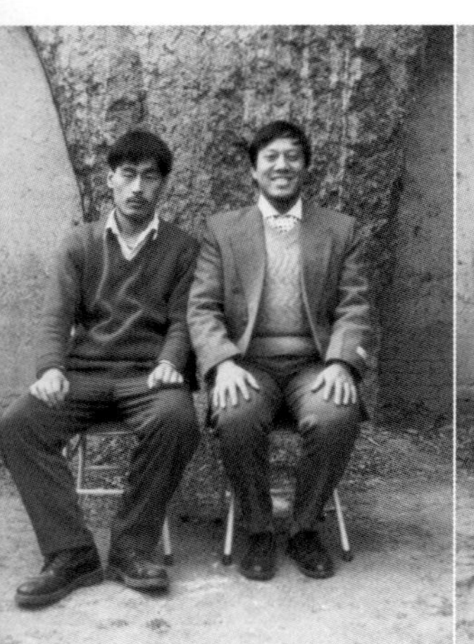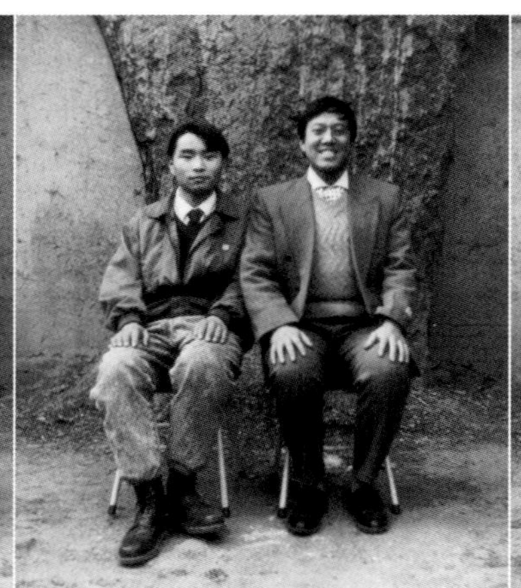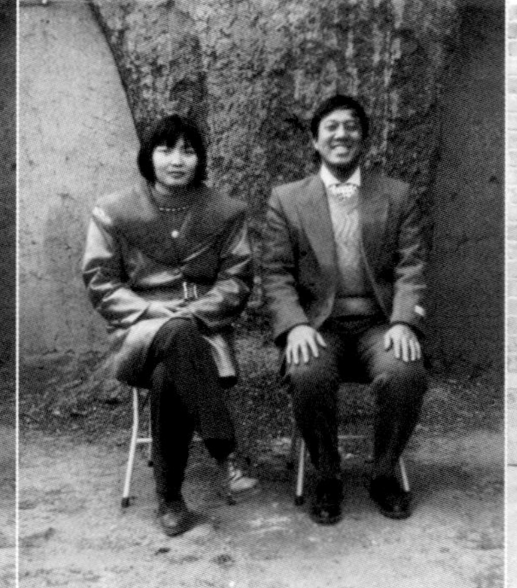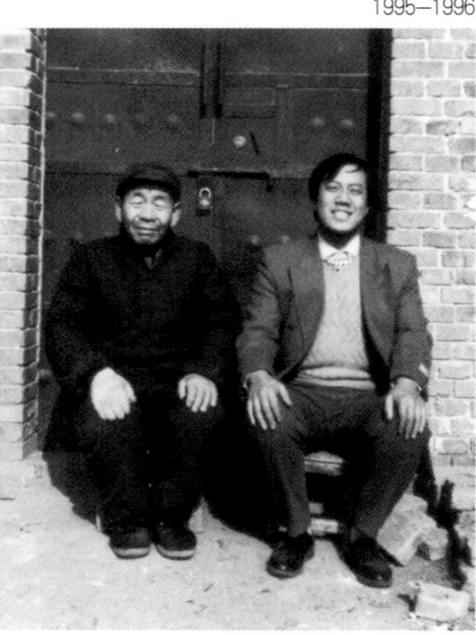

美丽这个词，在历次的艺术运动中被认为是保守落后和不识时务的东西，其实我们每个人对很直接的美的东西都有欲望，只是不敢承认罢了。现在中国当代艺术走得还是狭窄，不是很自信和开放。我把"十年"这些照片拿出来，同时想证明一点，就是美丽的东西还是美丽的。我每年夏季有一两个月时间去各地玩，很多东西让我感动，前后拍了几百个胶卷，其中一些是与朋友的合影，一些是个人生活，还有各地的风光和其他影像，这种情感的纪录对我来说是很重要的。那些阳光照耀下的山水，孩子脸上灿烂的笑容，都让我痴迷和留恋。我不避讳这些被称之为农民气十足的"粗俗"的情感，包括我在旅行的日子里，喜欢在火车上看小贩们兜售的低级杂志，到其它城市后看漂亮姑娘，逛洗脚中心等。有些画家借此形式反此意，被称之为"反讽"，我比较反感。如果有本事，自己可以编造一种情感，走另一条道路，没必要用自己的"有识"笑话百姓的"无知"。我要证明我自己的情感是这样，我需要这些，对活下来很重要。瀑布，美丽的风景，人，我都喜欢。

我对美丽的东西越来越感兴趣，可能从小受的苦难太多。在这"十年"作品中我很少挑选那些带有很强的社会意义的照片。实际上社会中的人随时都会有绝望的时候，我想自己绝望的情绪就让自己消化掉吧，不想带到这个社会里边。我也拍到过情绪很灰暗、很低落的东西，我不希望将它们拿出来，让别人再一次游历你的痛苦，我觉得这个世界上的人们活着已经很艰难了。还有我不希望别人在我作品前面去反思，最好是能给人一个直截了当的视觉刺激，我希望简单一点。

我不太敢以一个艺术家来自居，我更像一个艺术的劳动者，很多感动和震撼过我的艺术作品不是因为它们的构思和想法，而是因为上面凝结了人们的劳动，像云岗石窟、敦煌壁画、秦始皇兵马俑，给我神经上更大的刺激。这是劳动者对自然世界的认识和表达，是他们在精神和情感上的一种需要。我也希望自己的作品能够更多地显现出我的劳动，我的工作，而不仅仅是一些点子。我相信劳动能创造世界。

　　　　庄辉使作品的内容跟随生活中真切的兴趣和需要，艺术活动同时成为他生活的依托和意义。他的这一方式是经过时间的积累和不断的尝试、选择和凝炼的结果。这批作品的出现，显示了一个成熟的艺术家仍然对艺术的本质问题抱着探究和追问的可贵精神。不满足于现有的成功，不断地重新开始，不断地回到艺术的原始动机，寻找生活和艺术的真实需要，是一个艺术家难得的优秀品质。能够清醒地保持艺术的最初的感动力量的艺术家不会被社会表层上的过眼云烟所牵制，也不会被艺术潮流中的起伏波动和流行风尚所羁绊。

　　　　庄辉对艺术的态度和实践为我们对当代艺术的习惯理解提出了一个严肃的挑战。在一个特定的范围内，我们已经过分地为了艺术而艺术，为了作品而艺术，而丧失掉了作为主体的独立和自由的意志。艺术首先是个体的事情，人类的天性有艺术的趋向，是应该庆幸的事情，而如果艺术的需要超过人真实的需要，那就是做作和虚假。生活的质感在于独立的人性，庄辉的作品可以启示我们认识真实的生活，拒绝强权的愚弄和奴役，抵制利益的引诱，在闻风而动和众口铄金的环境中维护自身的完整和健全。

　　　　如果说这些照片只对作者个人有更多的意义，那么我们可能忽略了作品产生的语境。在当代艺术趋向异化的背景中，展出庄辉的这批作品，应该称作是一种破冰式的举动。

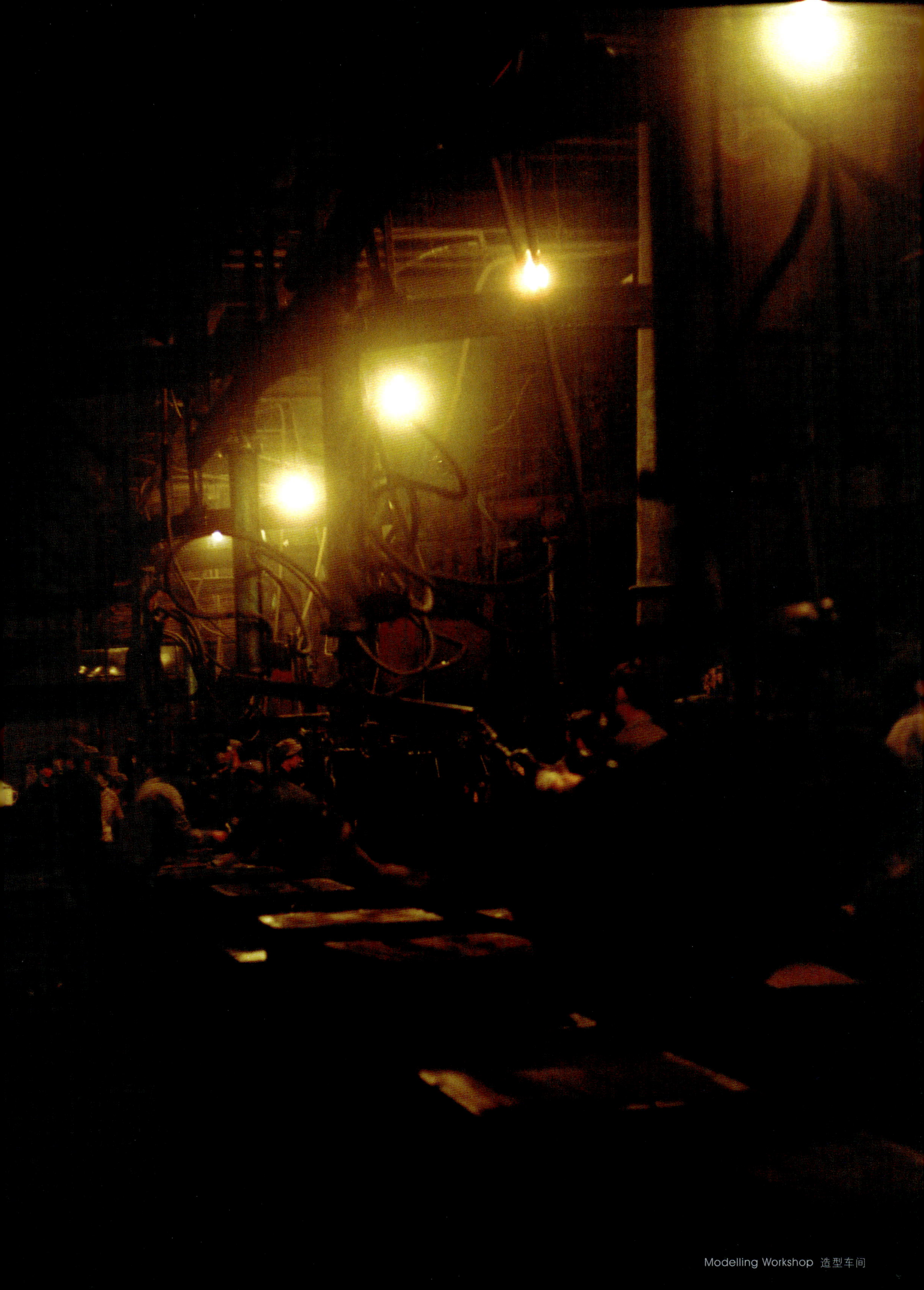

Modelling Workshop　造型车间

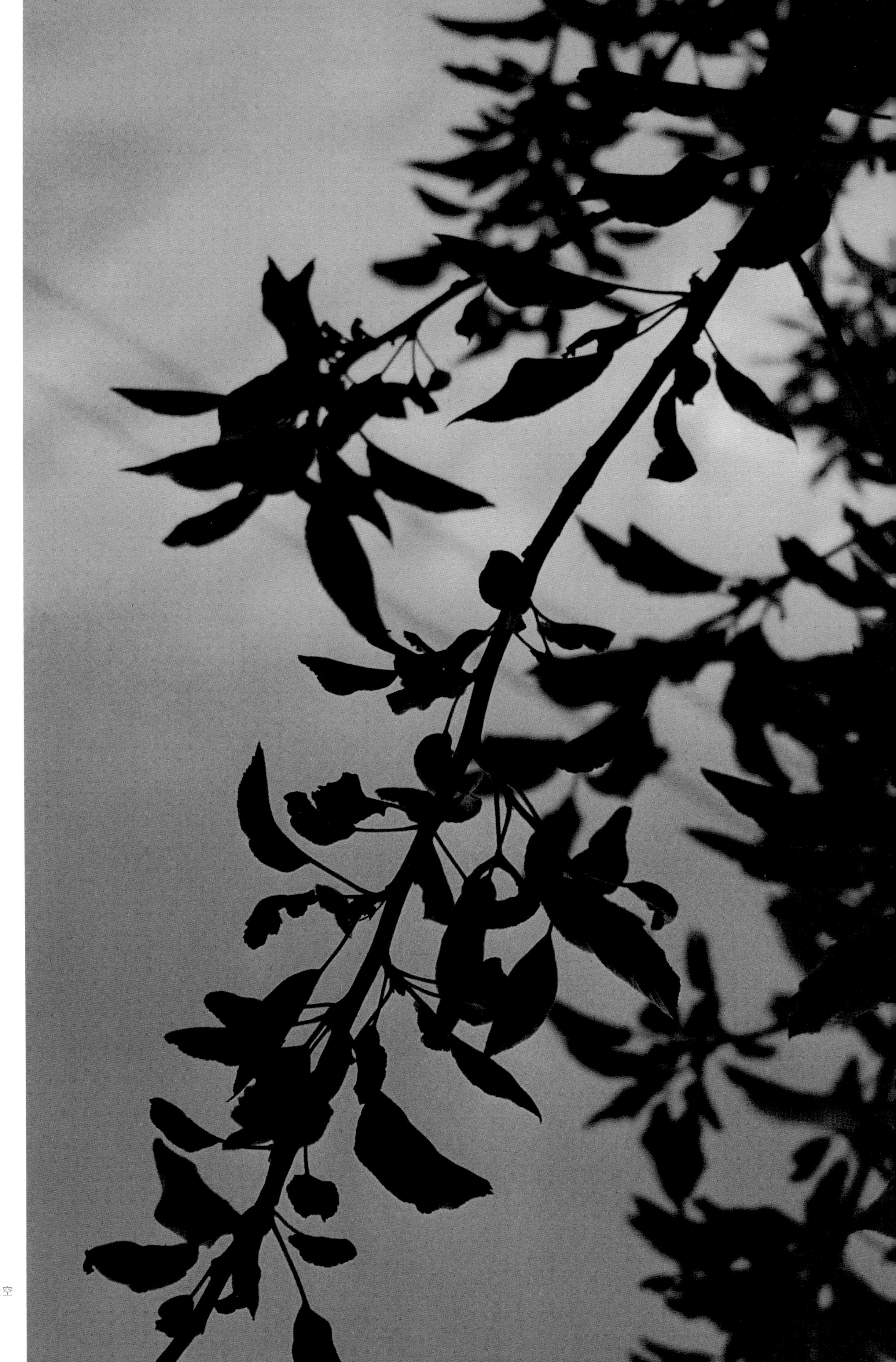

Sky 天空

At Yumen 在玉门

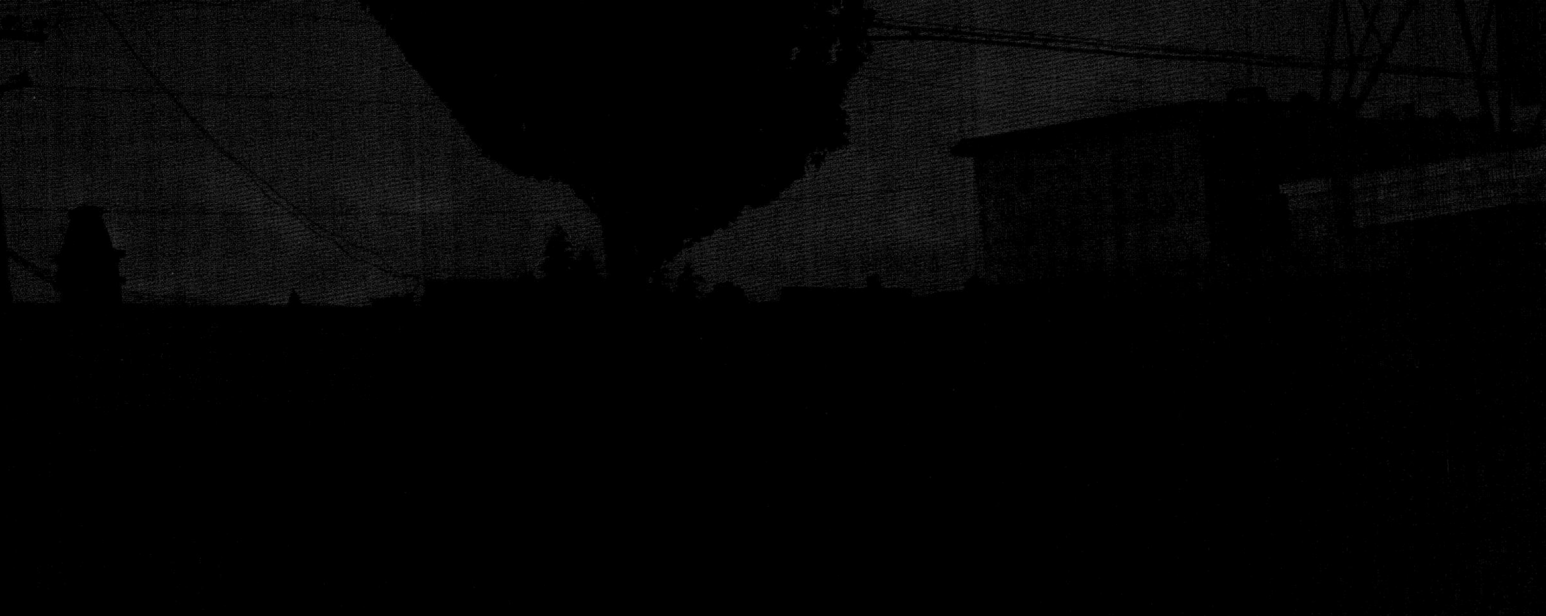

Sunset 日落

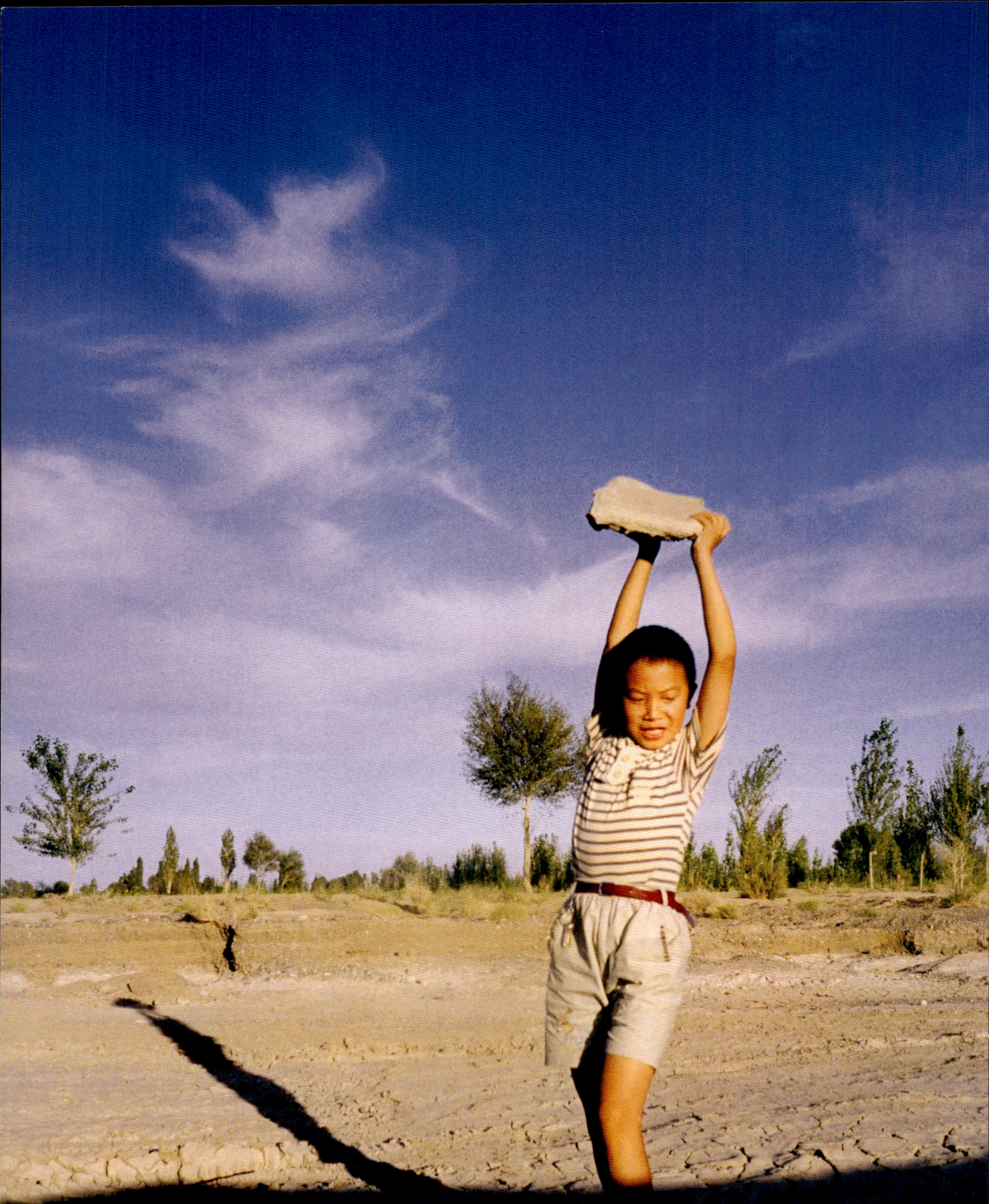

angyang 羊羊

Treetop 树梢

Yumen 玉门

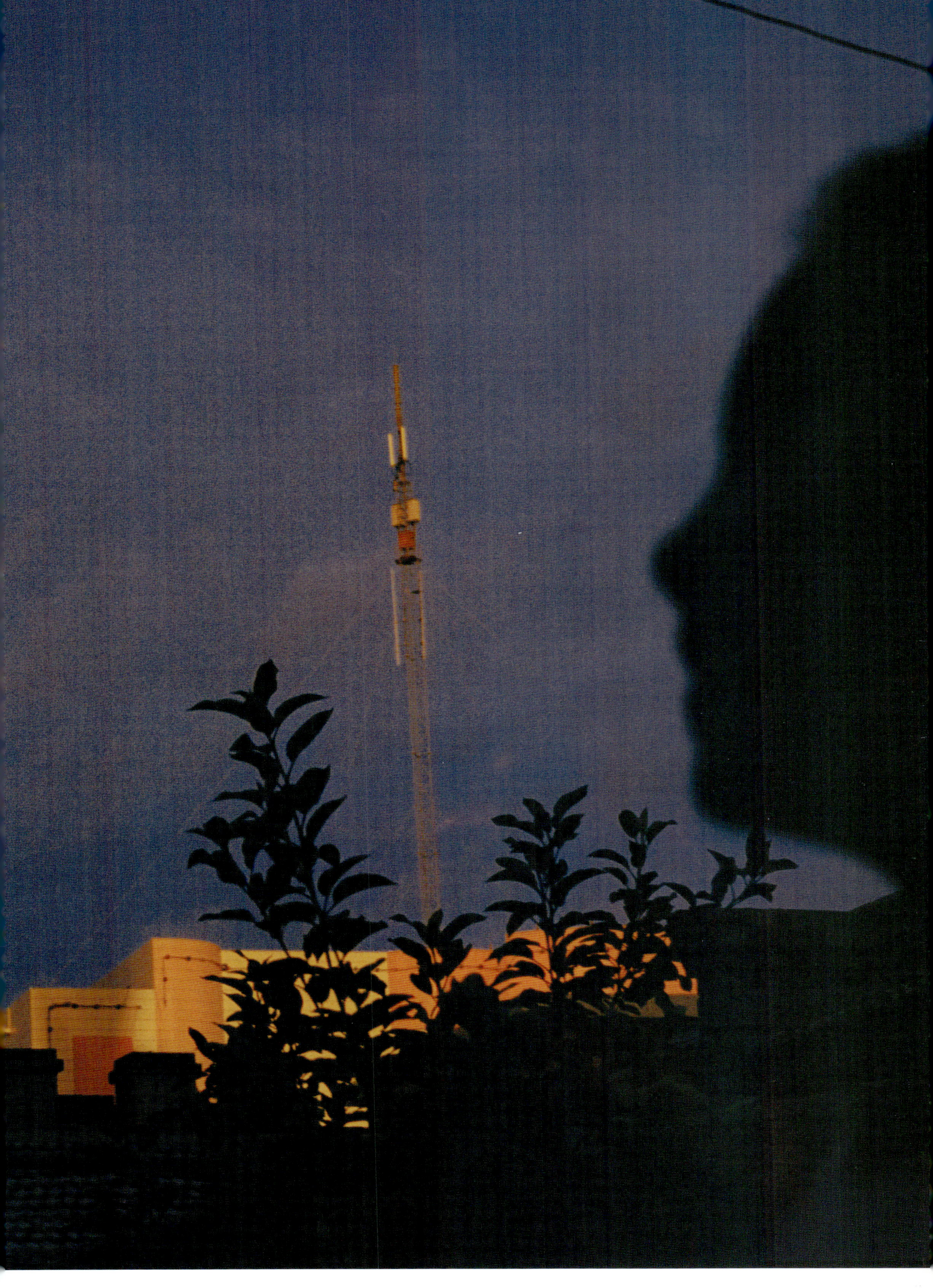

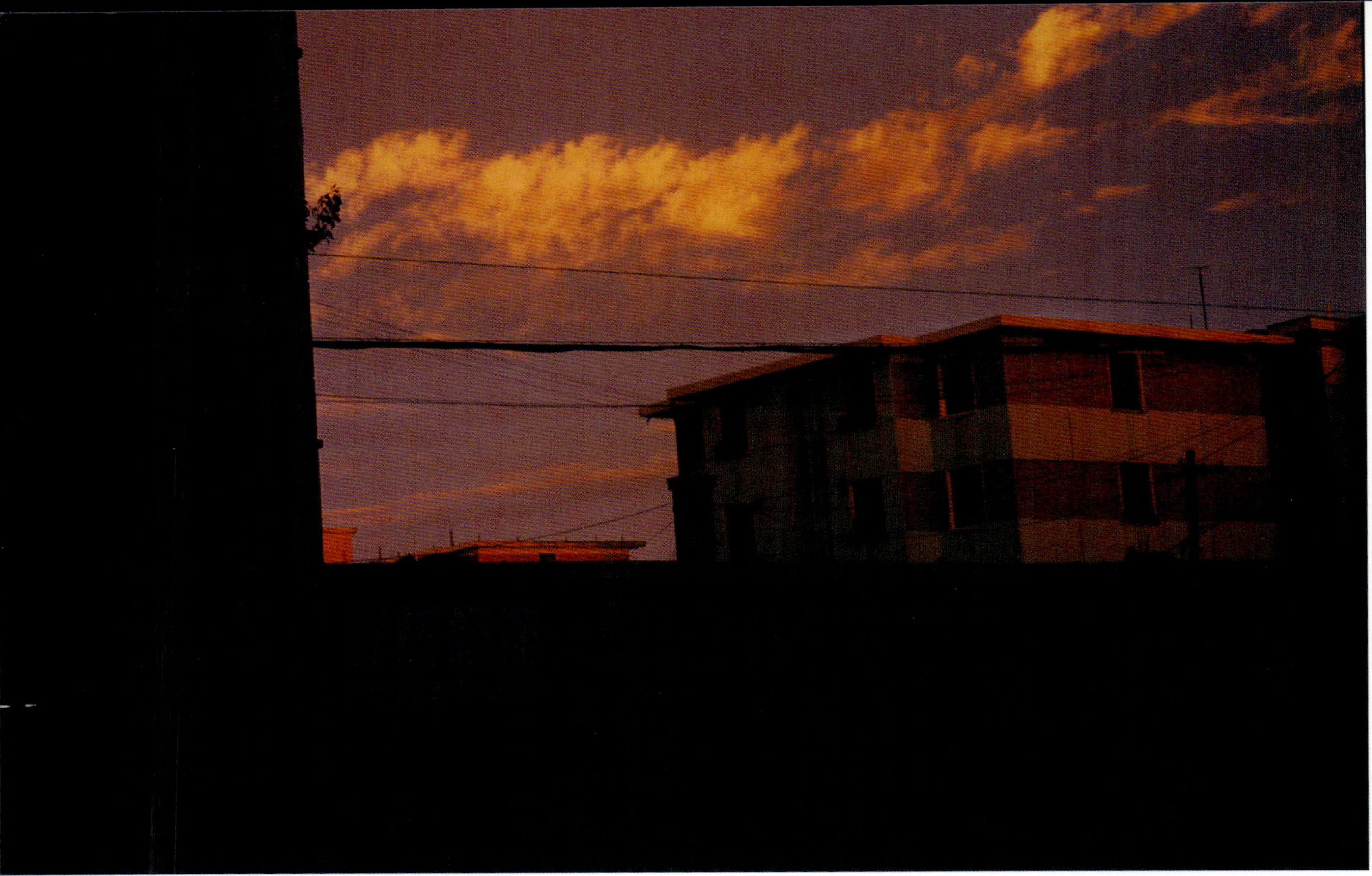

Sunset Glow 晚霞

At Yumen 在玉门

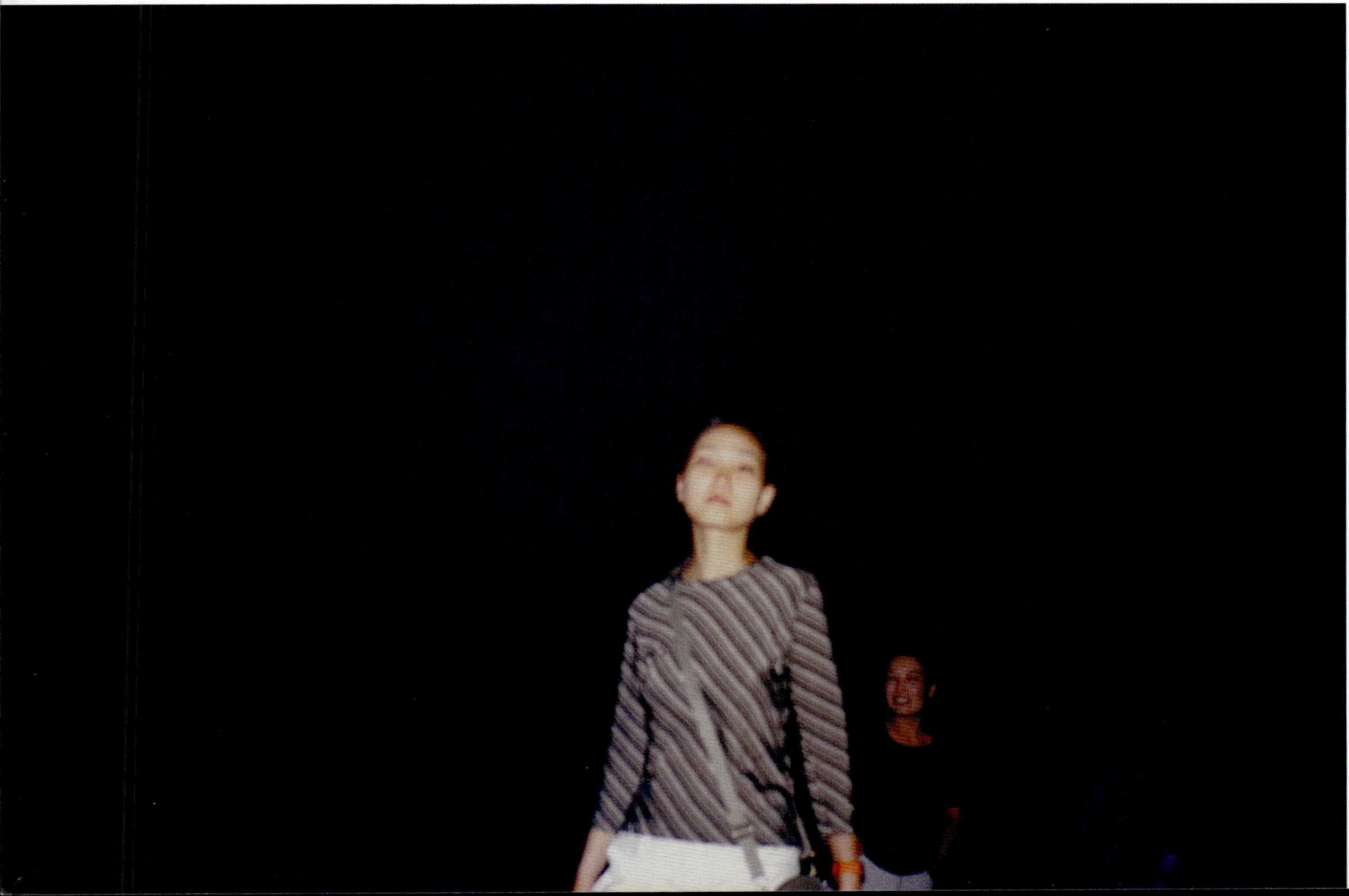

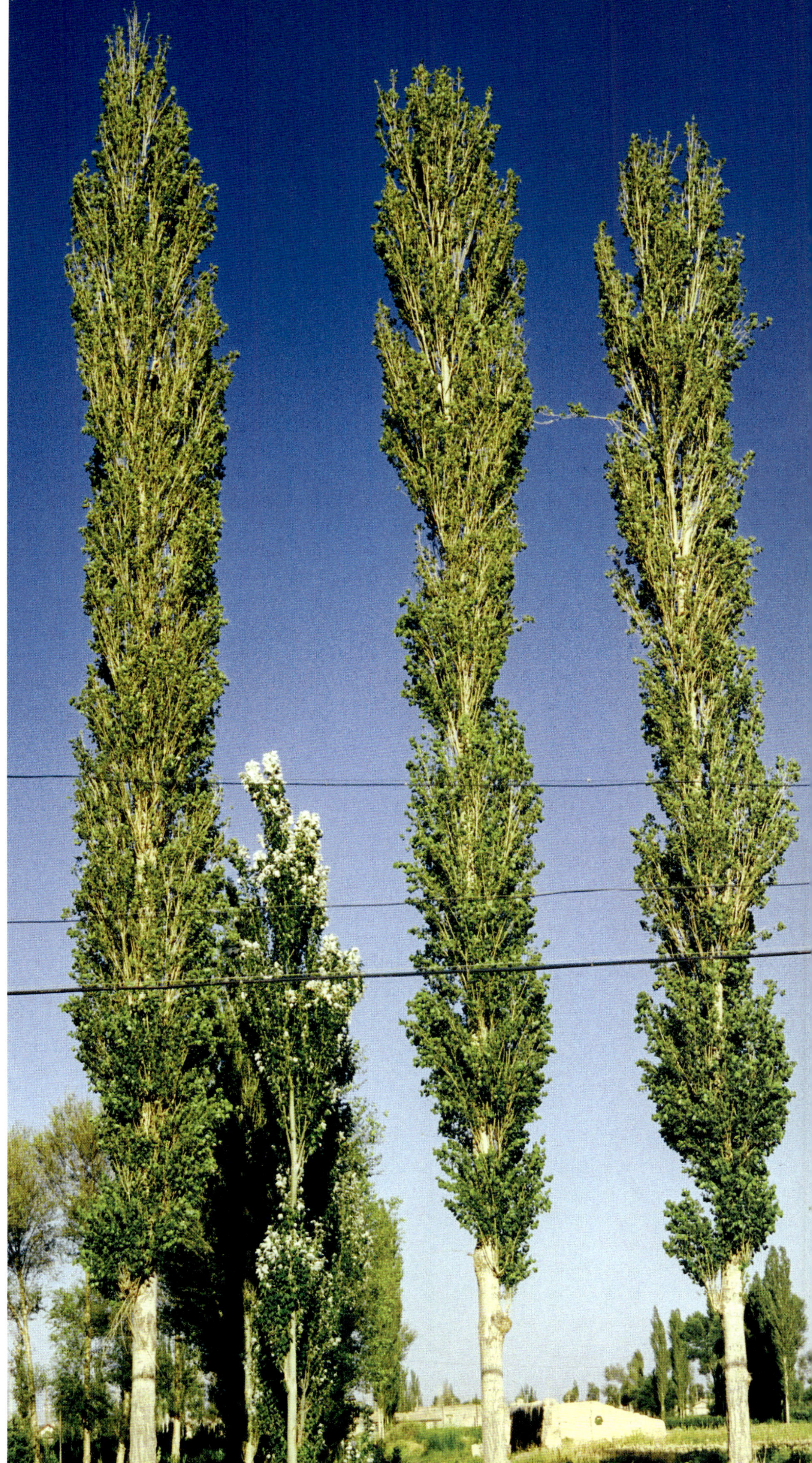

Three Trees 三棵树

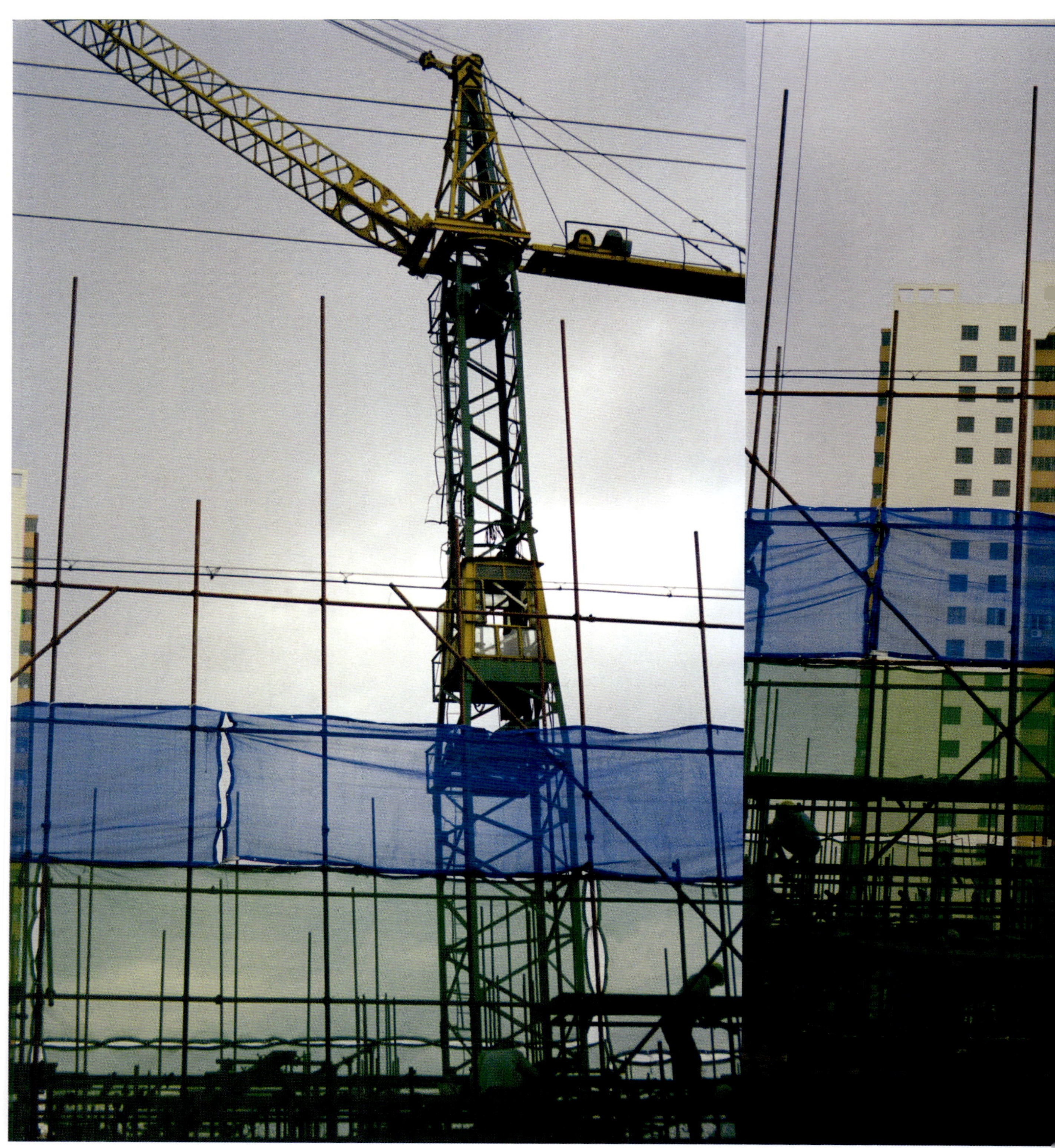

Shuanglong District 双龙小区

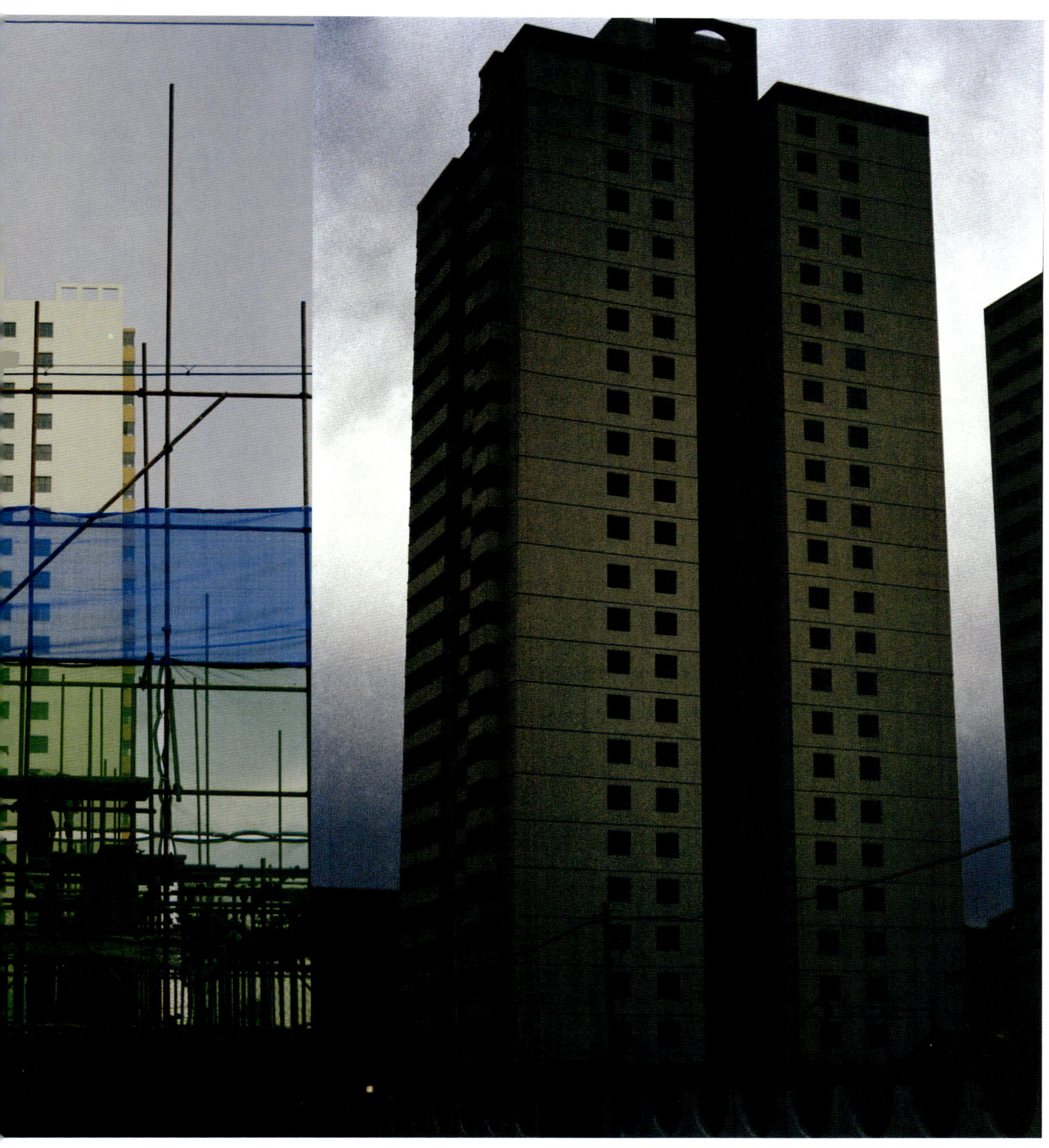

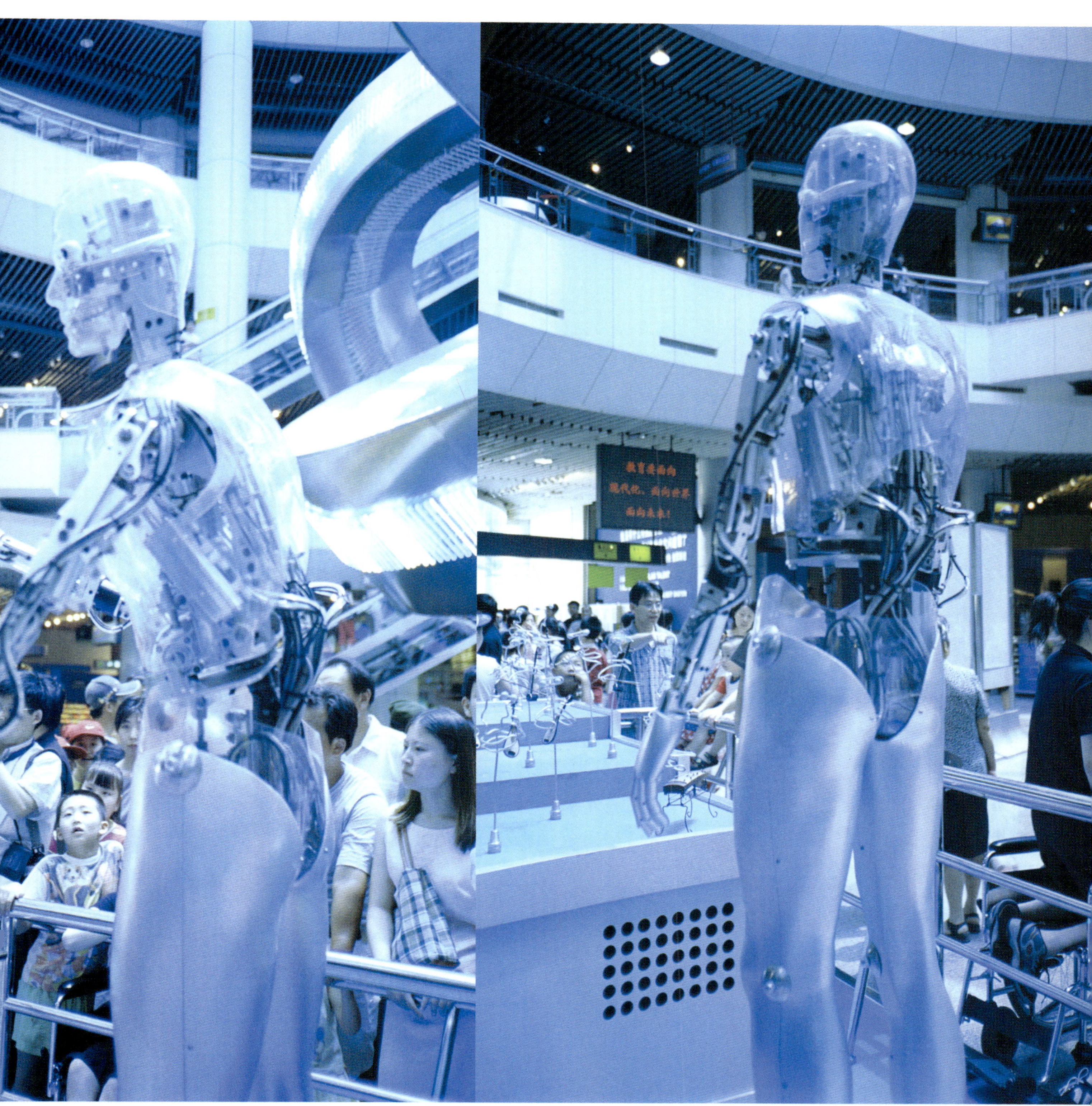

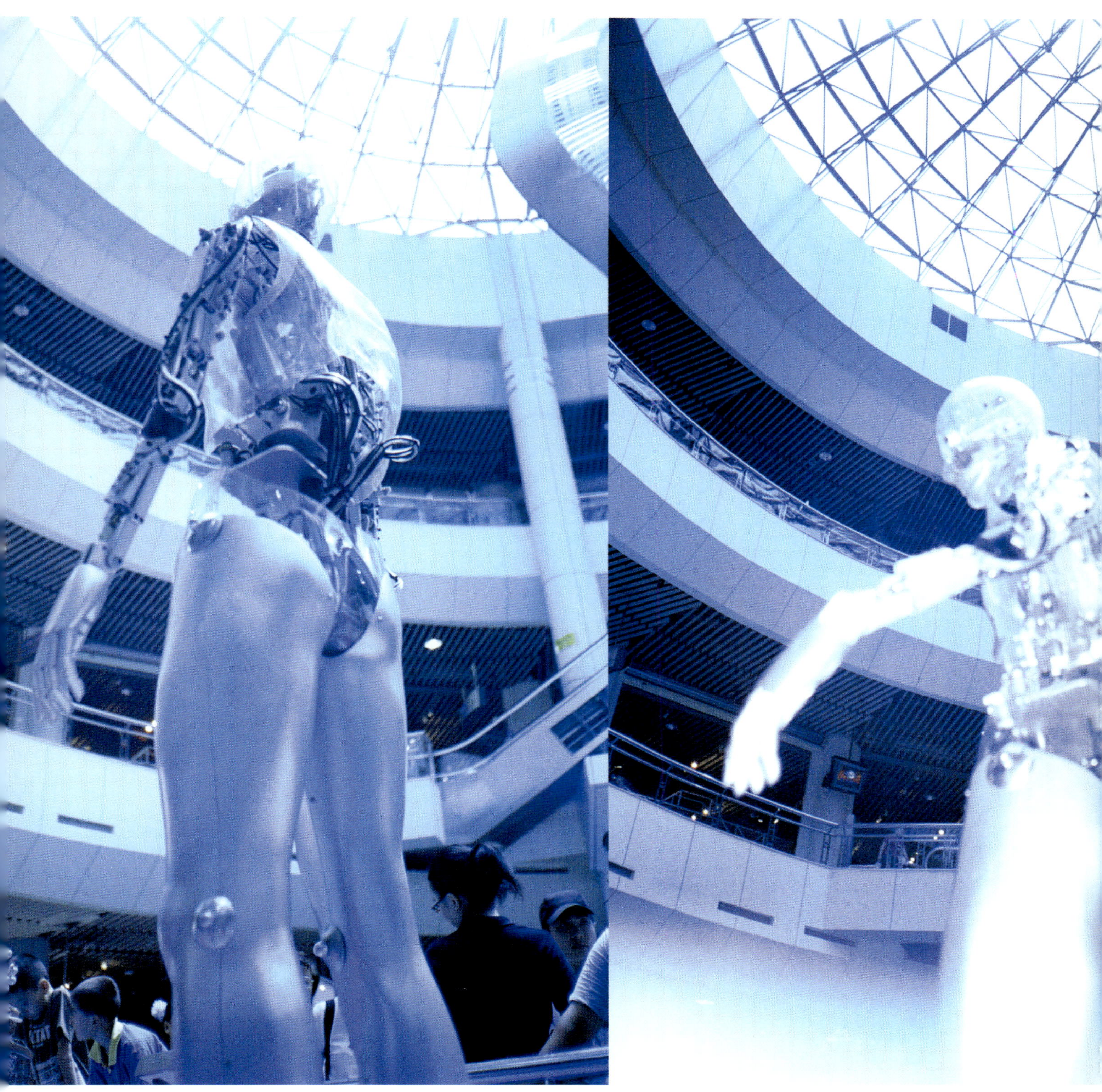

ot 机器人

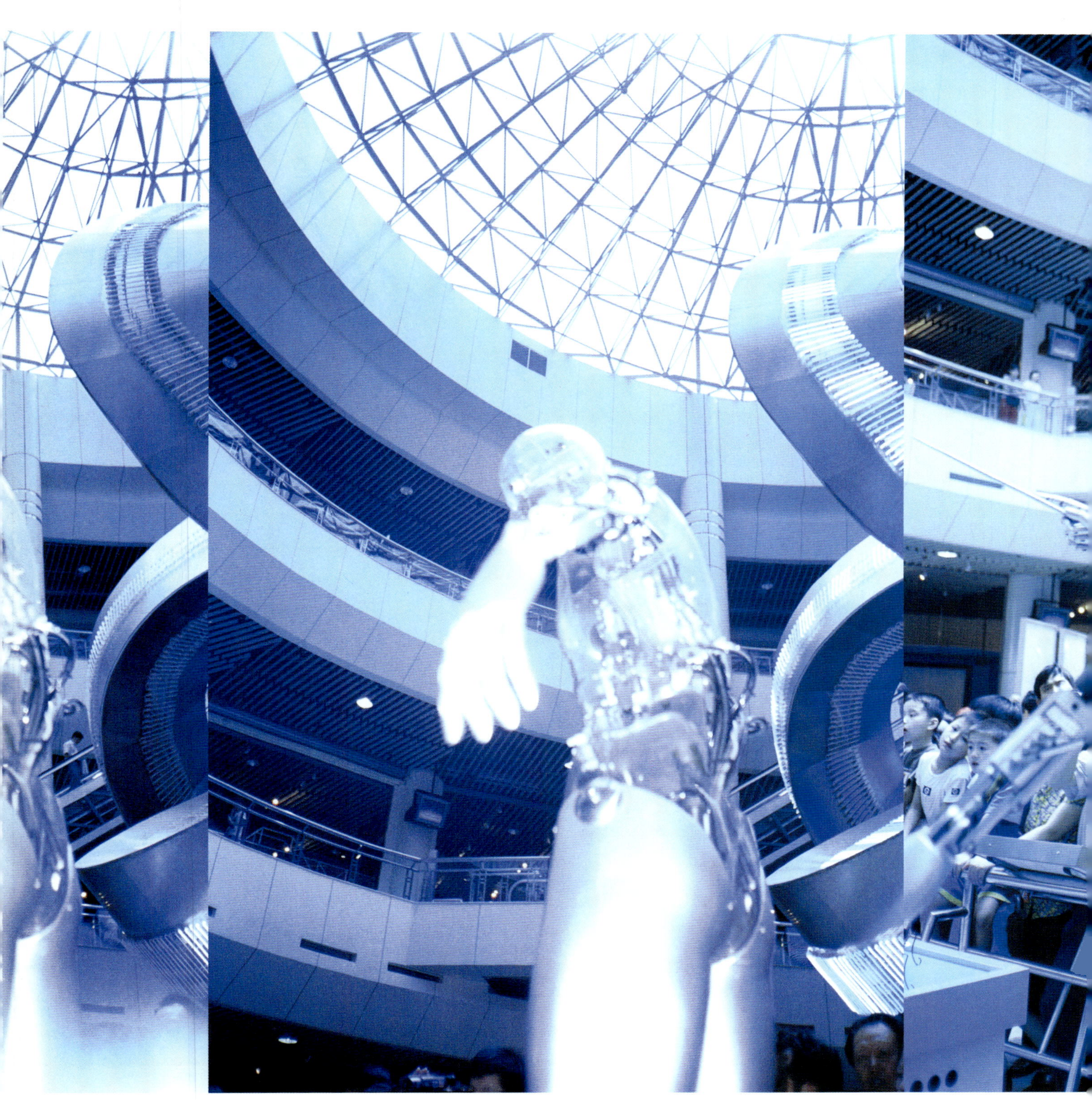

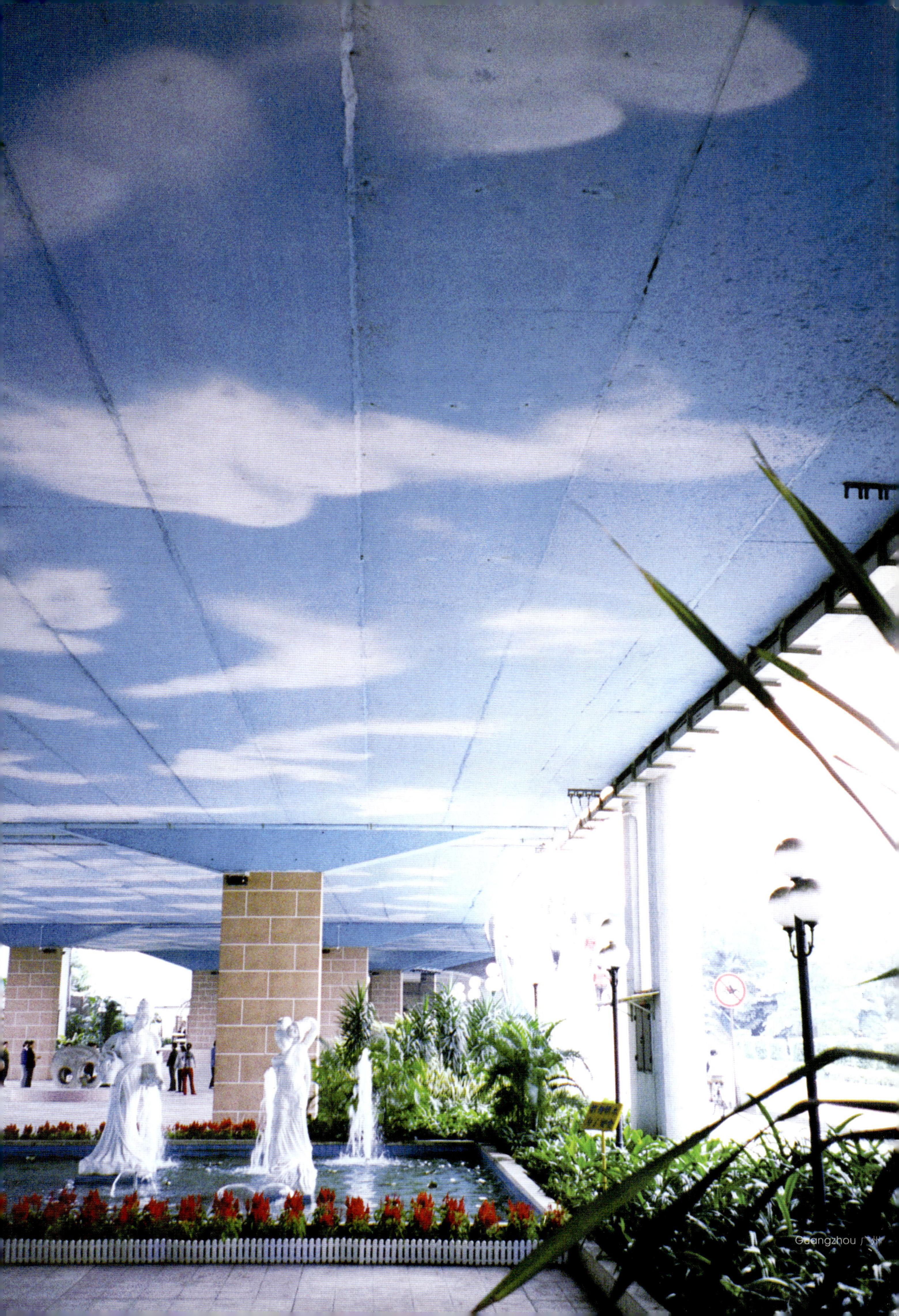
Guangzhou 广州

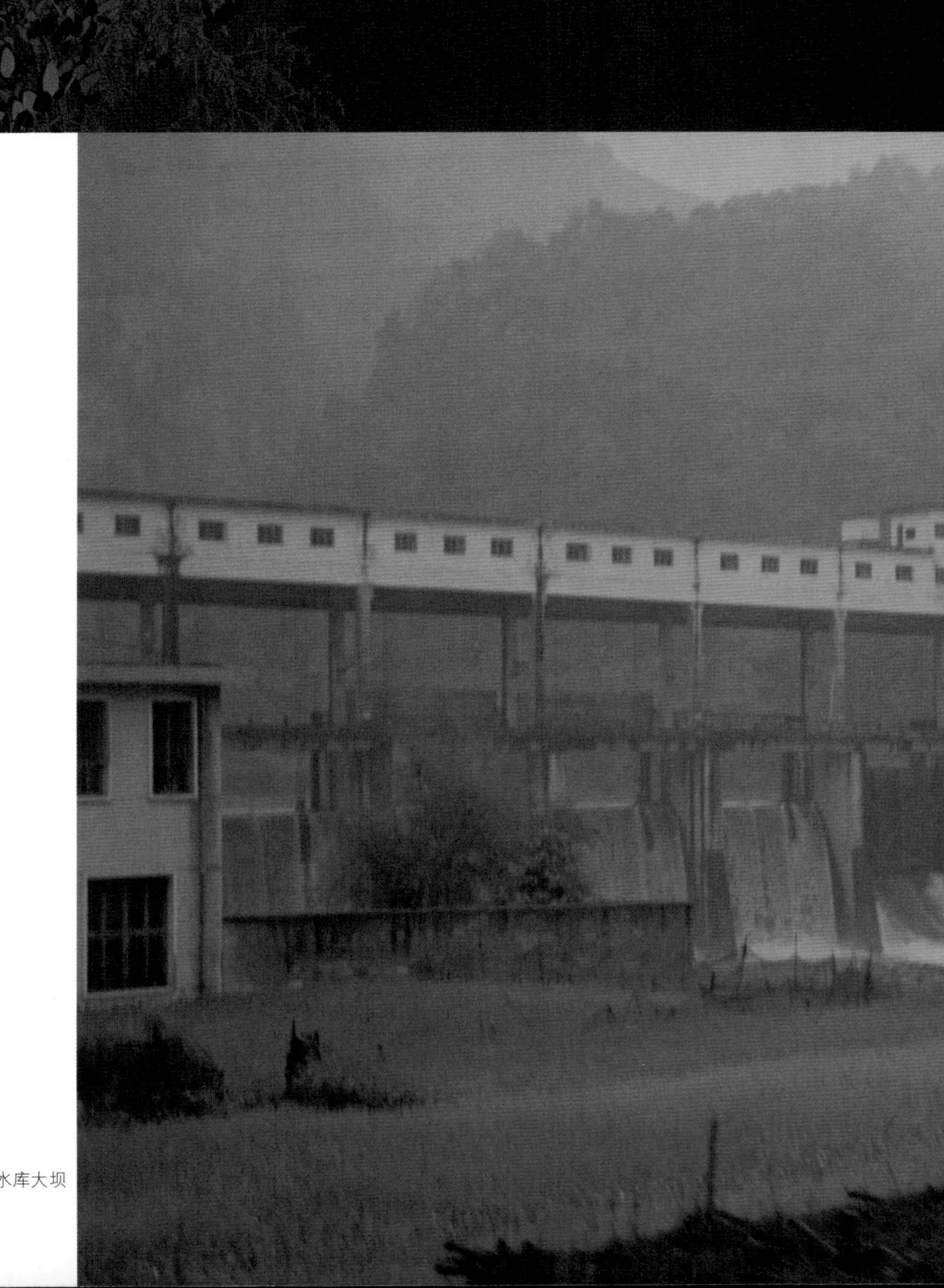

Tree 树

Reservoir Dam 水库大坝

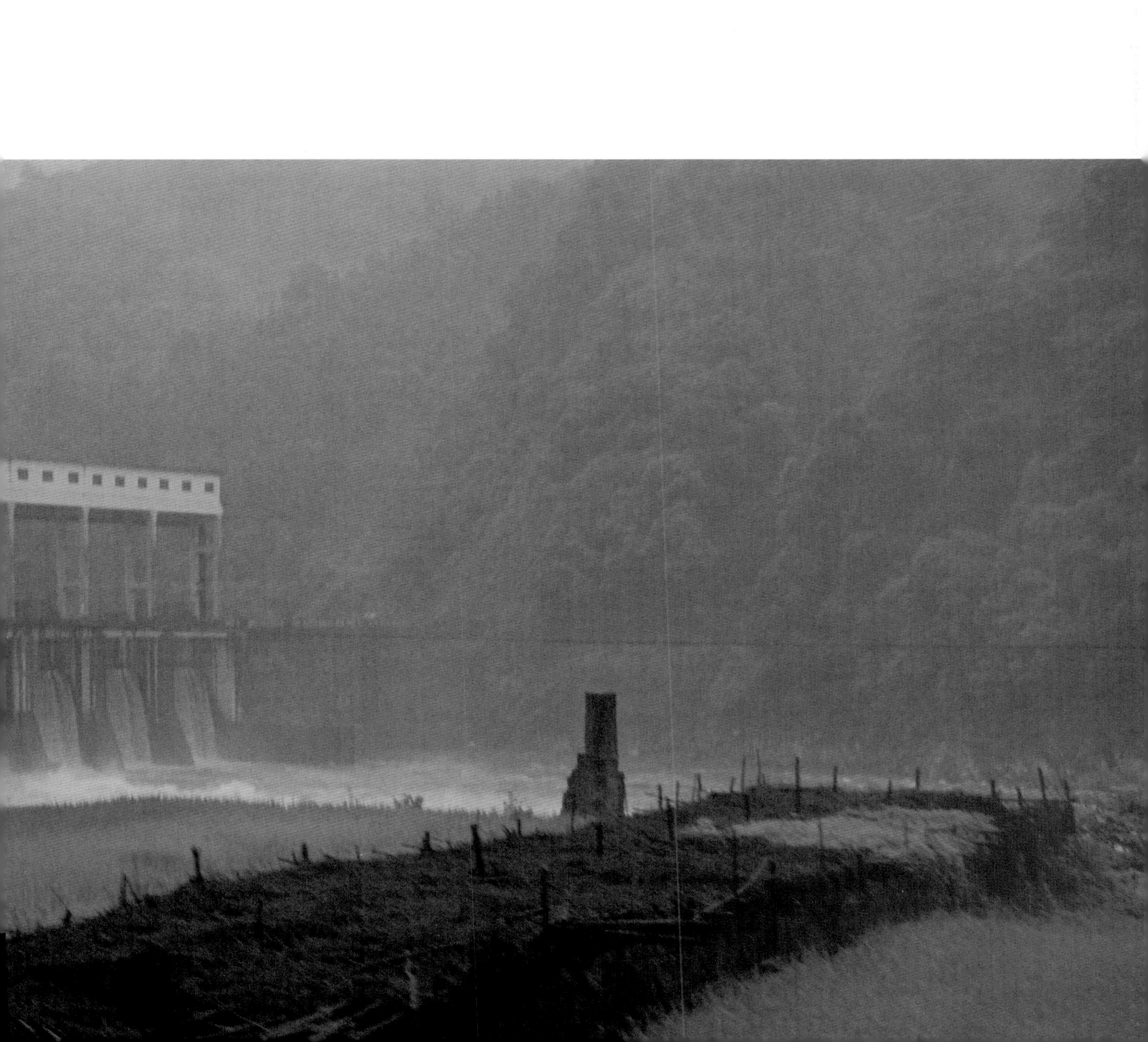

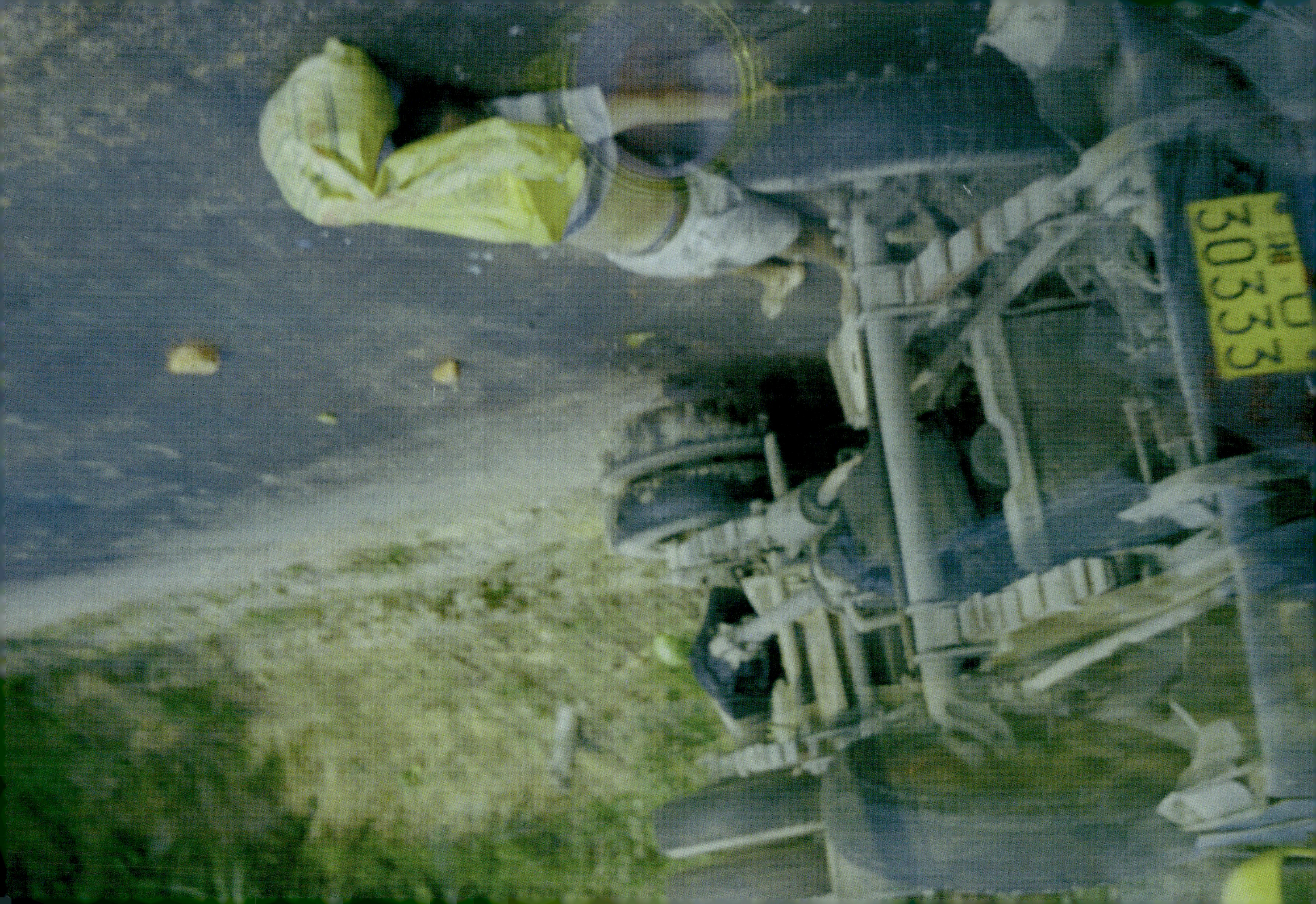
HI U
30333

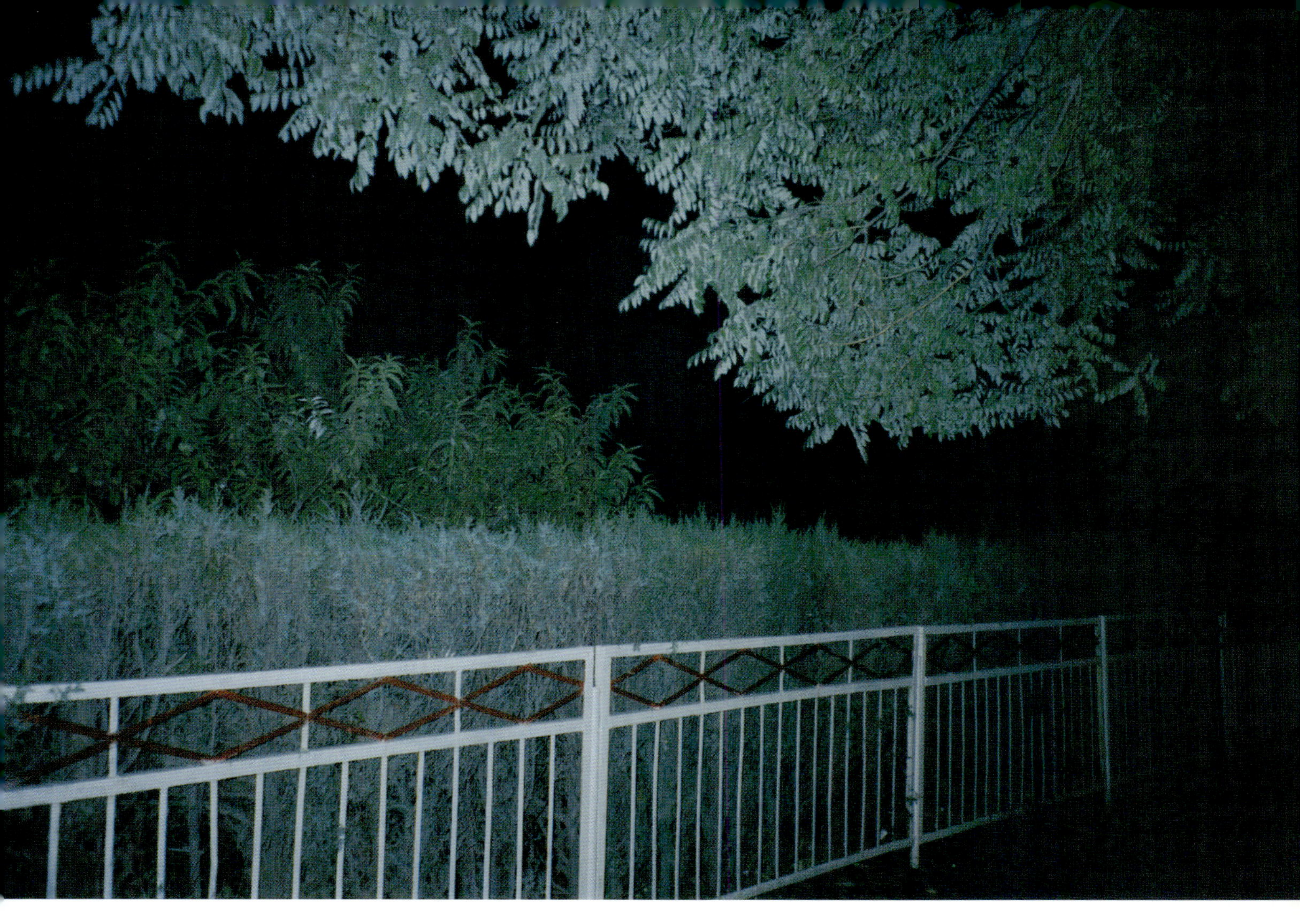

Guoyuan Roundabout 果园环岛

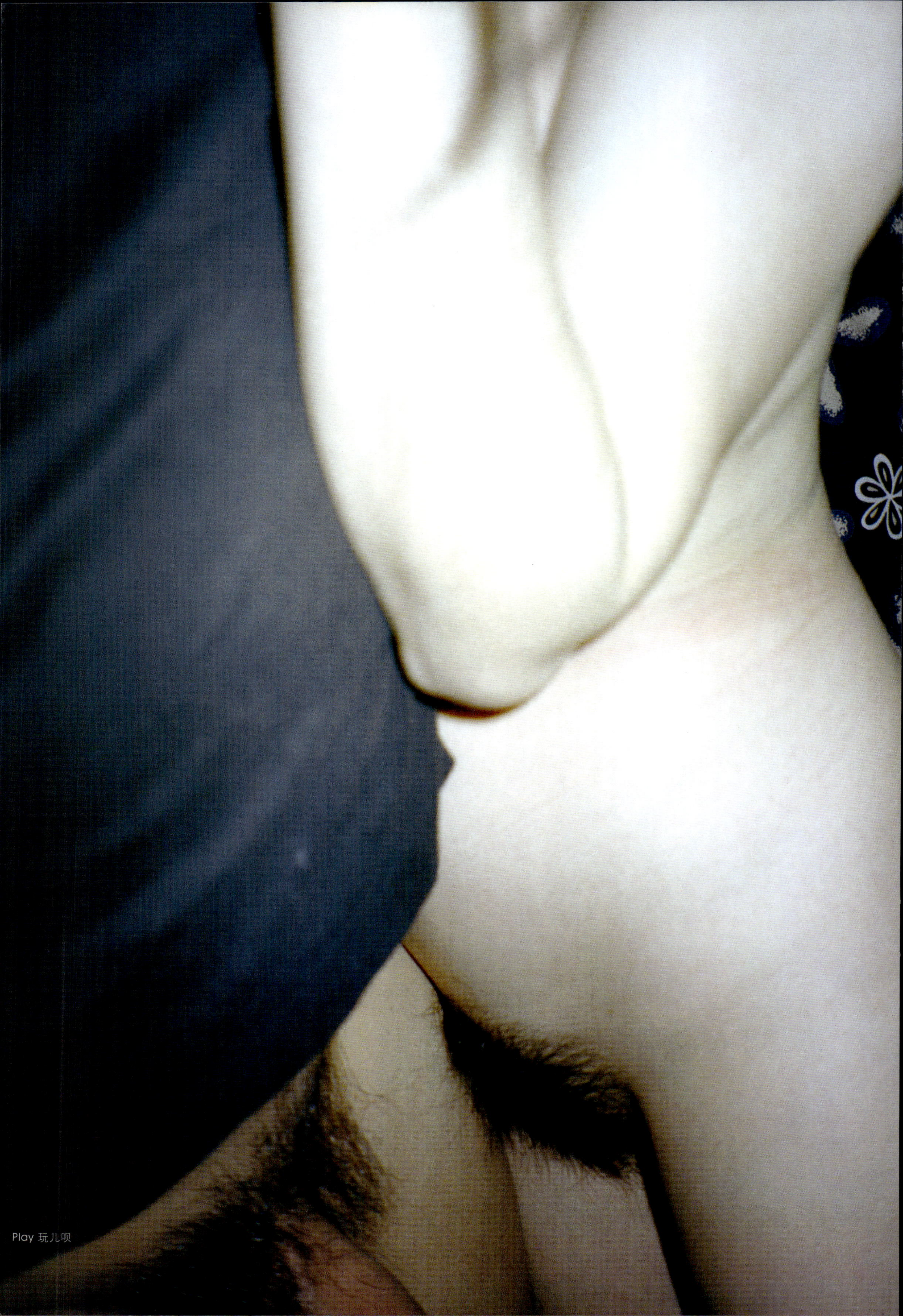

Play 玩儿呗

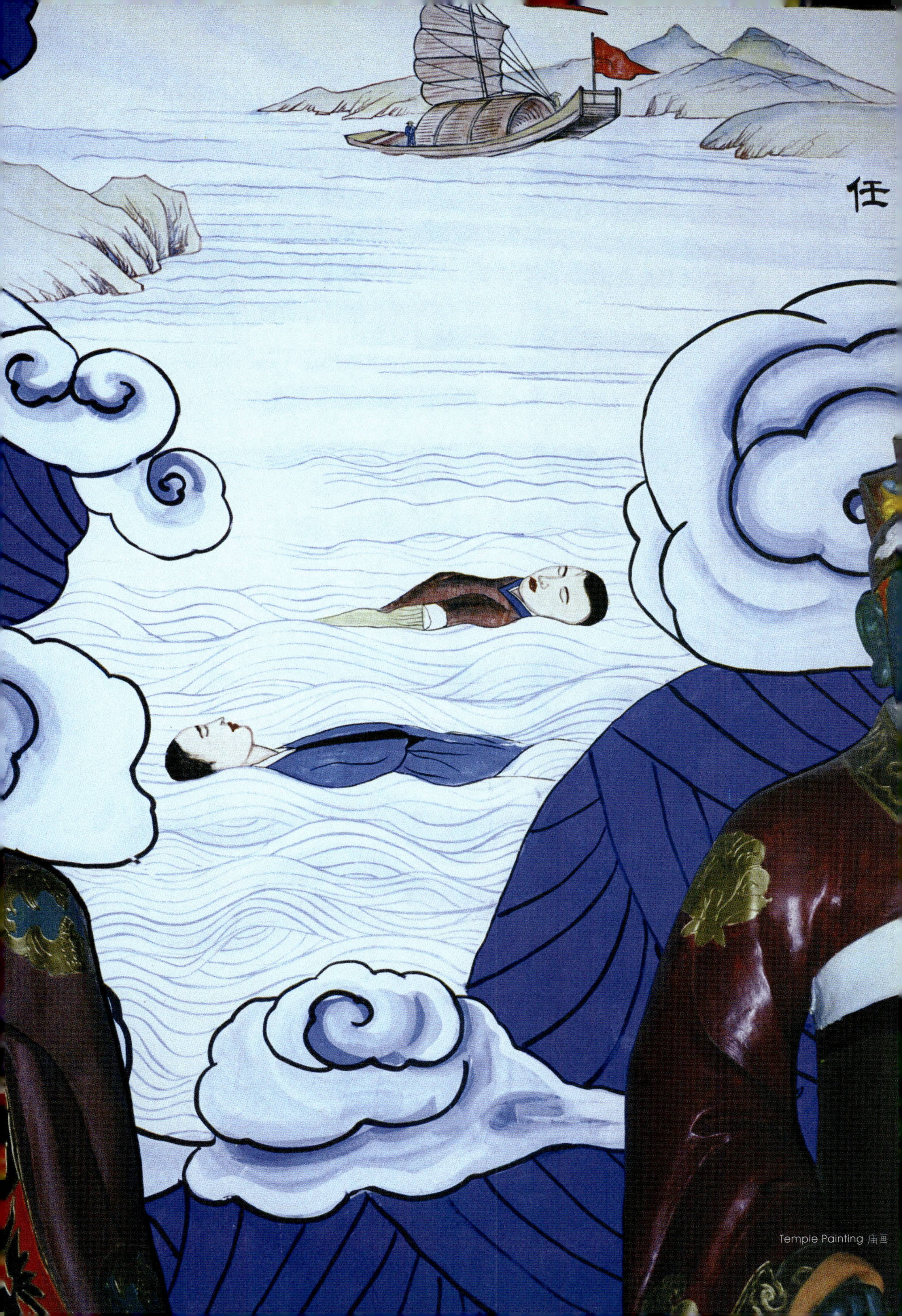

Temple Painting 庙画

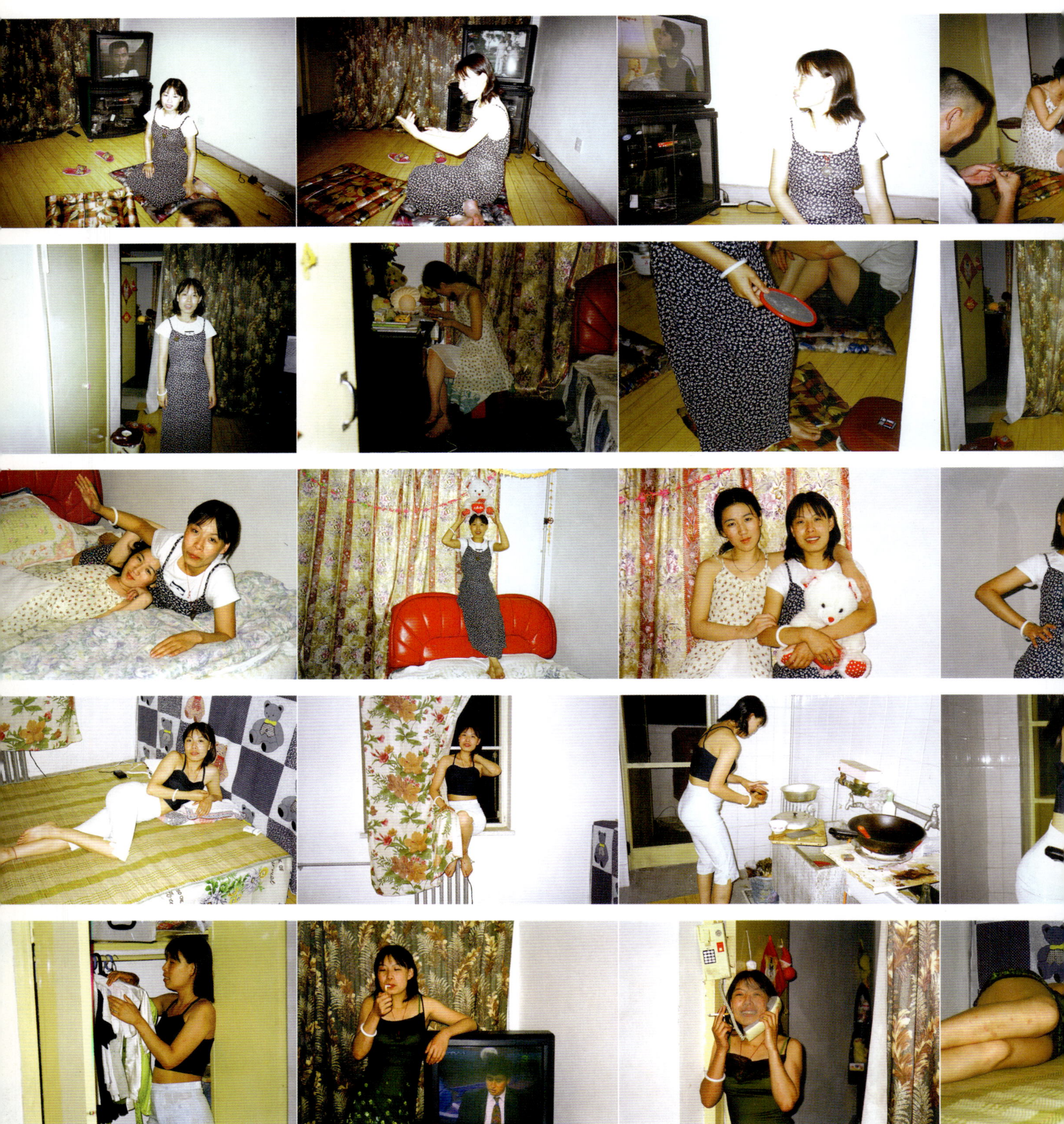

Two Girls from the North-East 两个东北姑娘

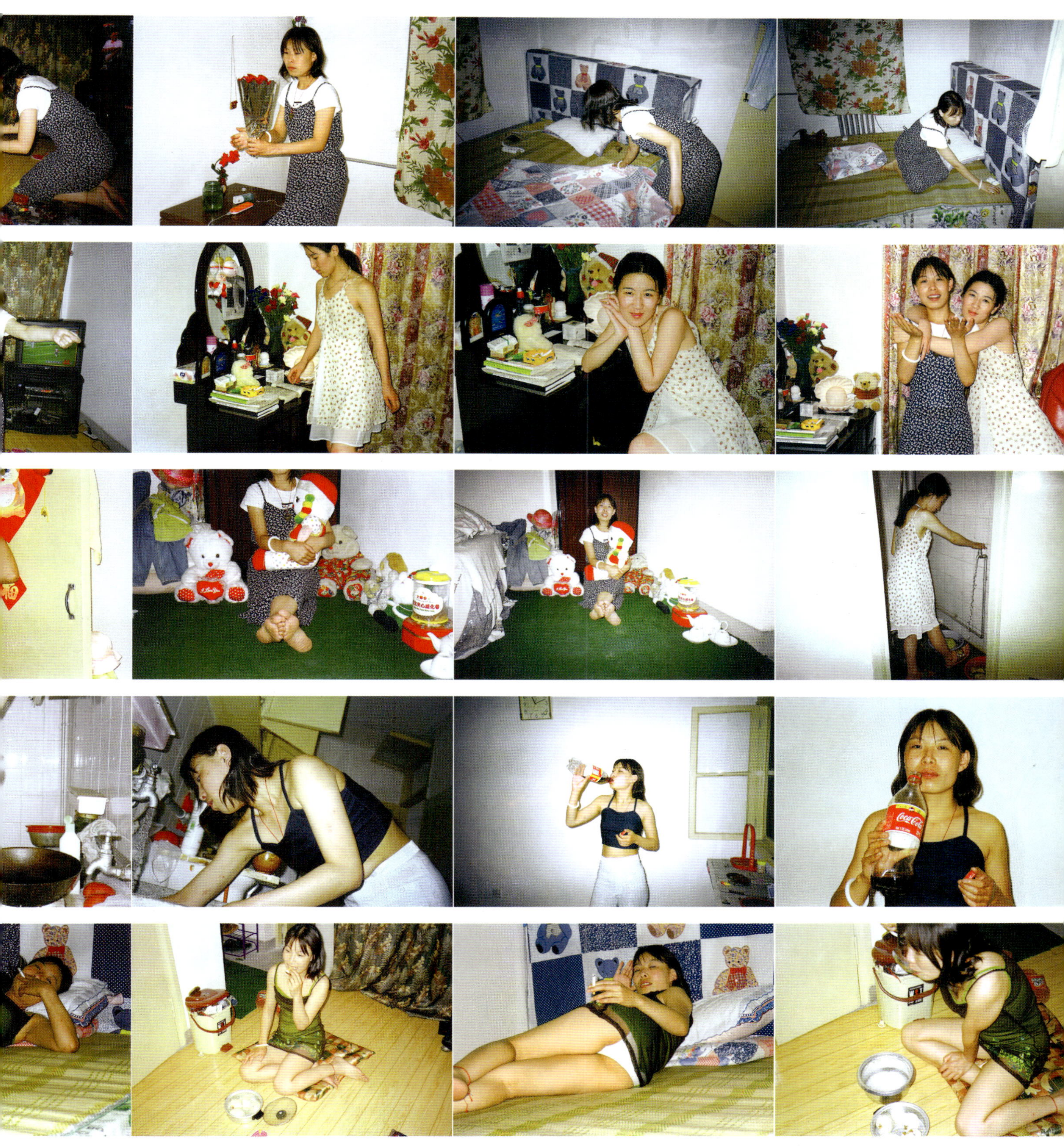

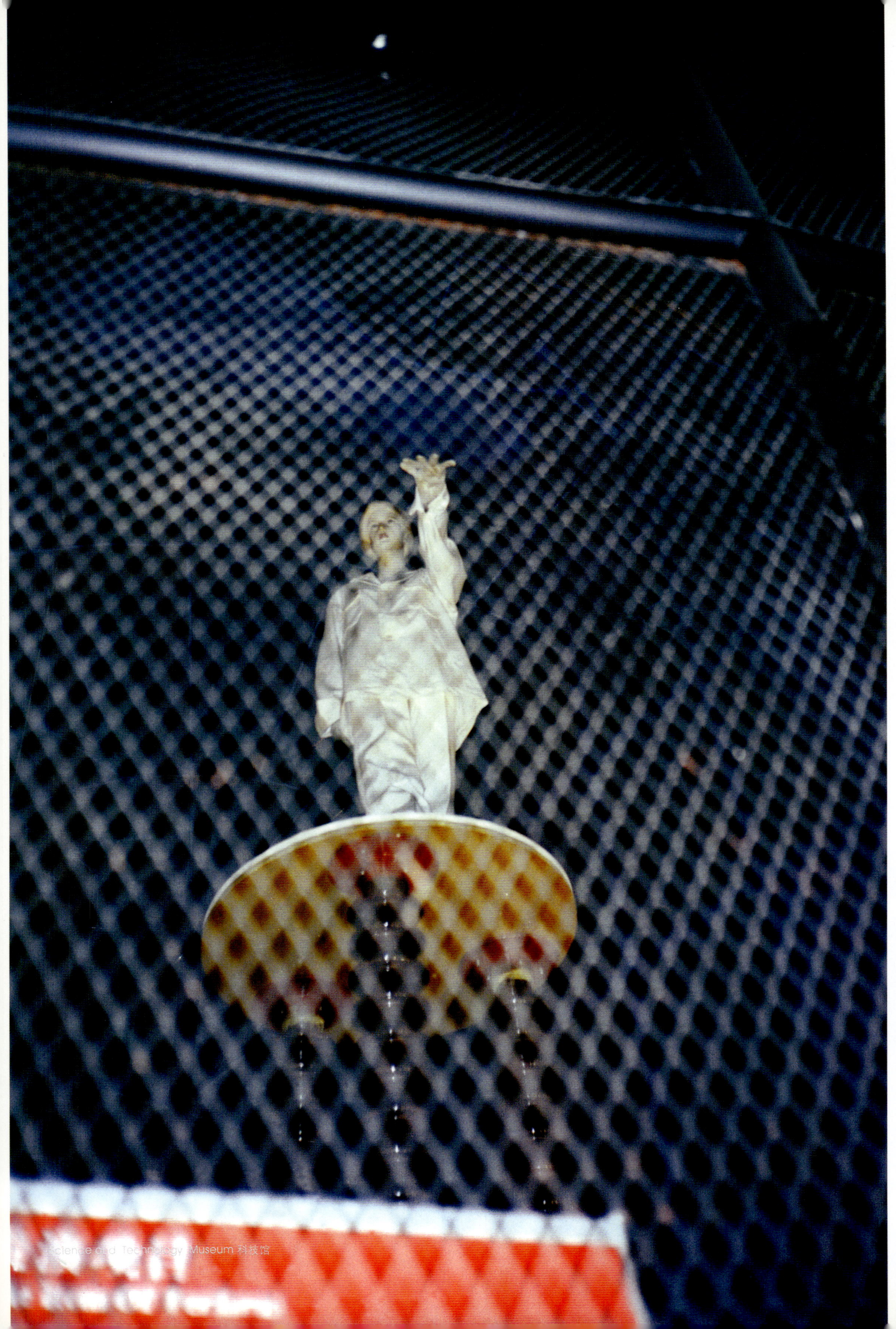
Science and Technology Museum 科技馆

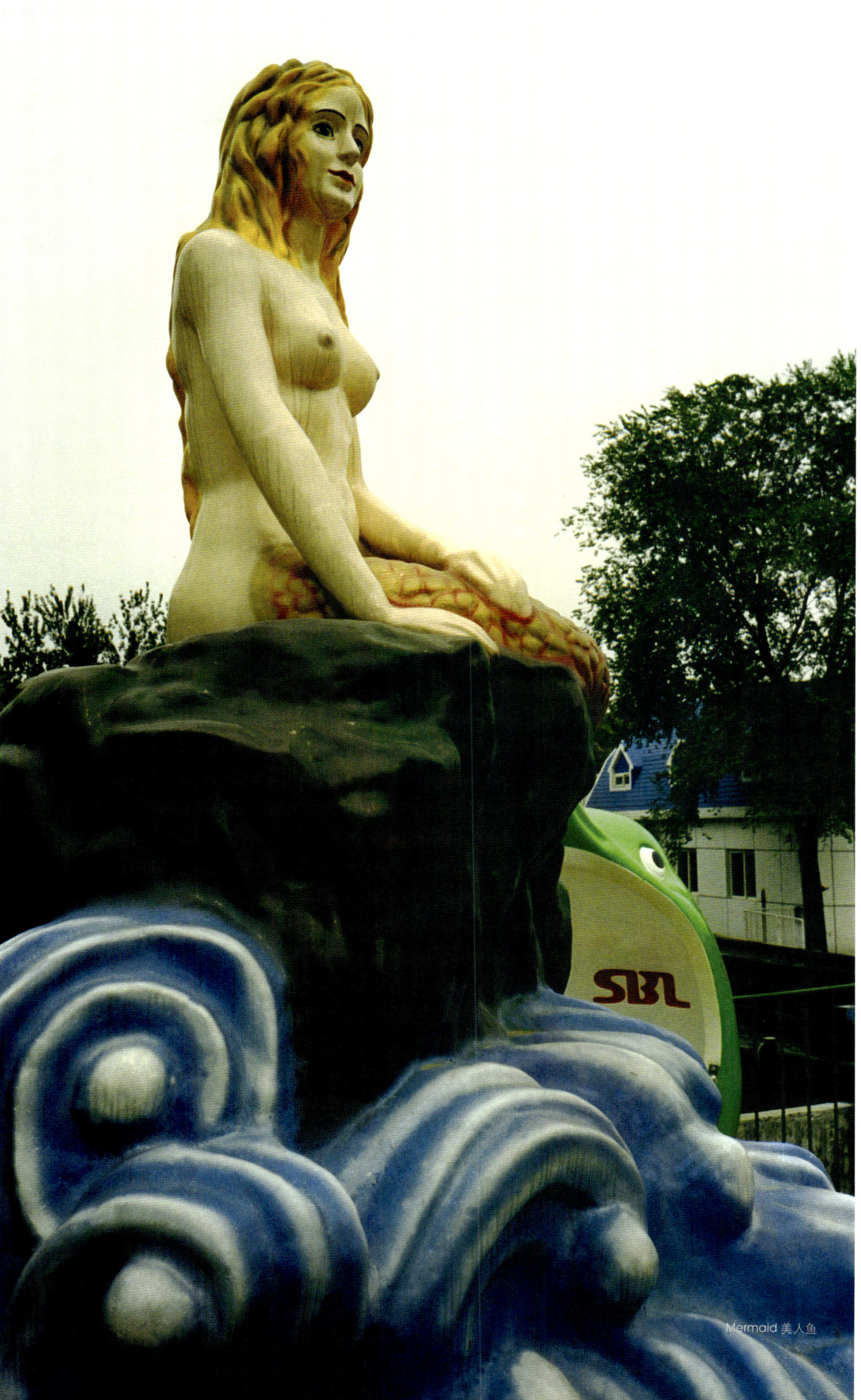

Mermaid 美人鱼

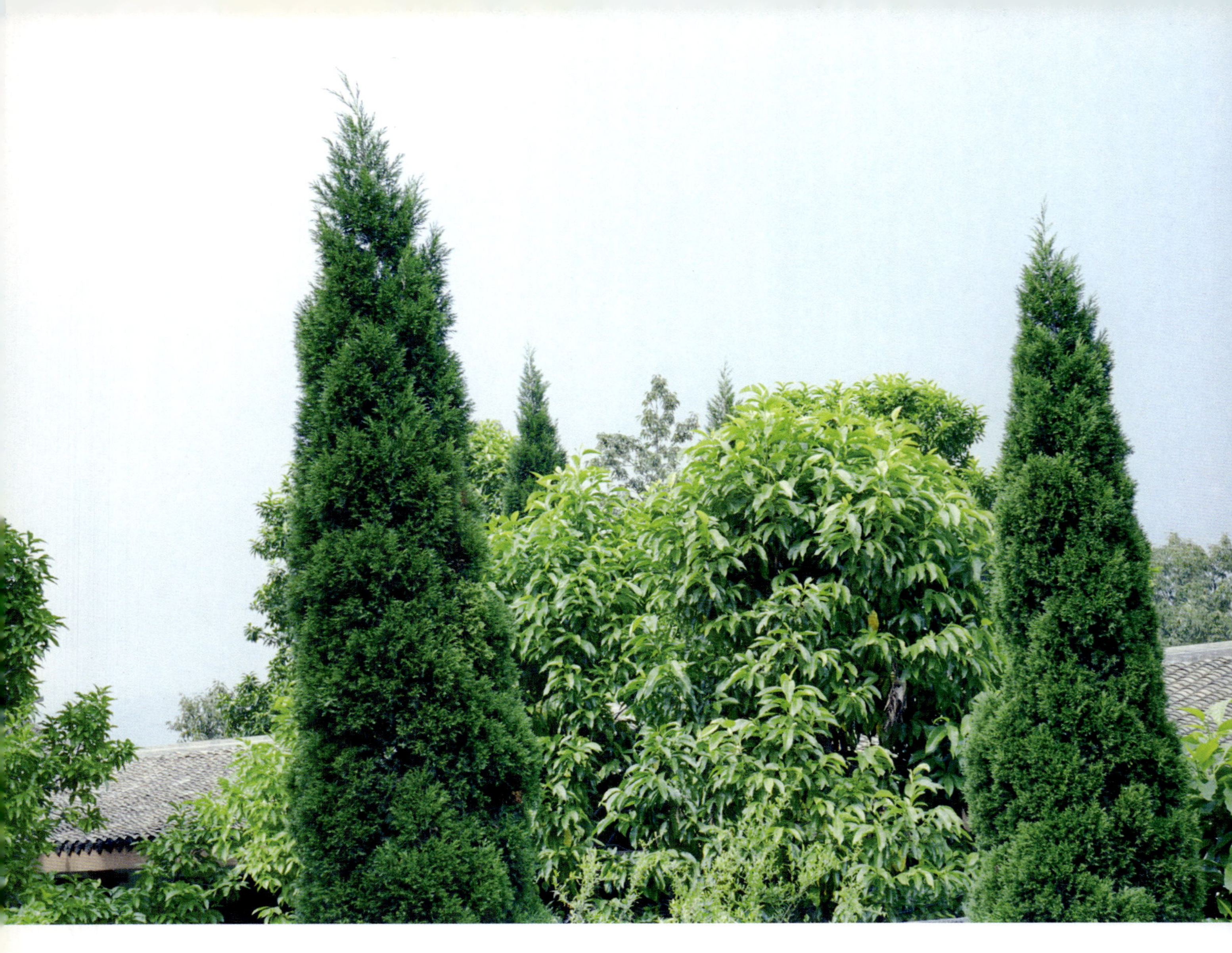

Family Garden 庭院

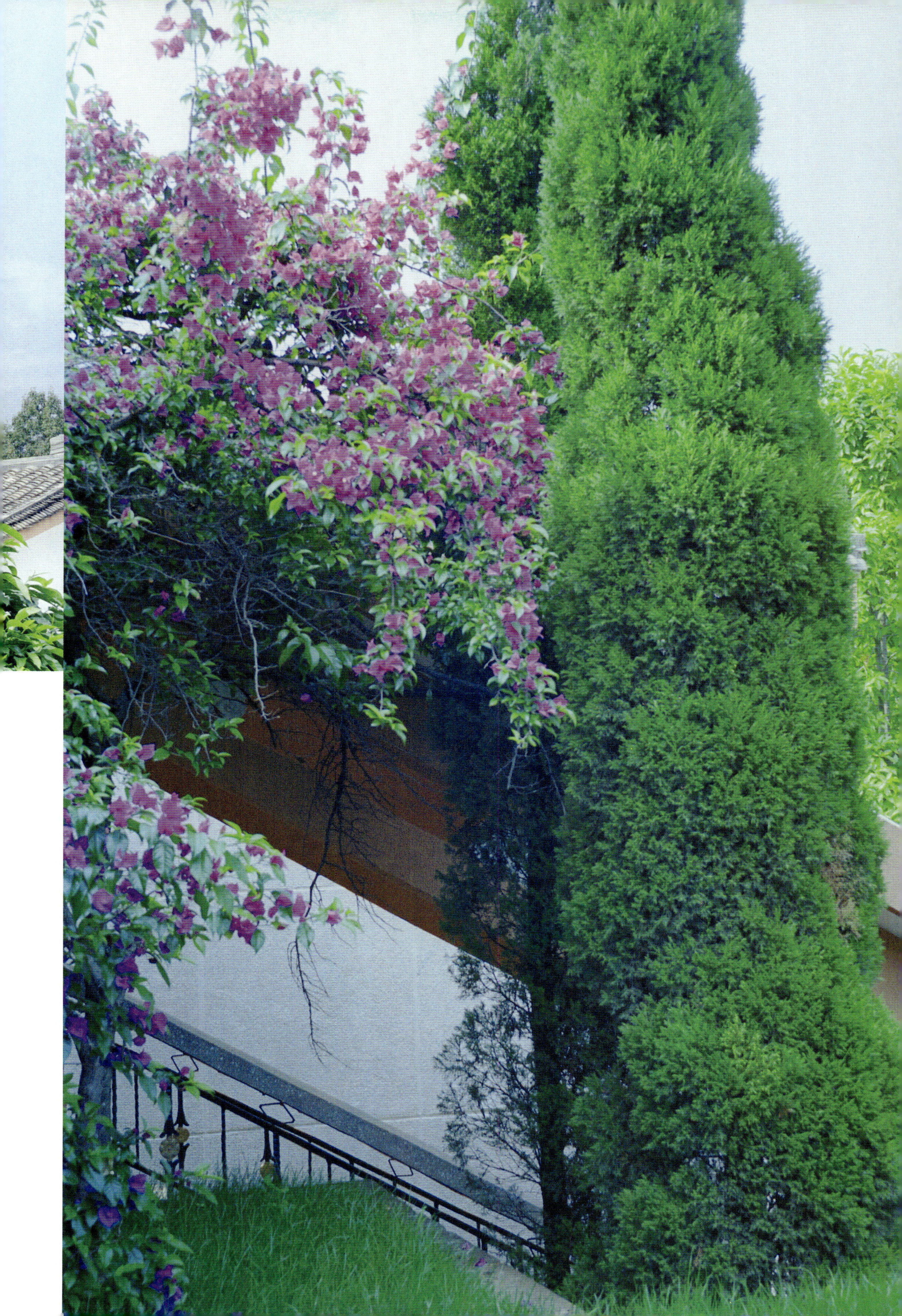

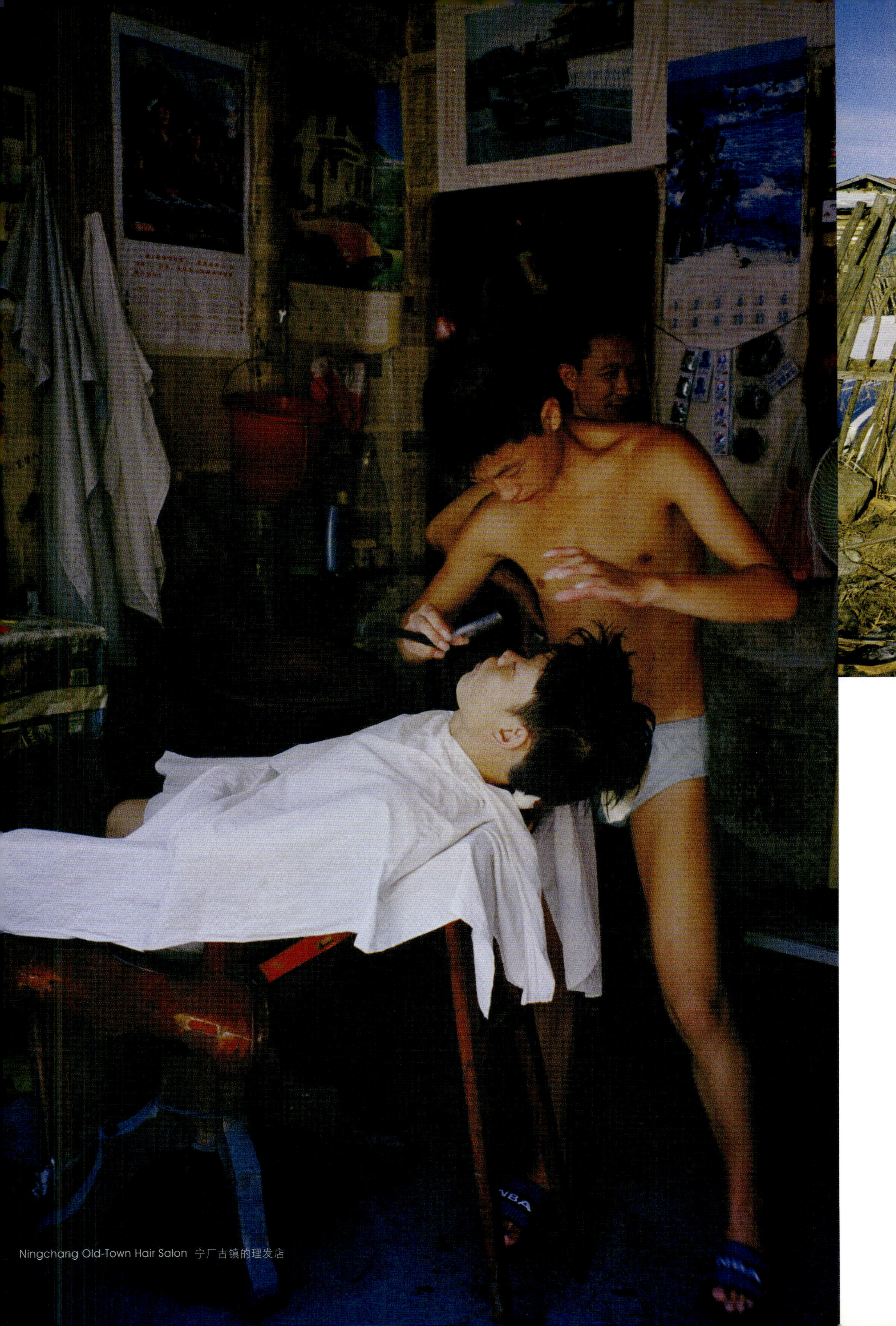

Ningchang Old-Town Hair Salon 宁厂古镇的理发店

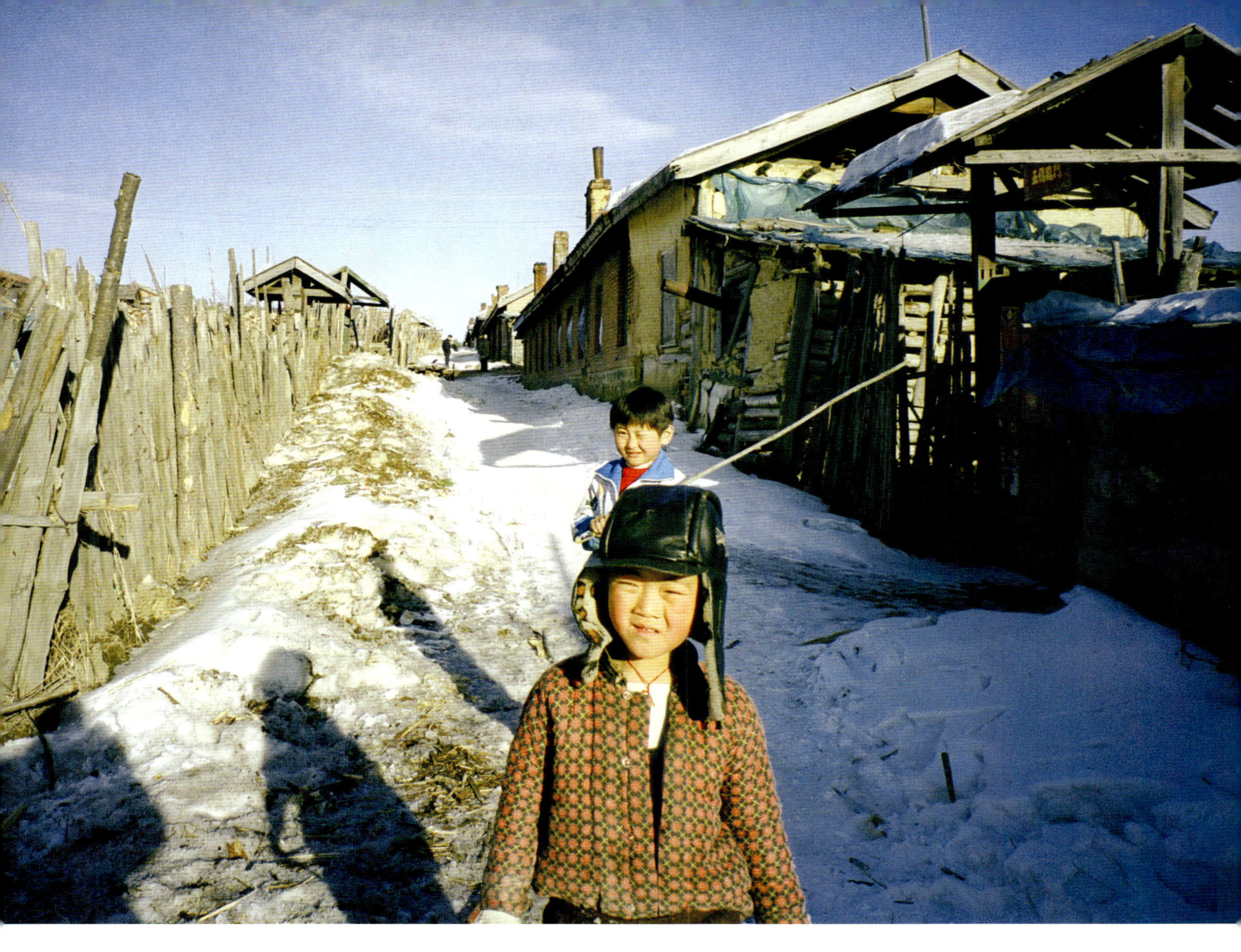

Song Jiang River State Forest District 松江河林区

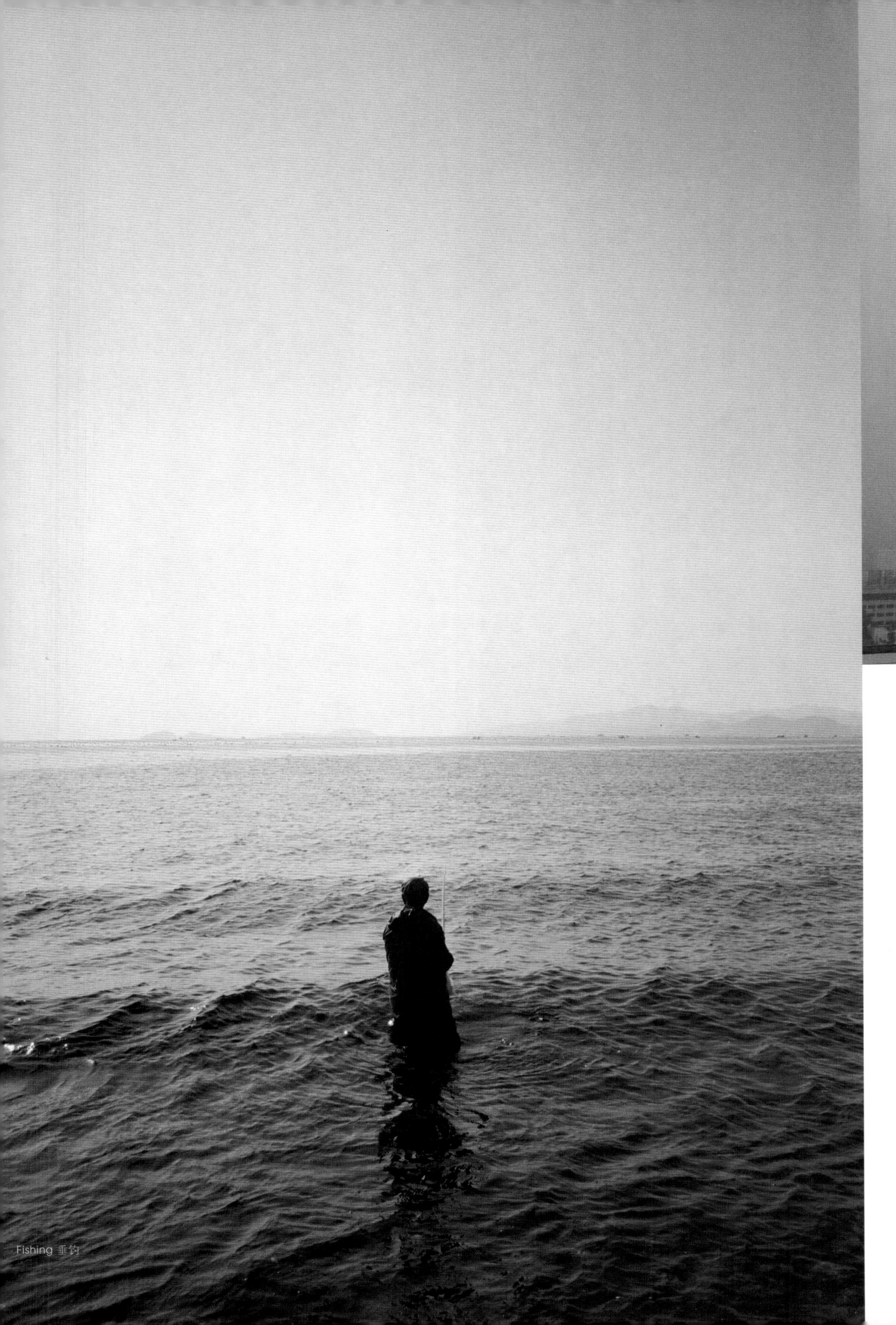

Fishing 垂钓

Luoyang 洛阳

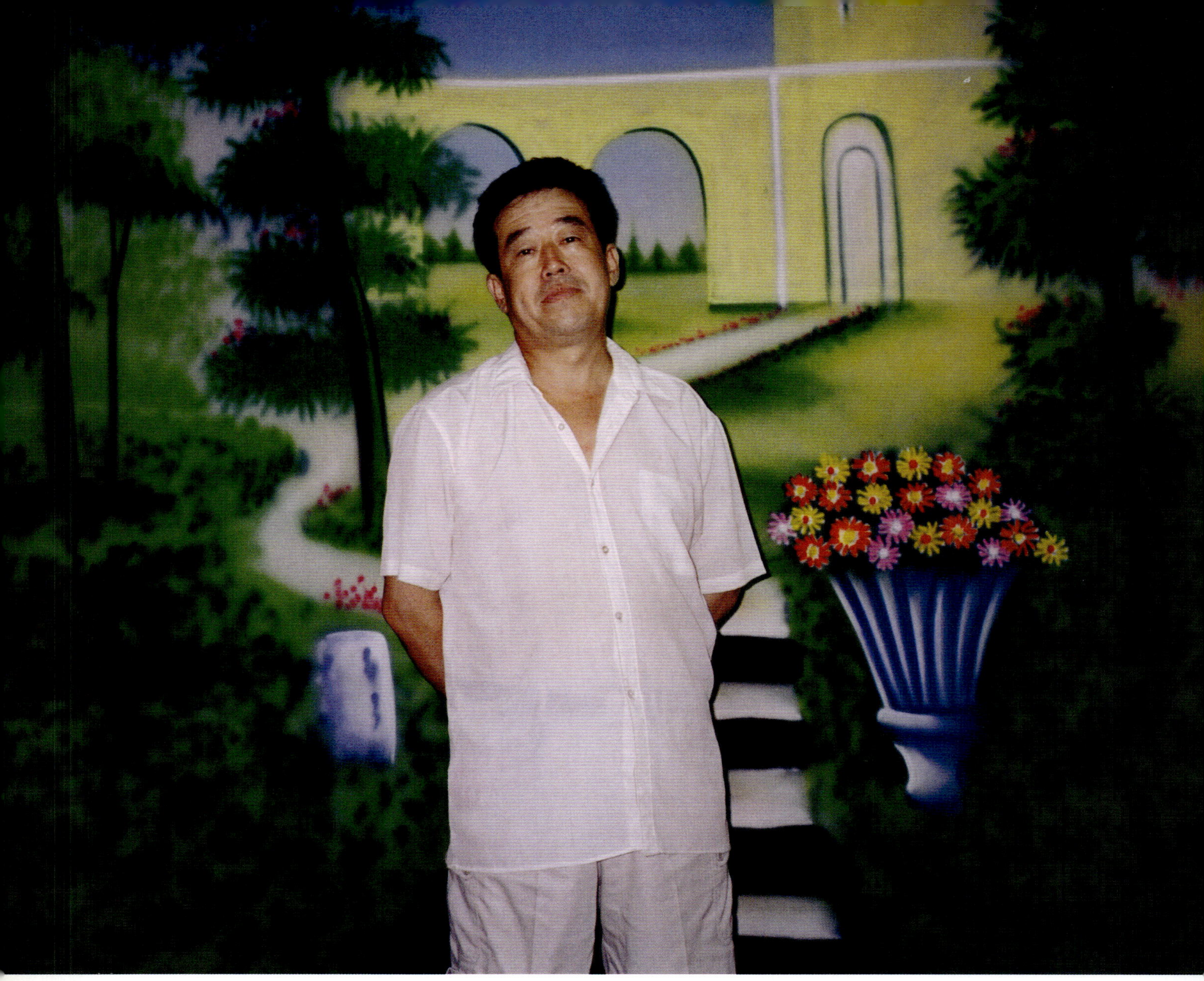

Wu Pu Country Photo Salon 吴堡镇上的摄影师

Shui Lu Temple Lotus Pond 水陆庙前的荷

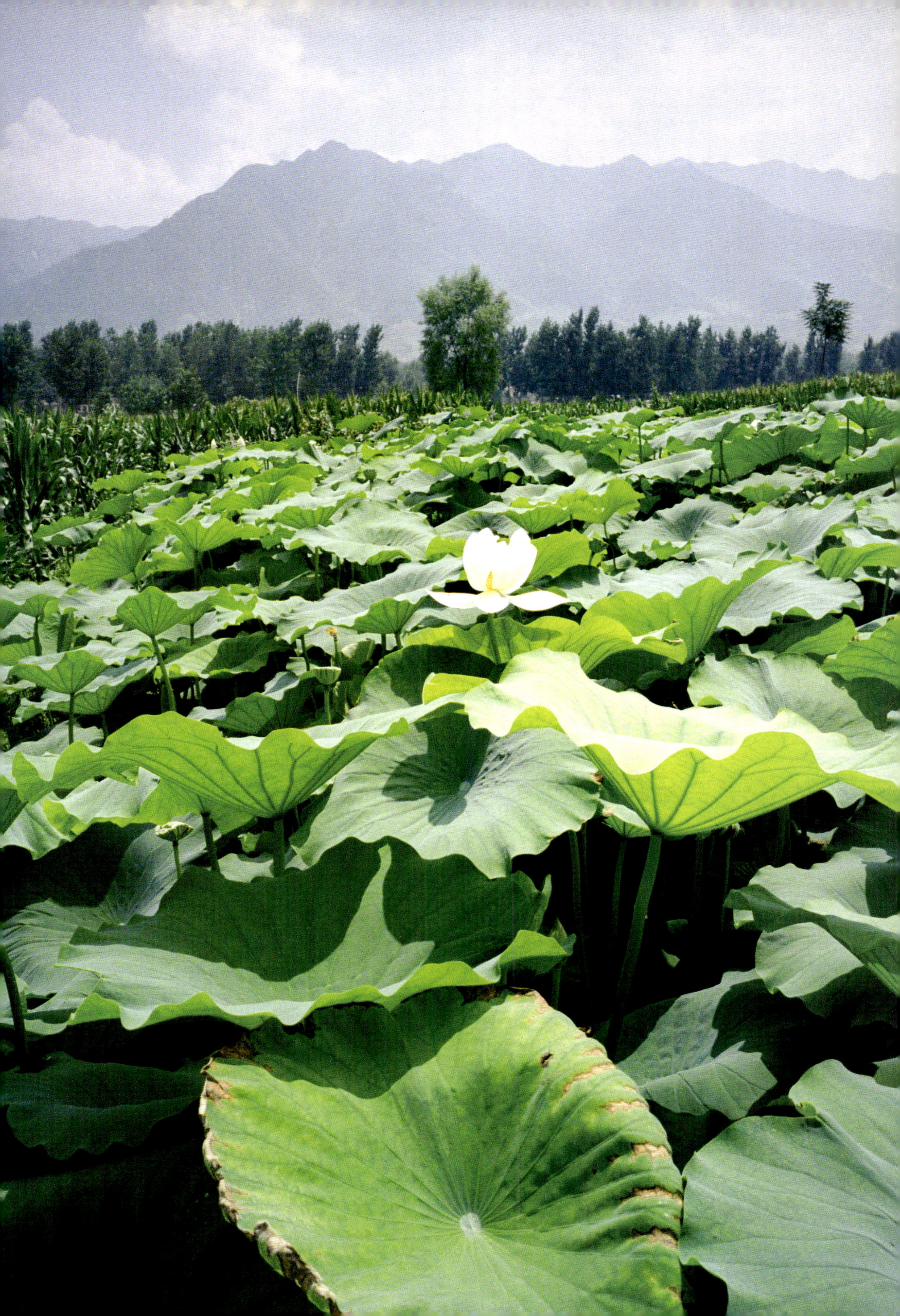

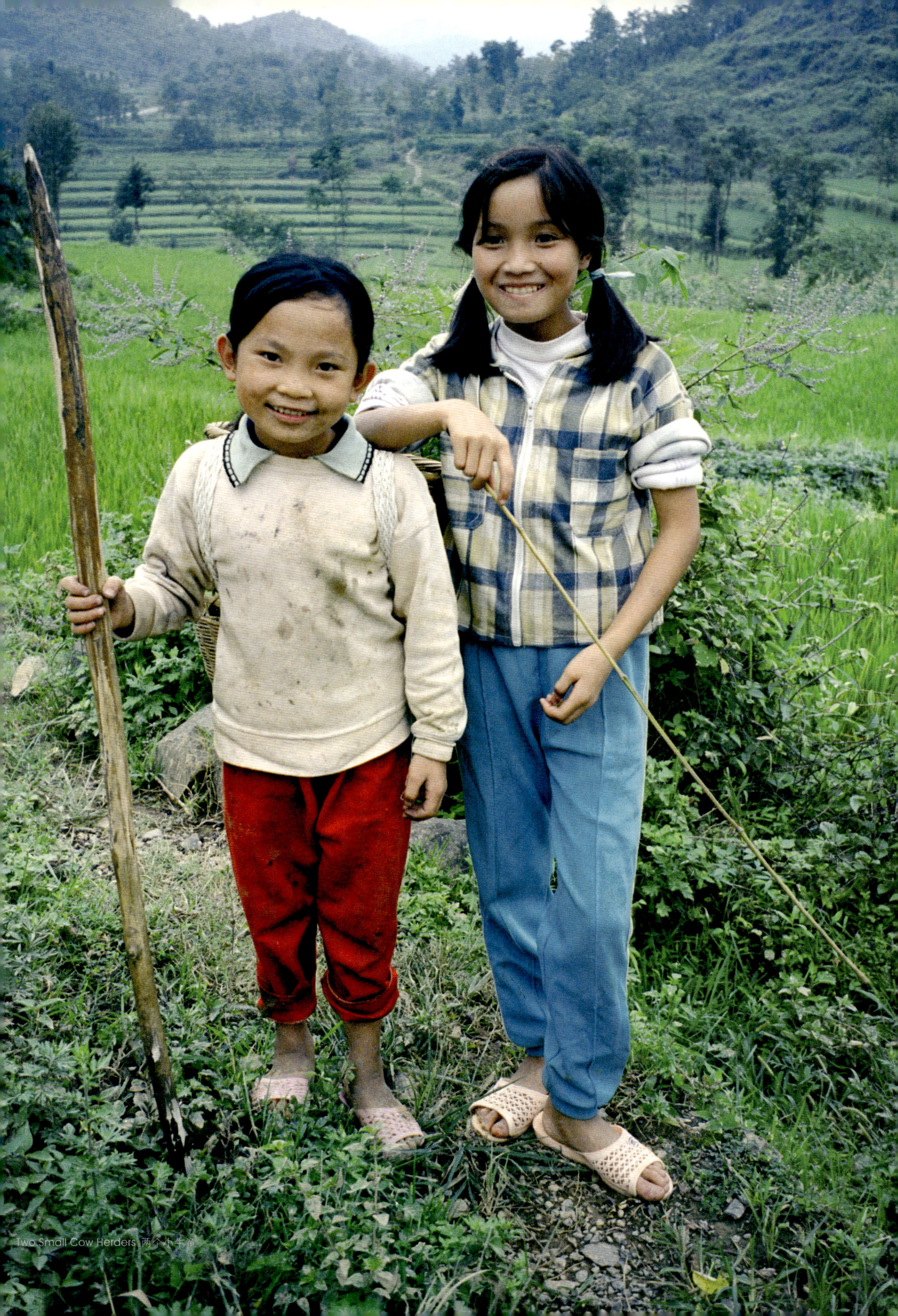

Two Small Cow Herders 两个小牛倌

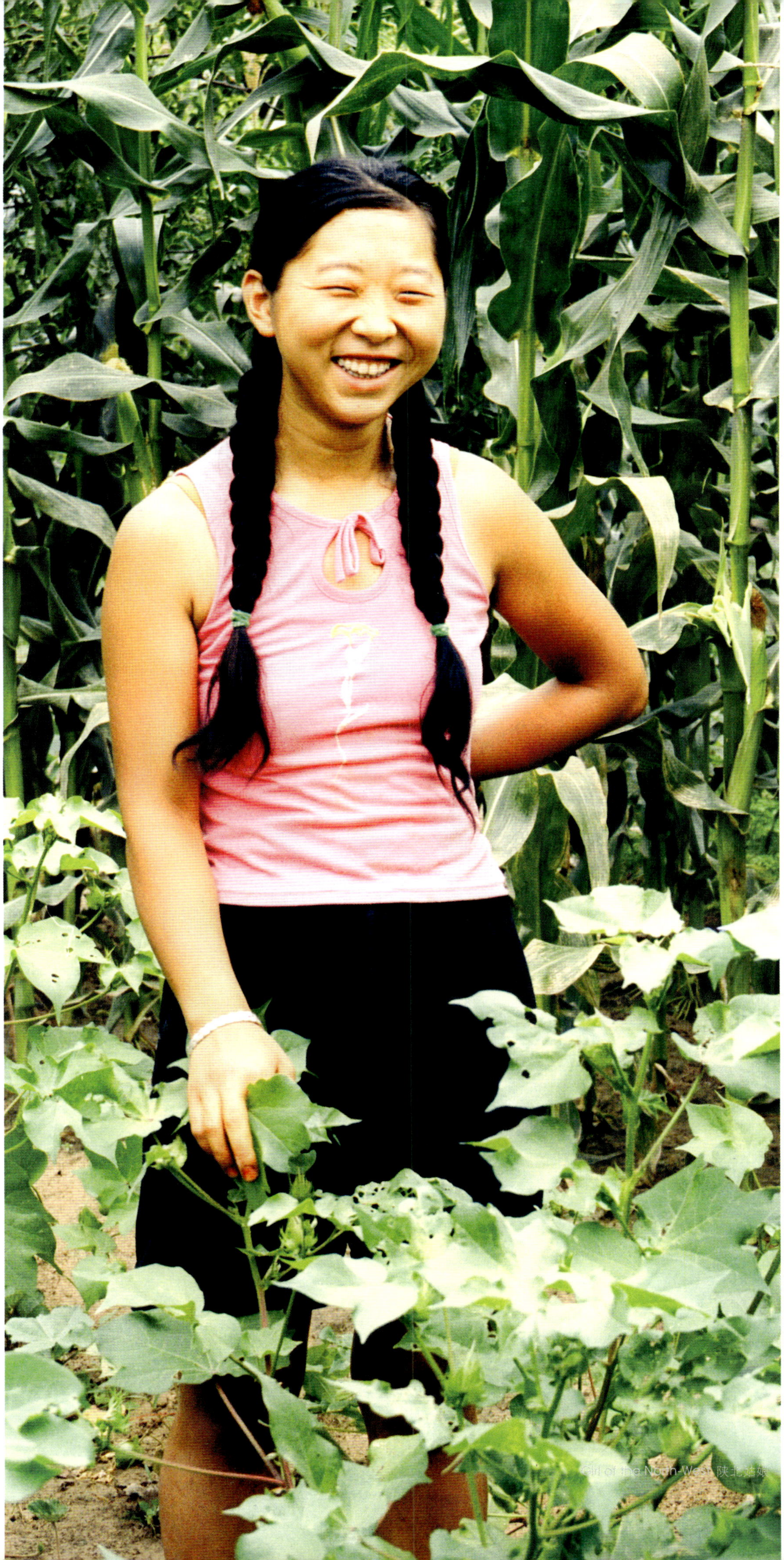
Girl of the North-West　陕北姑娘

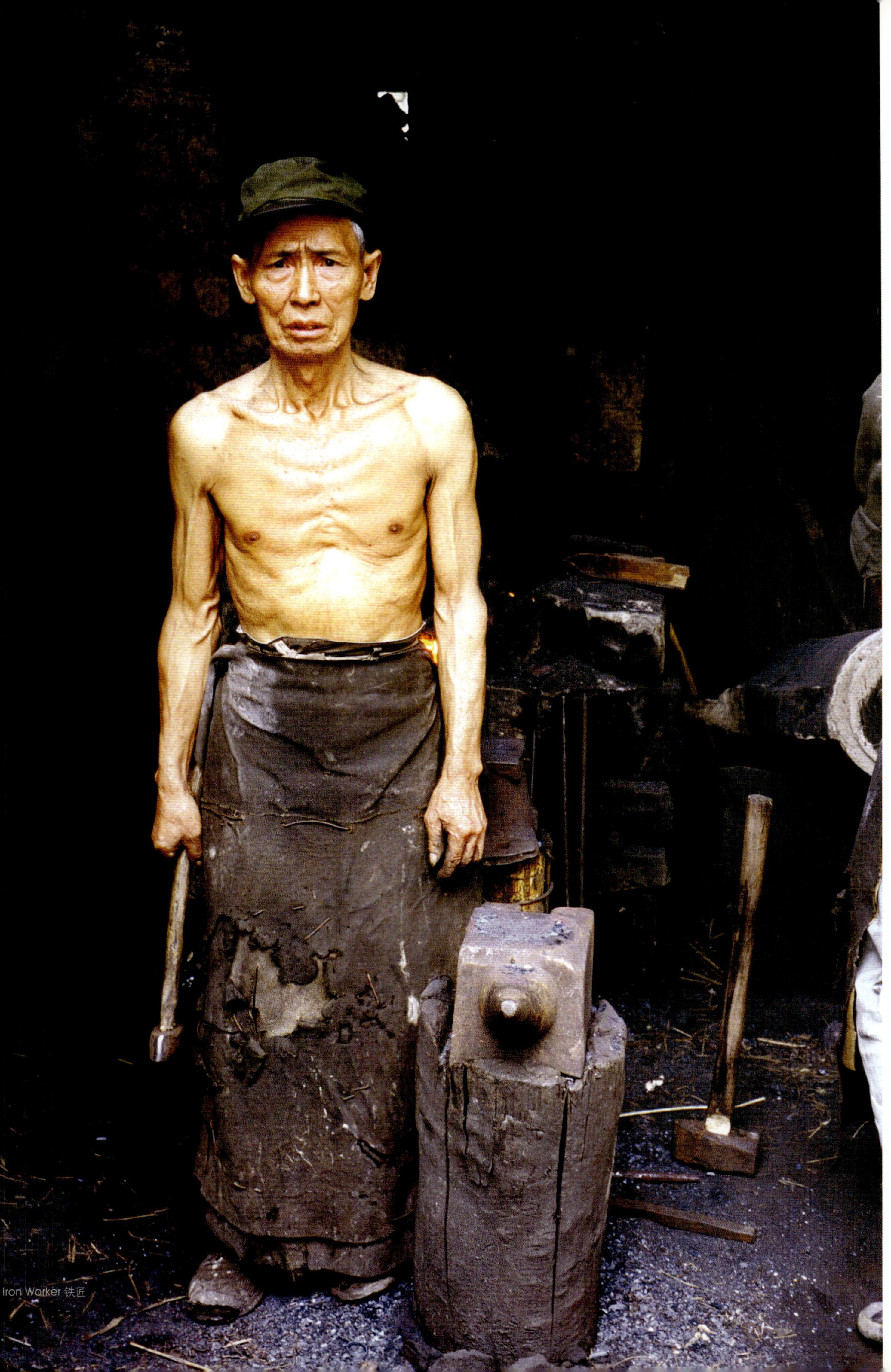

Iron Worker 铁匠

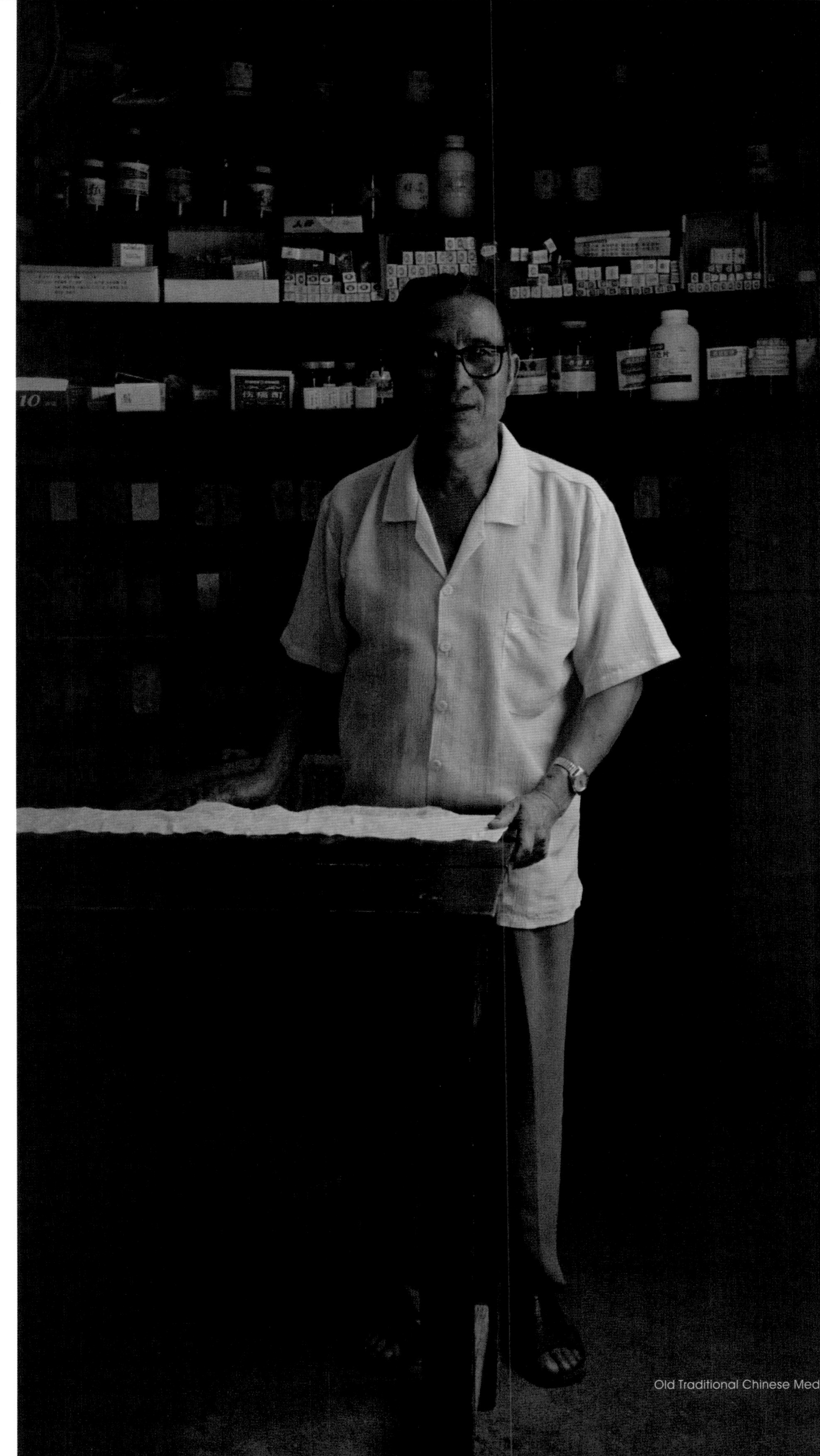
Old Traditional Chinese Med

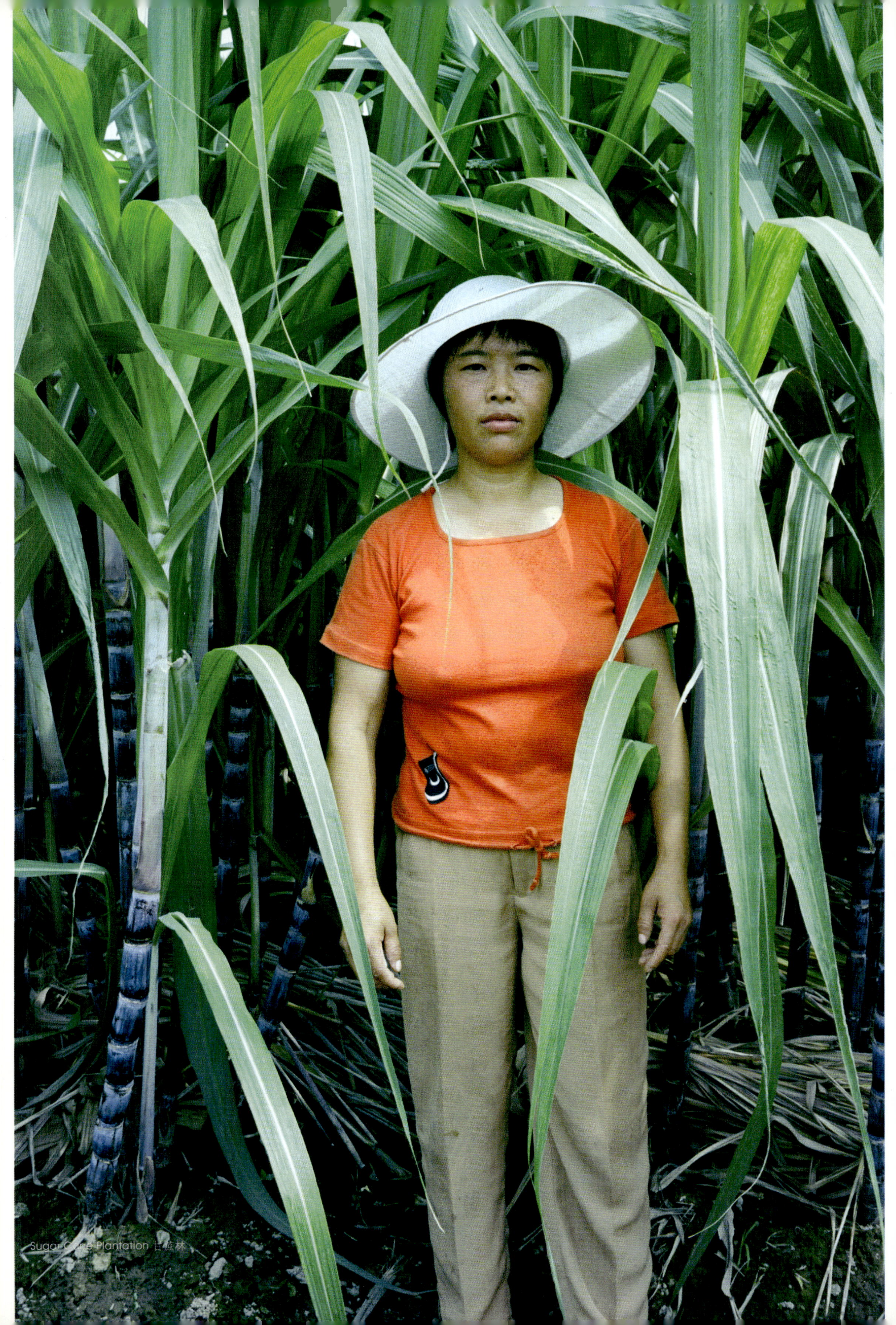

Sugar Cane Plantation 甘蔗林

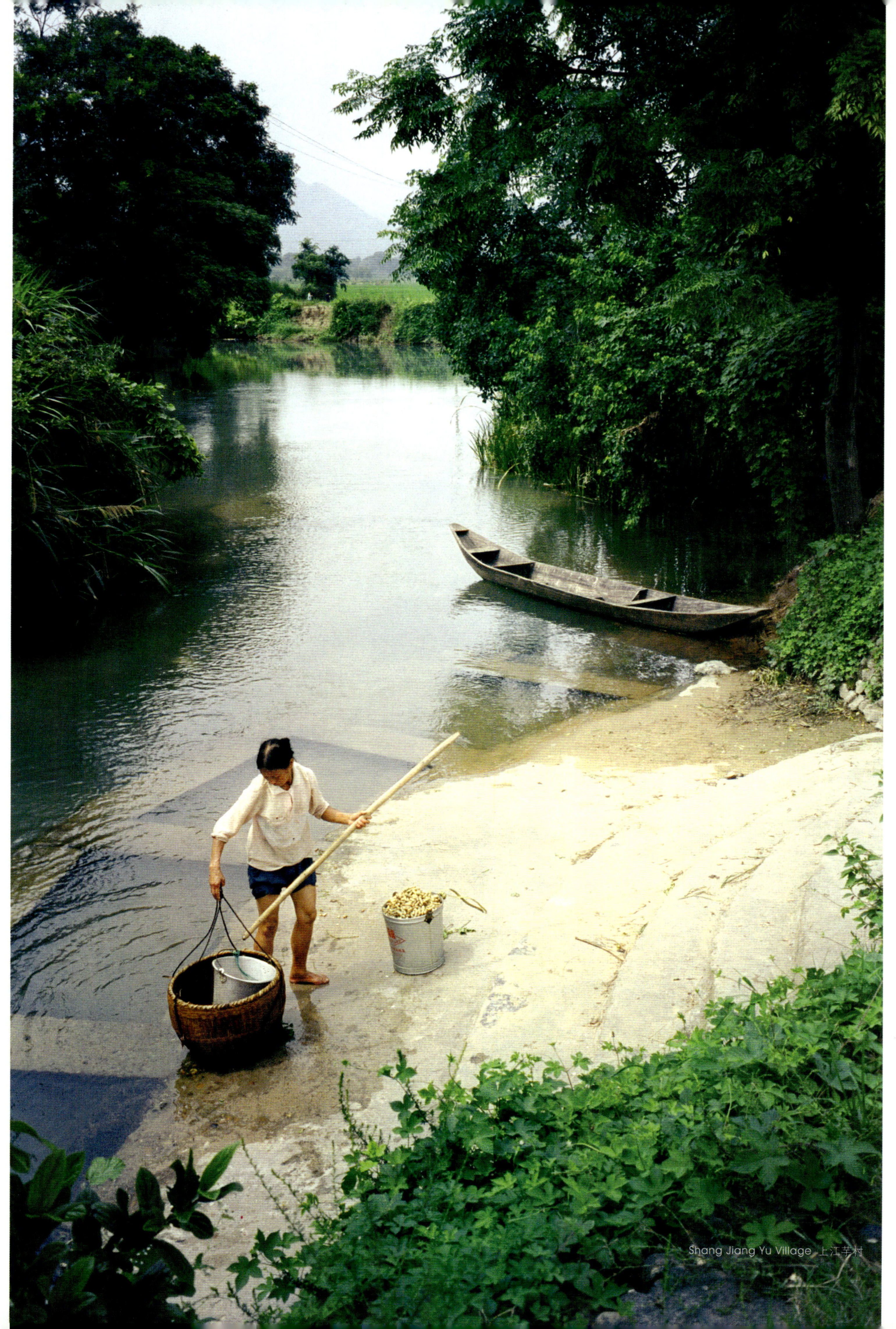
Shang Jiang Yu Village 上江芋村

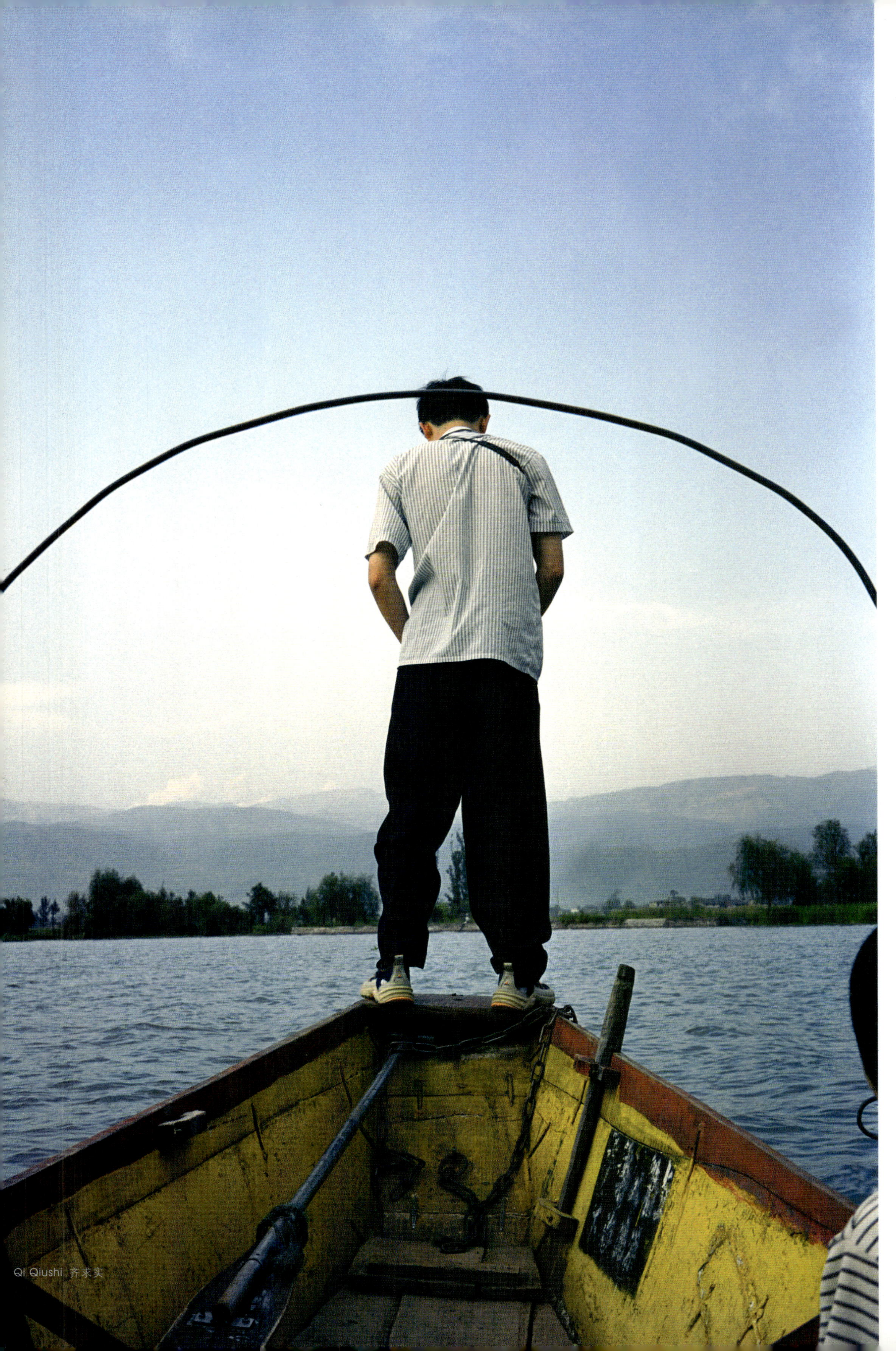
Qi Qiushi 齐来实

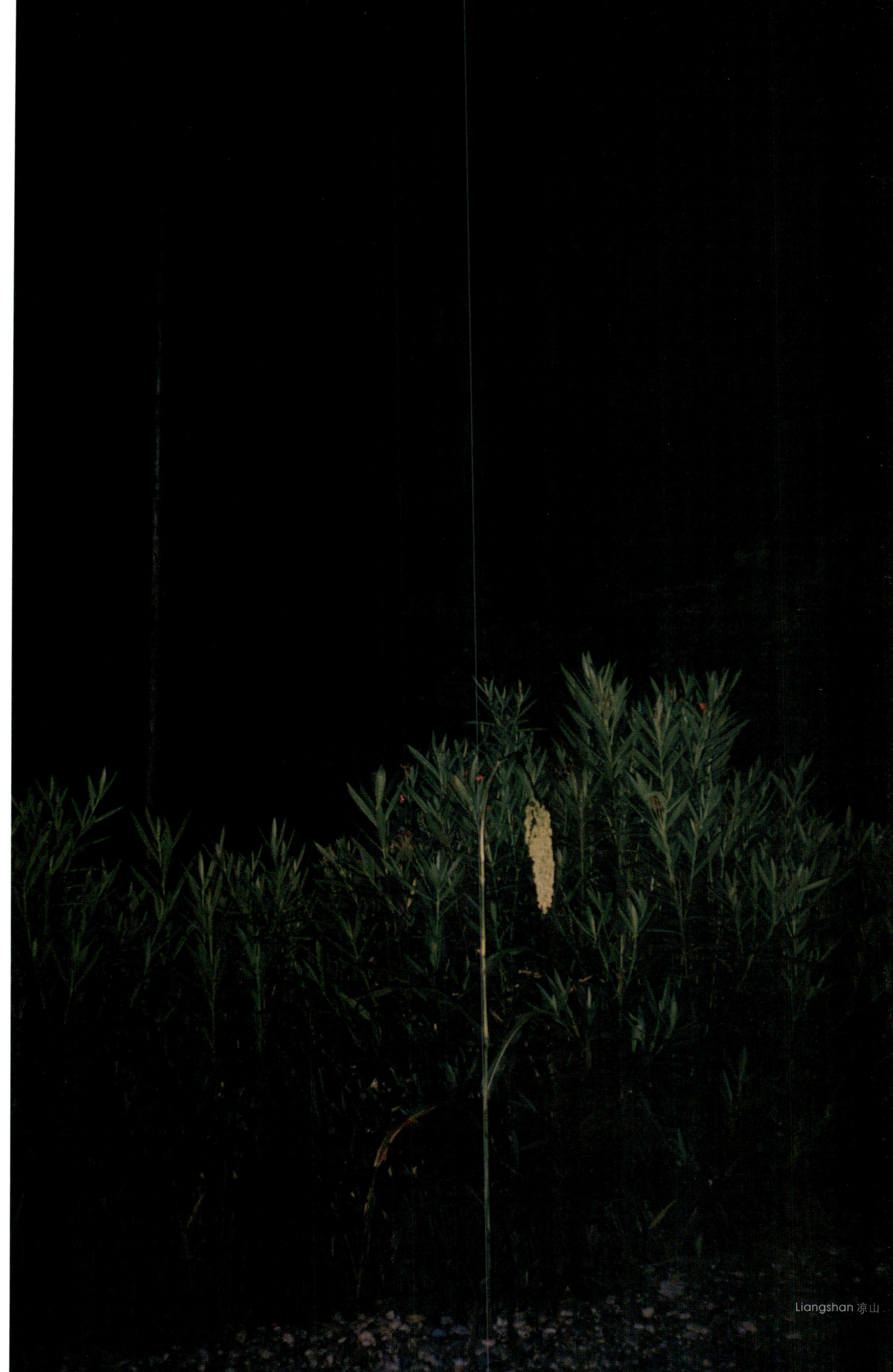
Liangshan 凉山

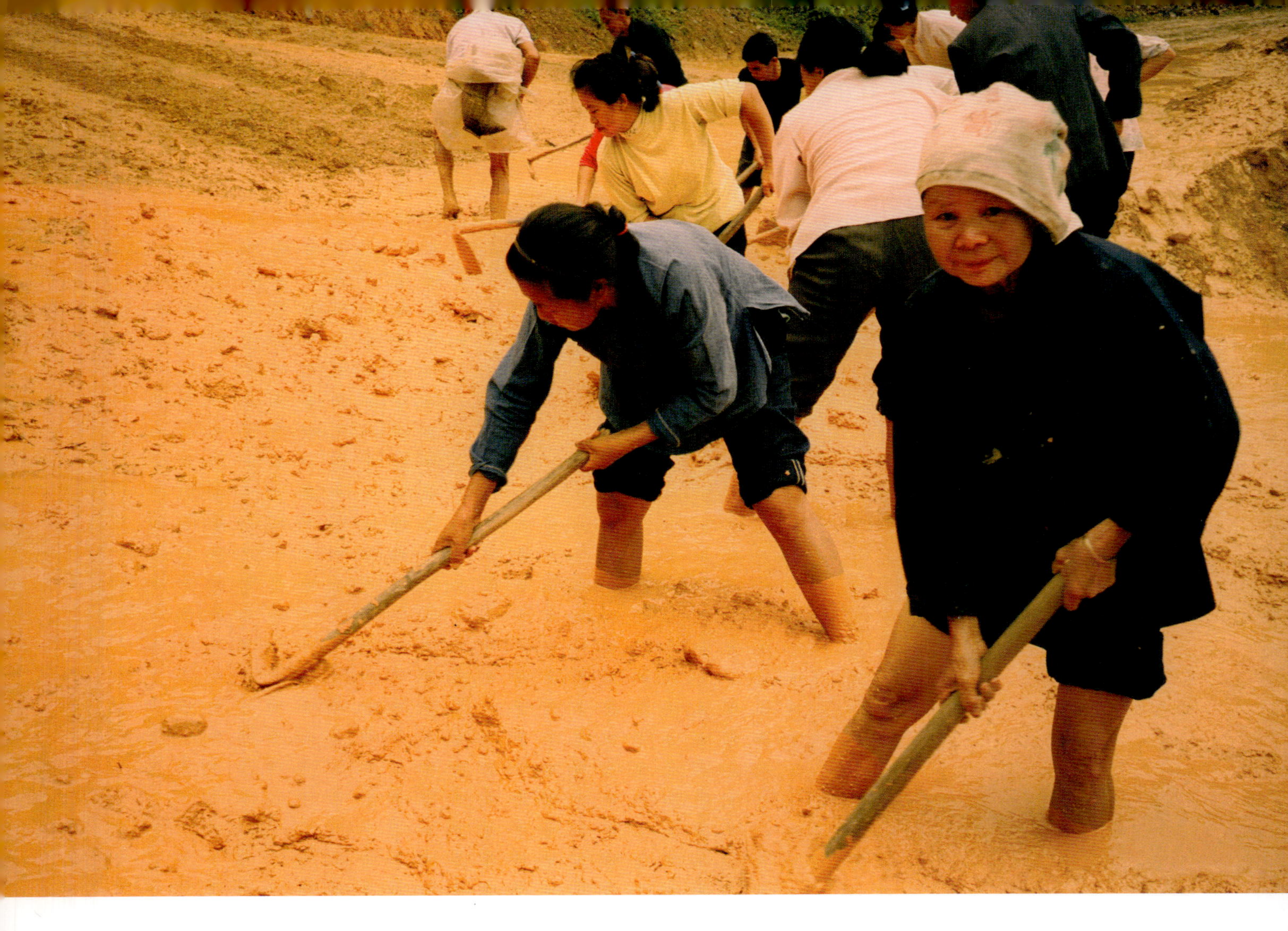

Emergency Road Repair 抢修公路

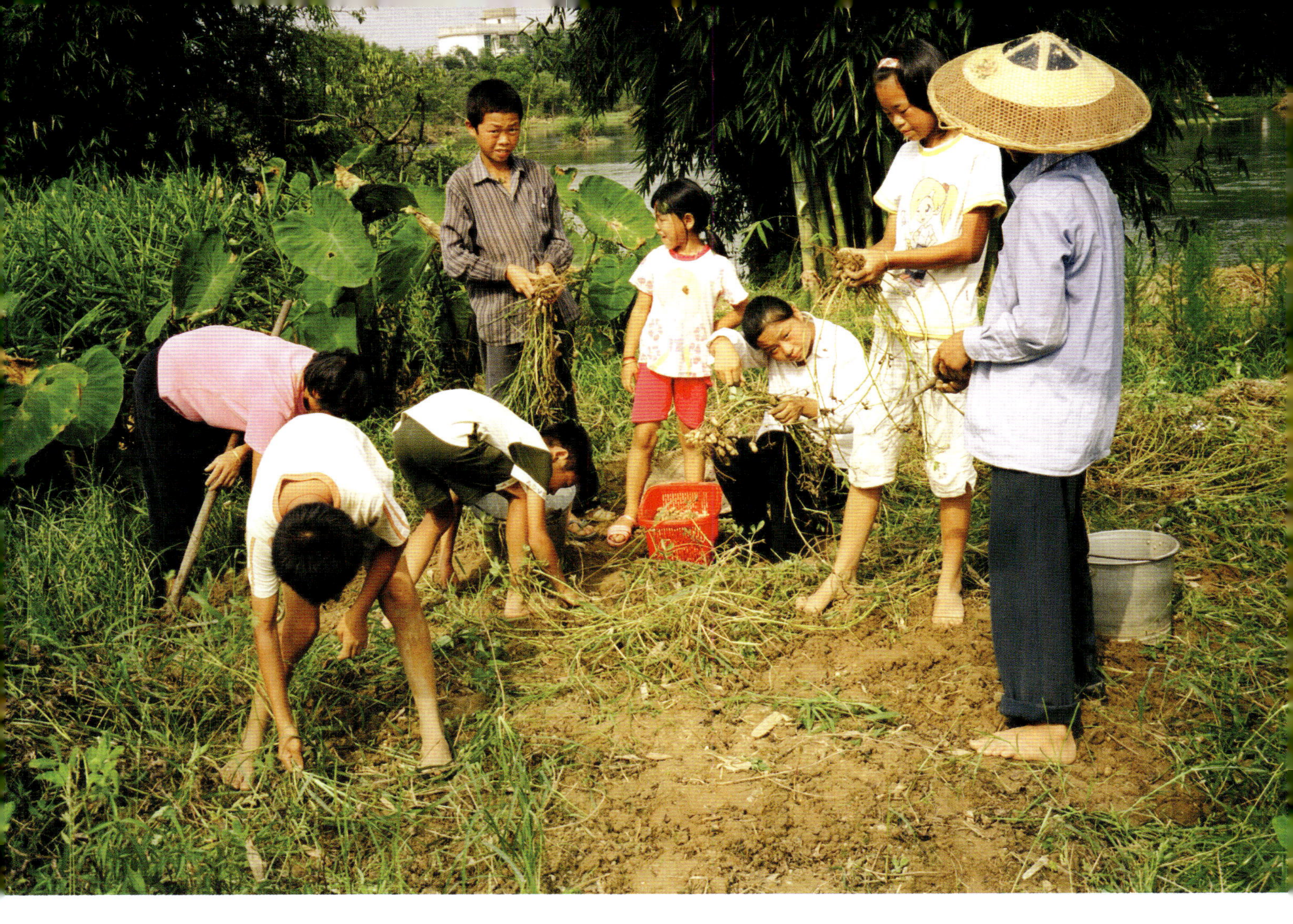

Peanut Harvest 收花生

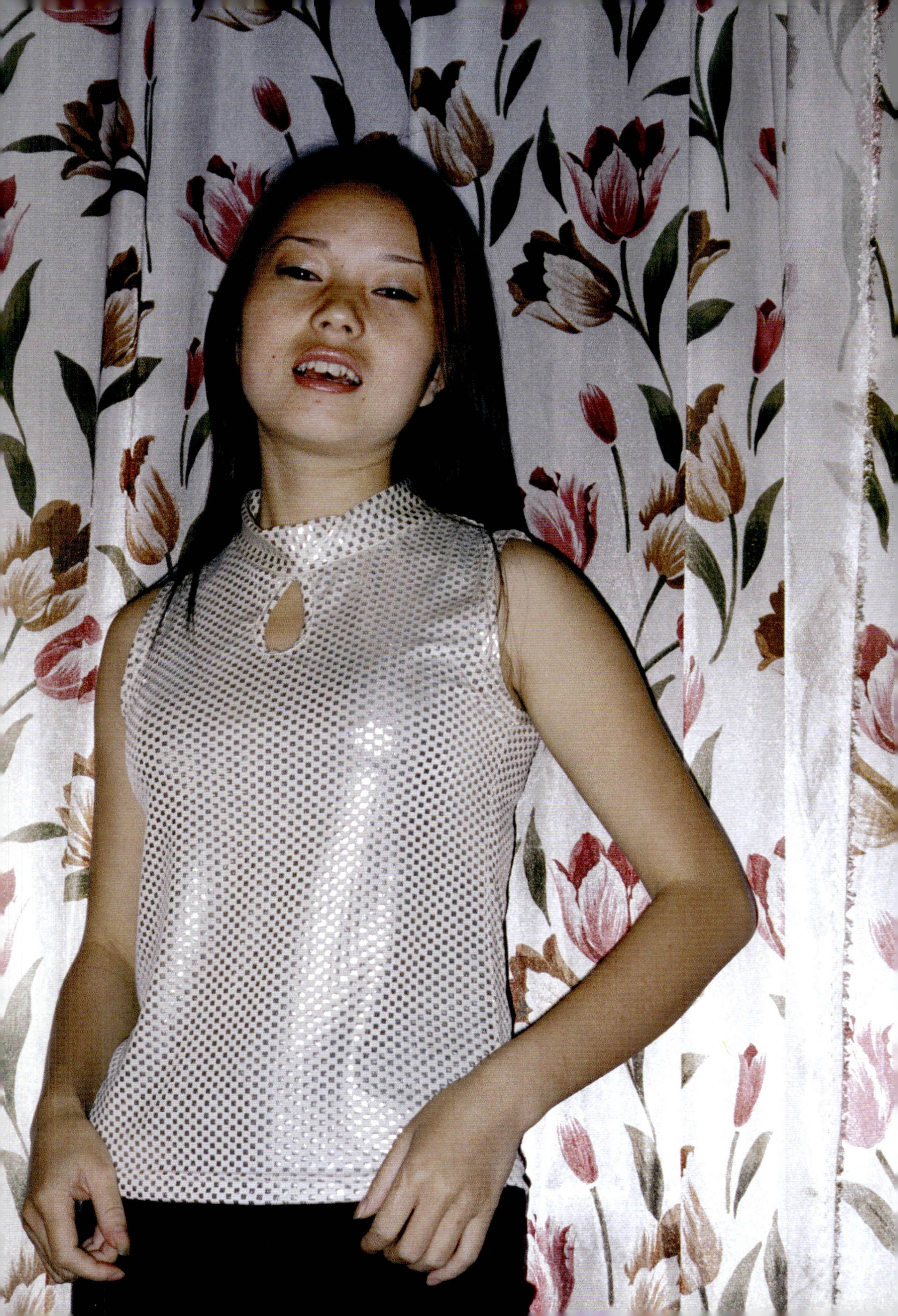

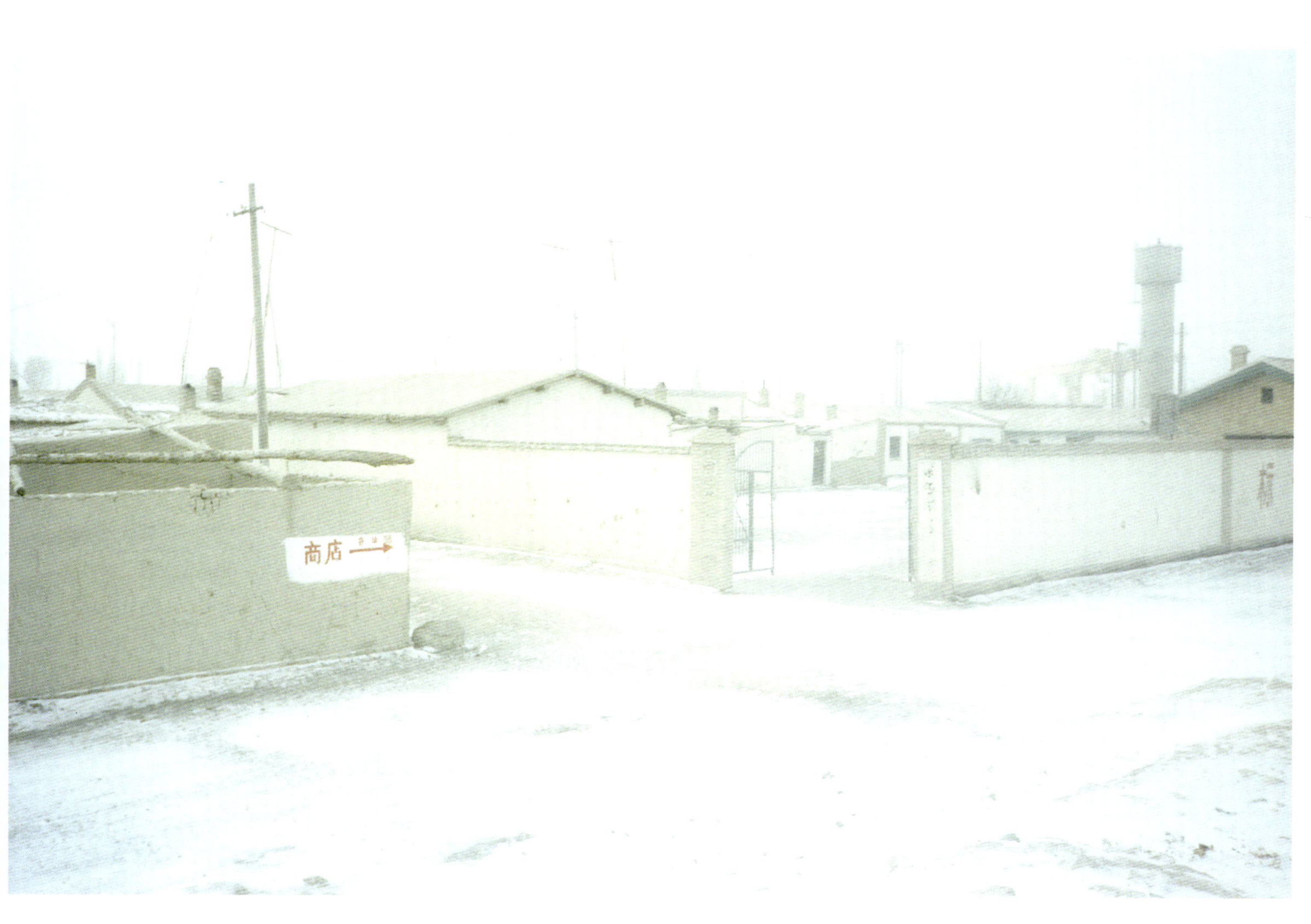

Girl from Fenghuang District 凤凰县的姑娘

Hometown 家乡

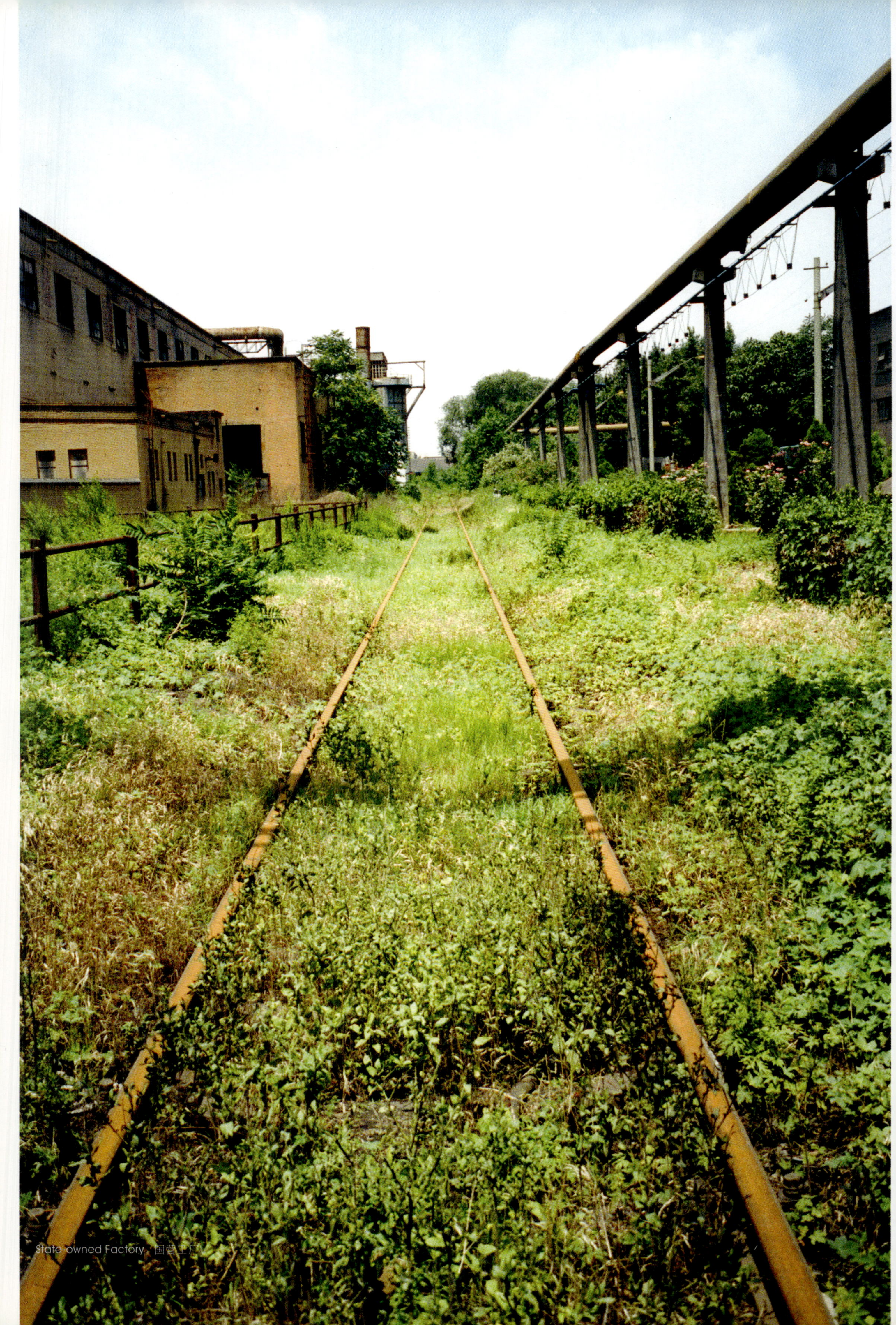

State-owned Factory　国营工厂

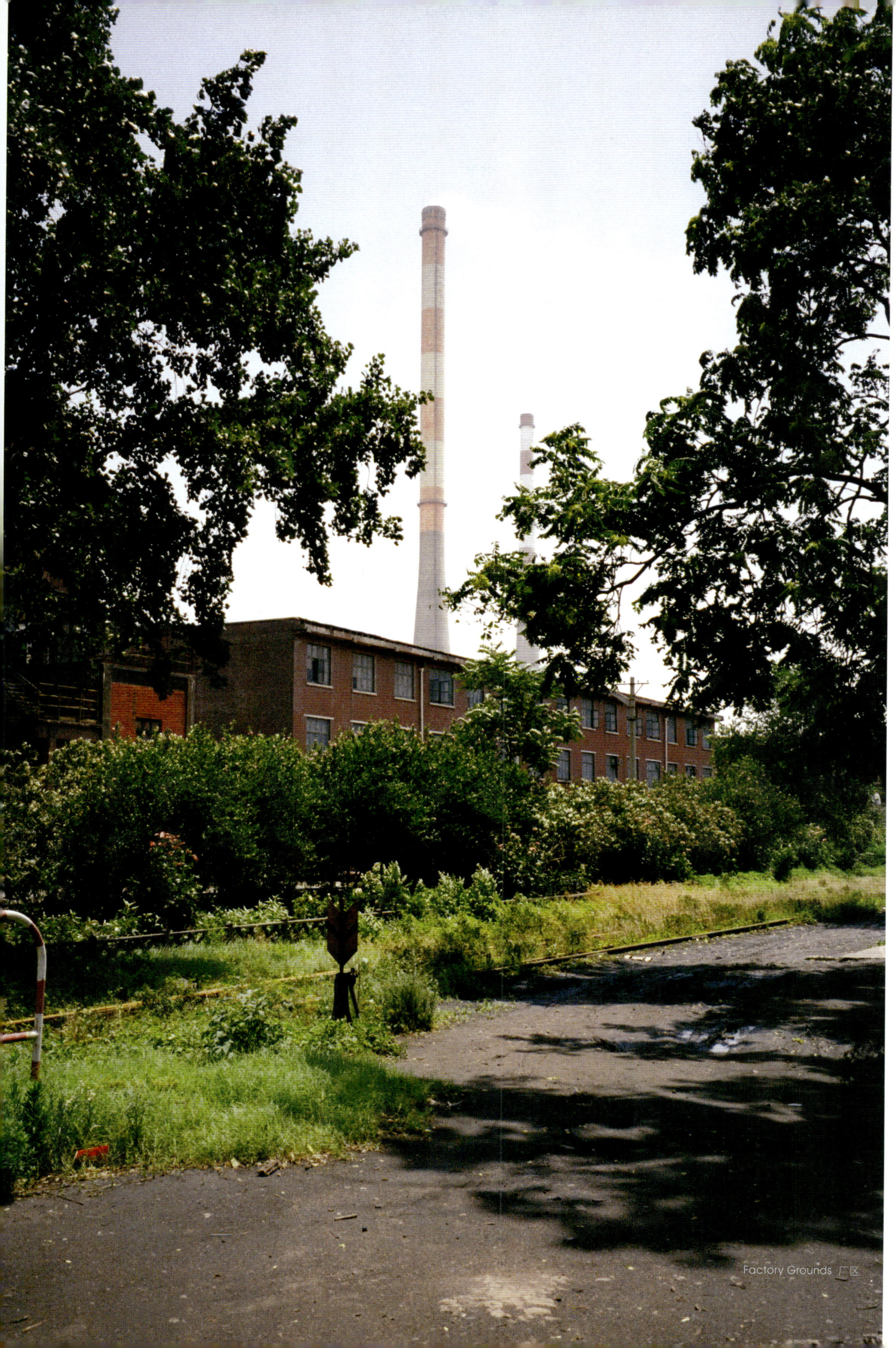

Factory Grounds 厂区

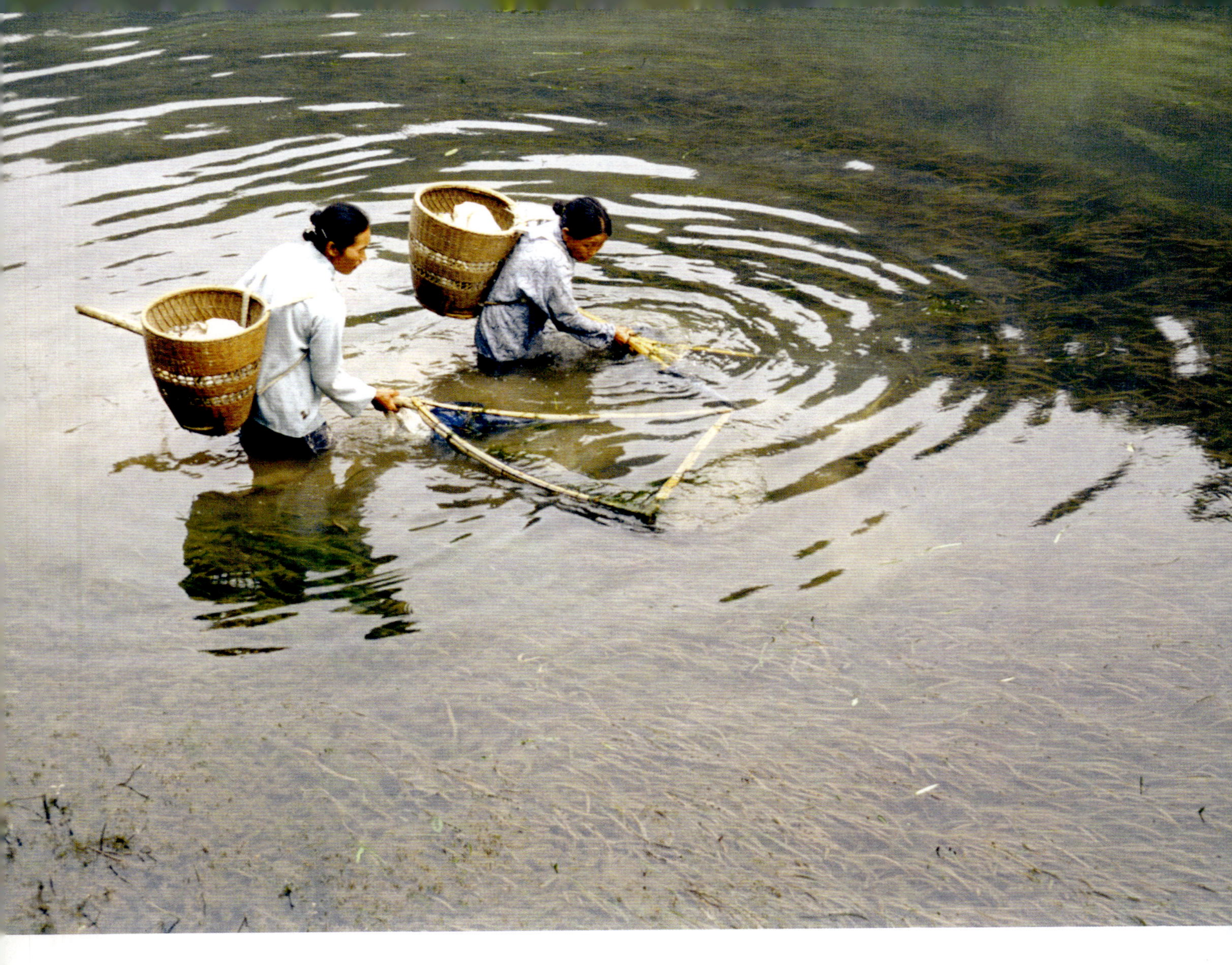

Shrimp Fishing 捞虾

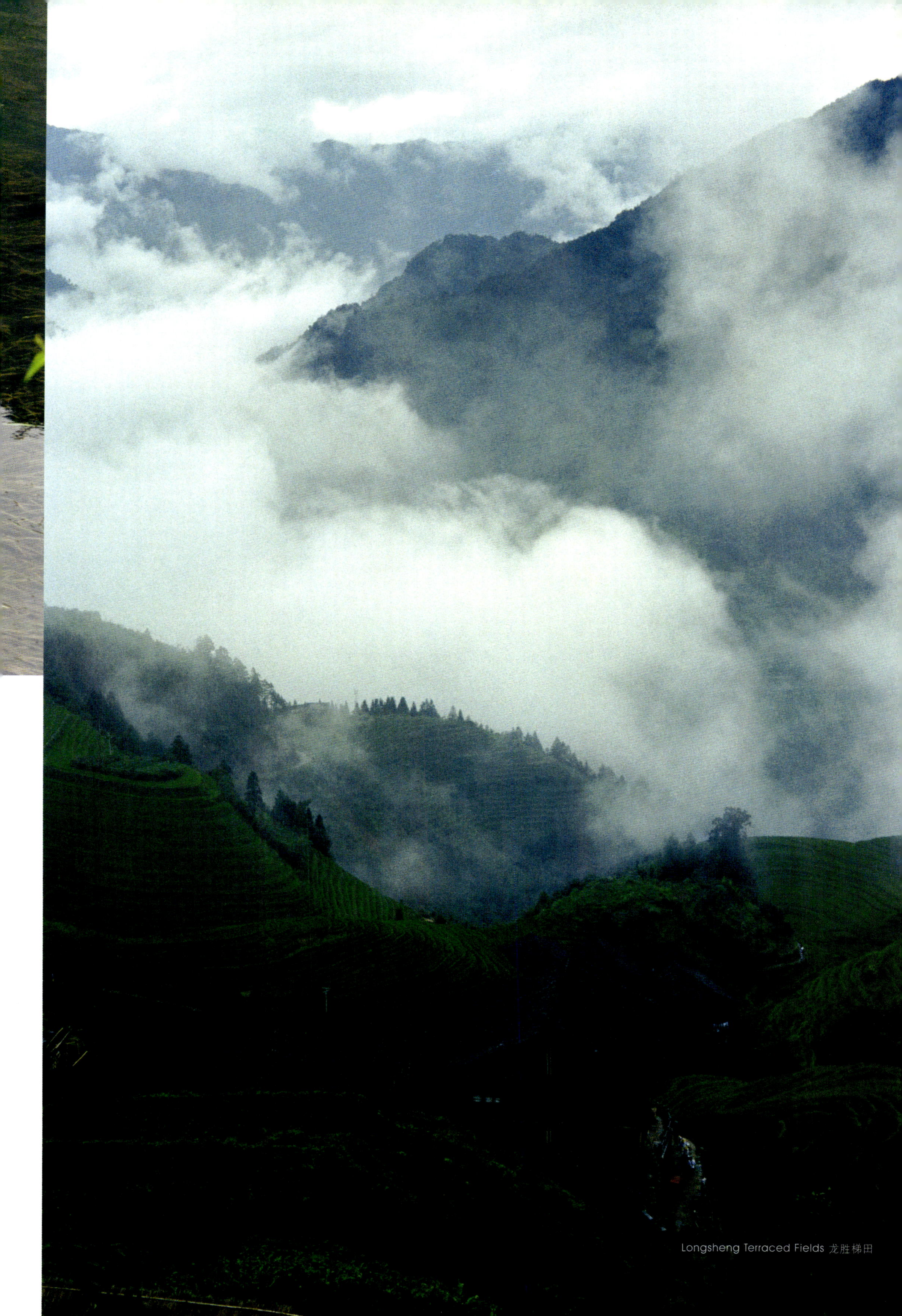

Longsheng Terraced Fields 龙胜梯田

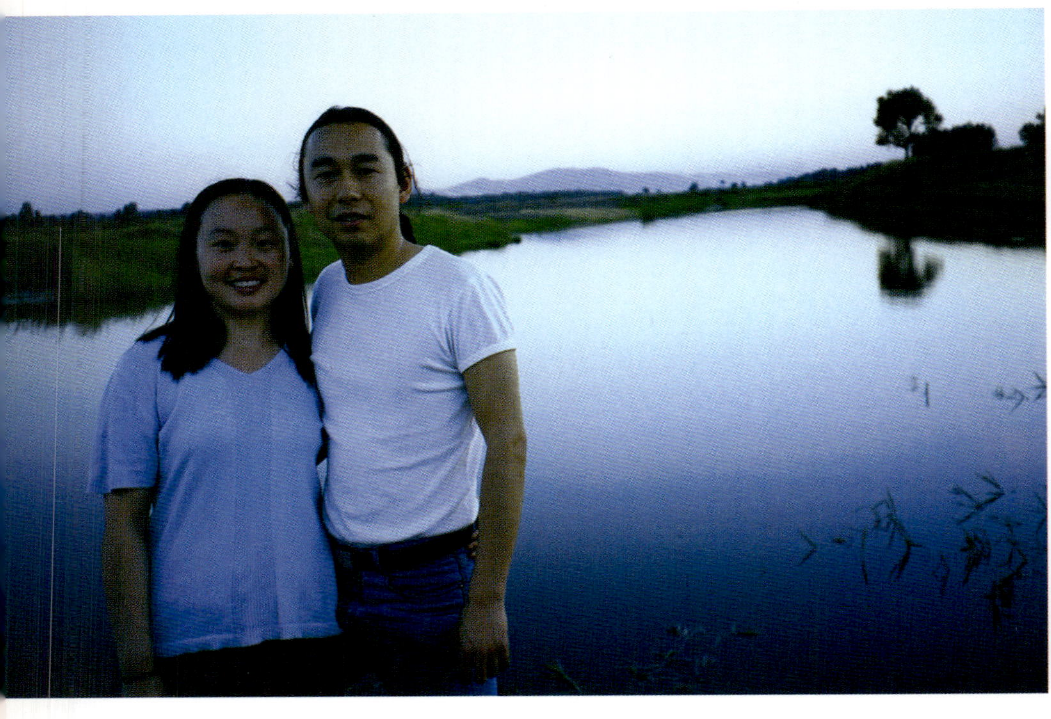 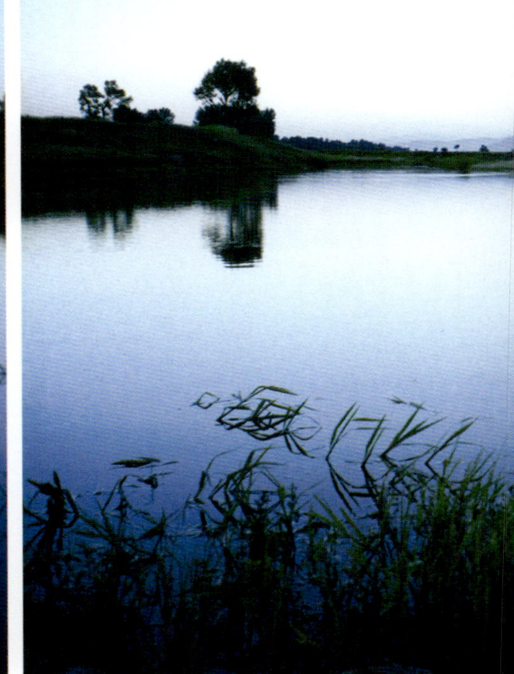

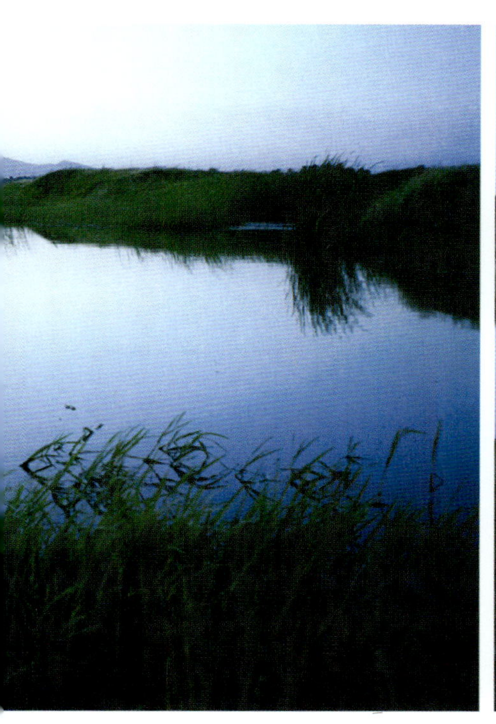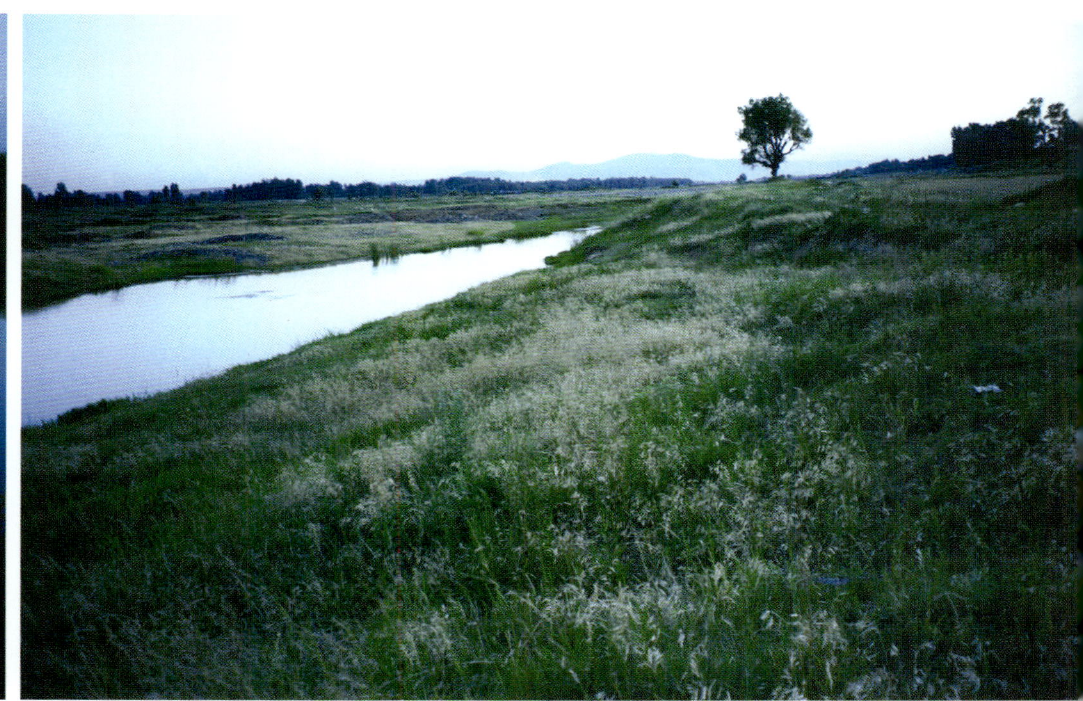

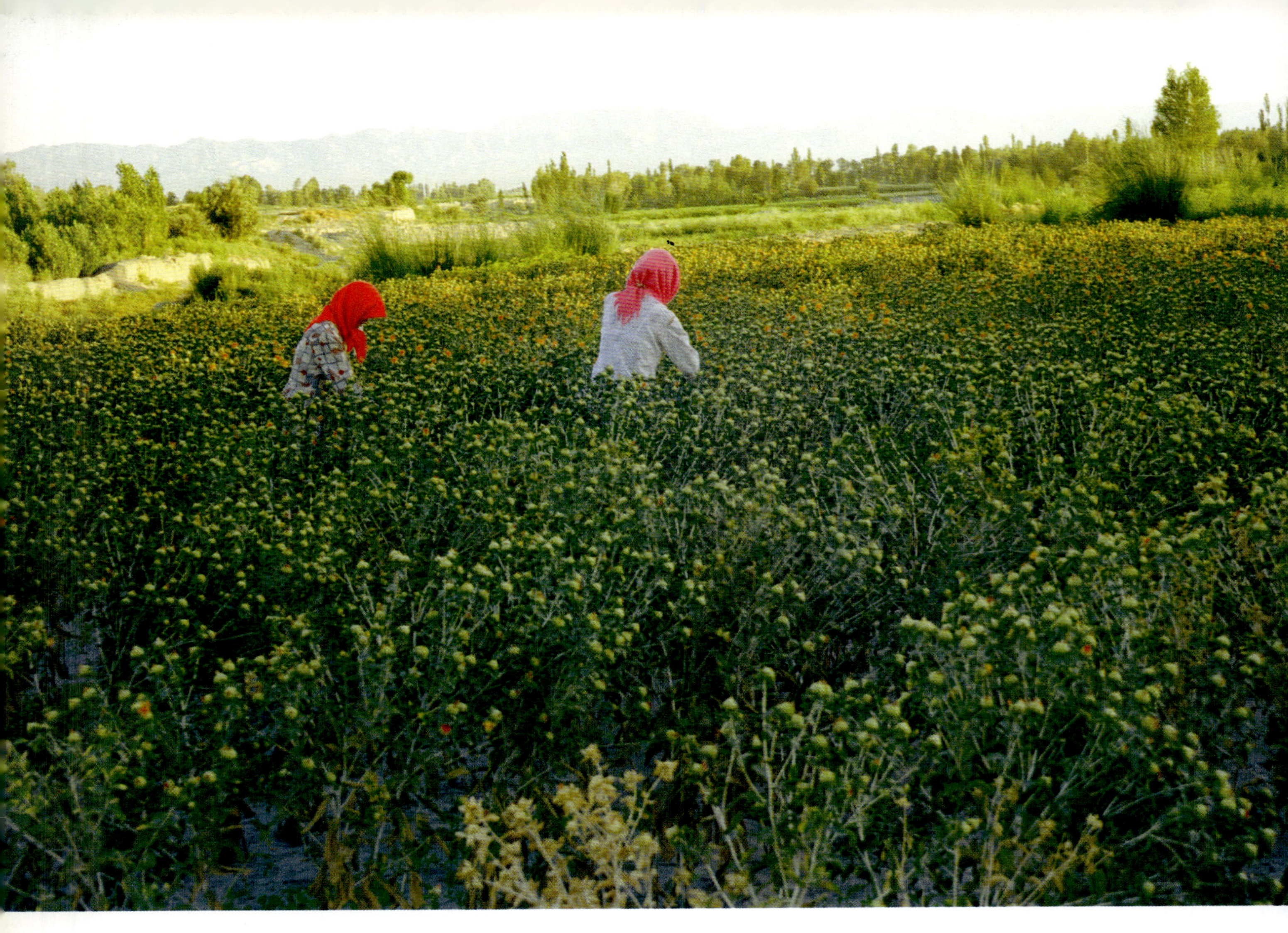

Gathering Flowers 摘花

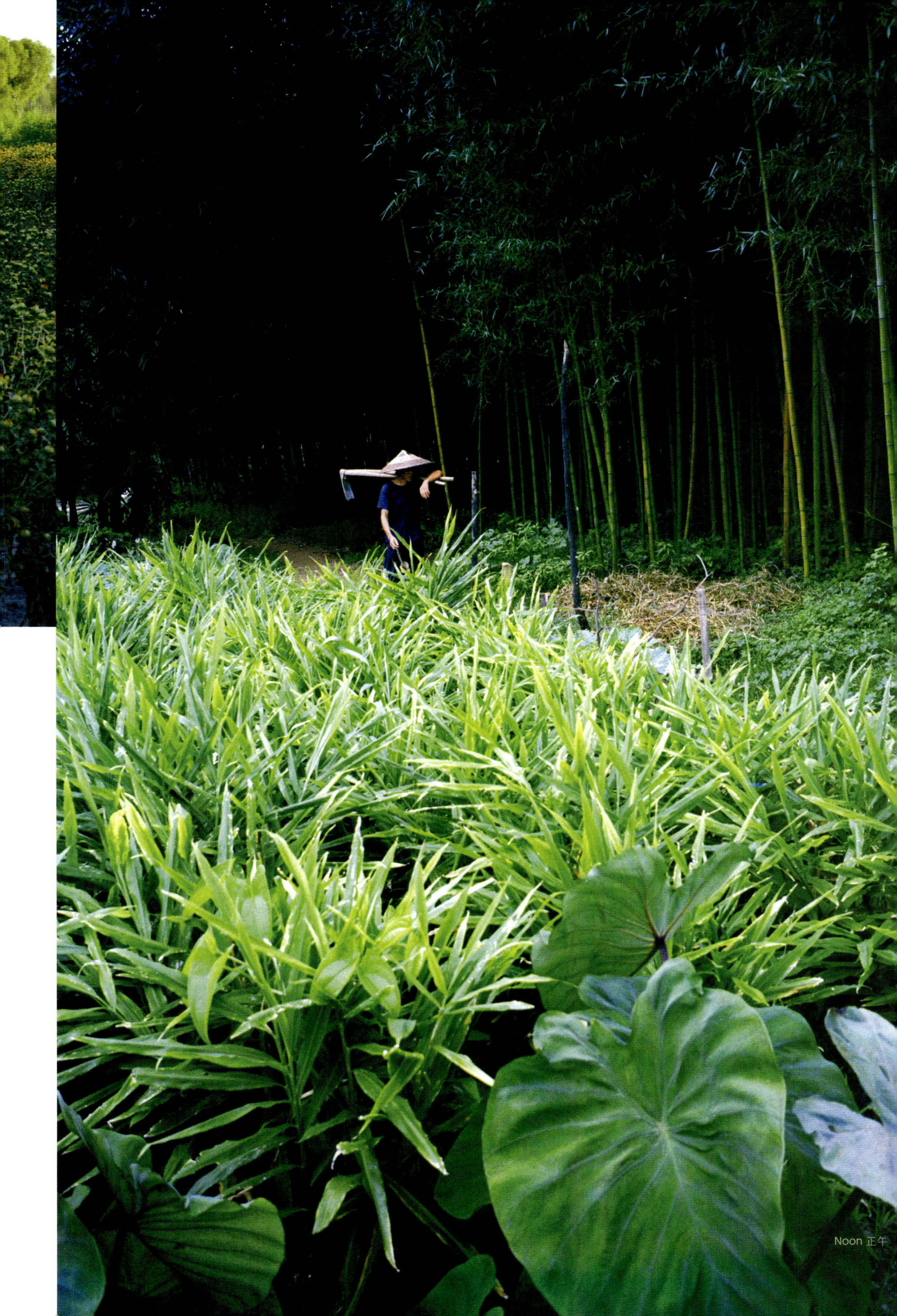
Noon 正午

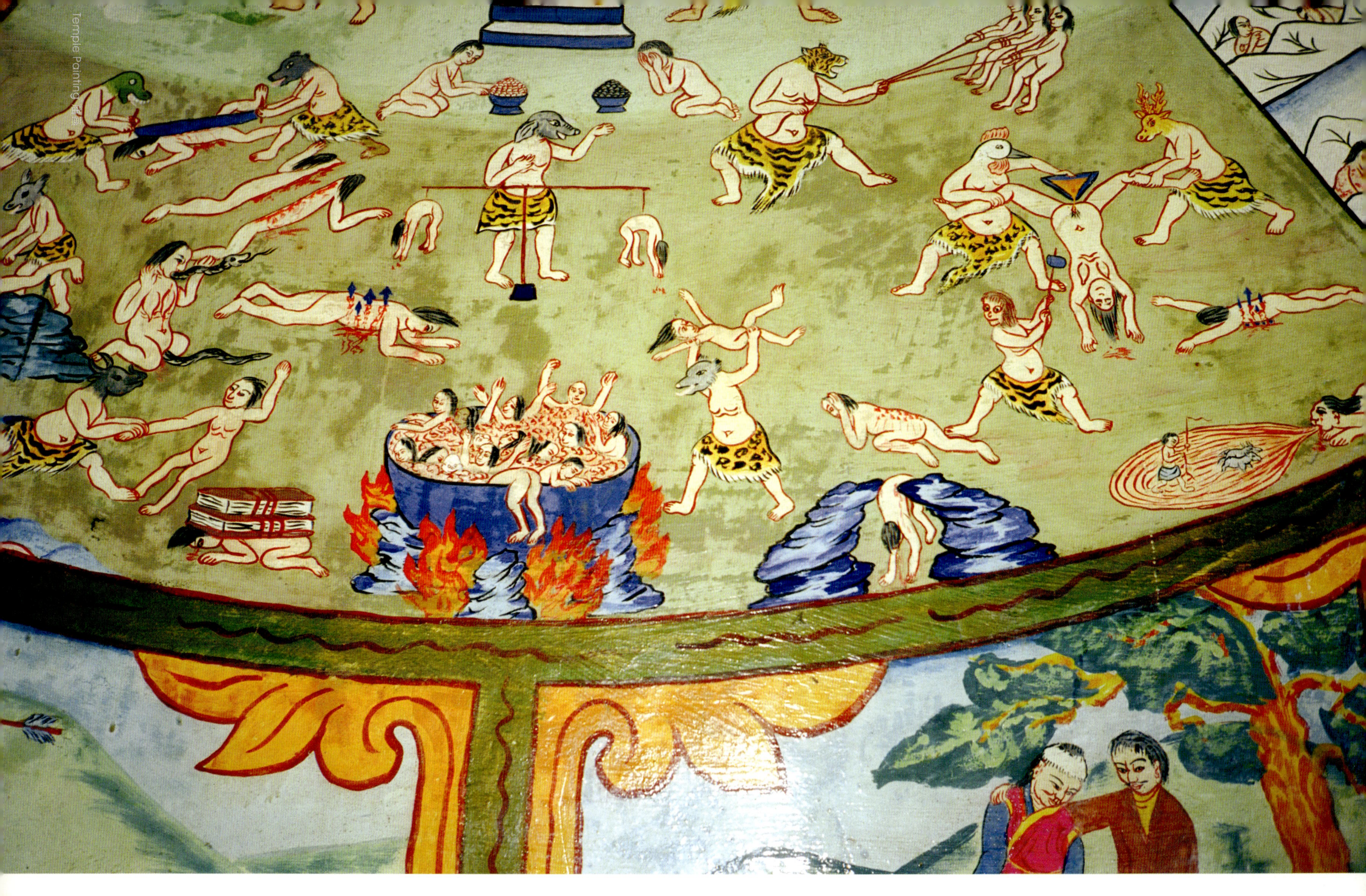
Temple Painting 壁畫

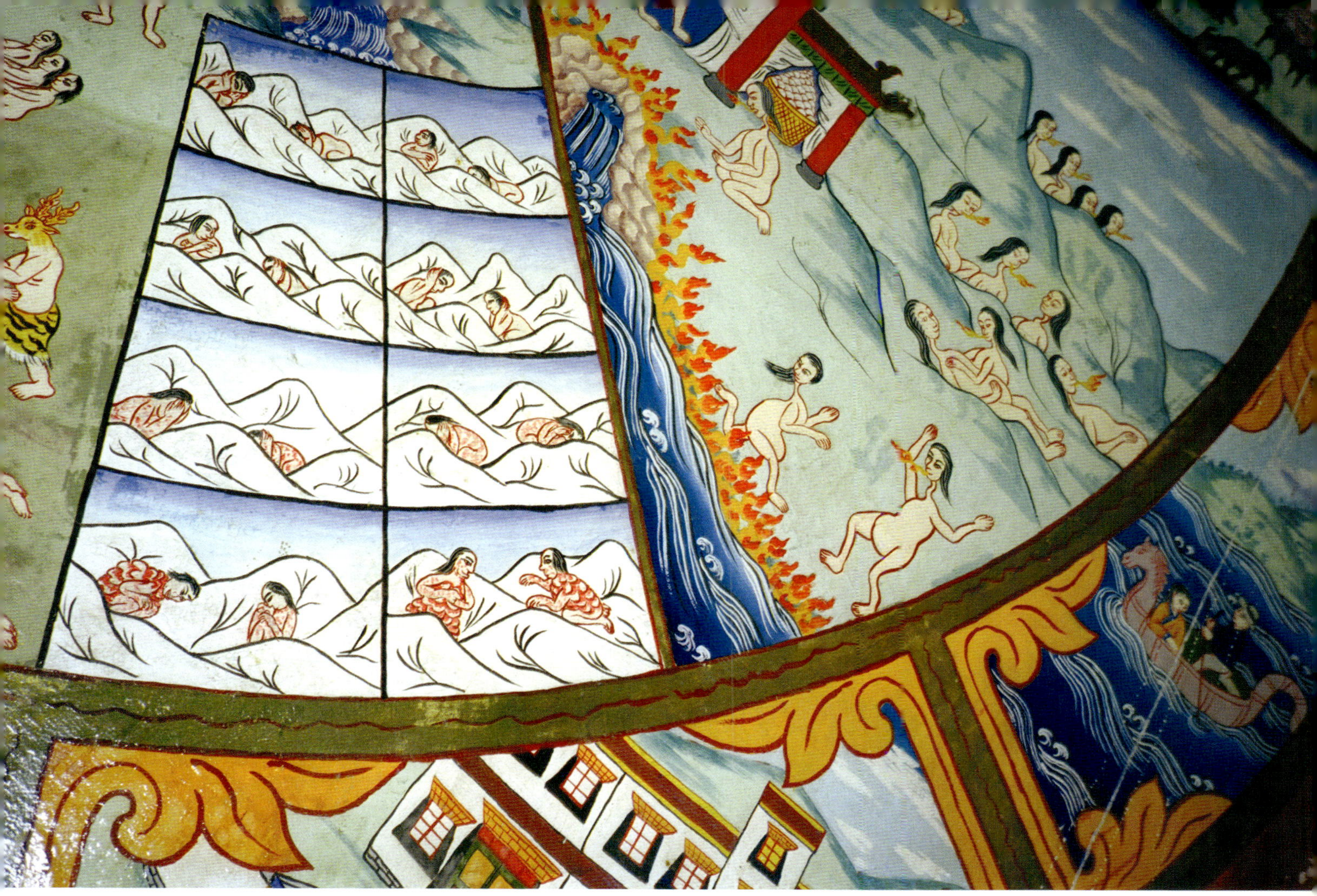

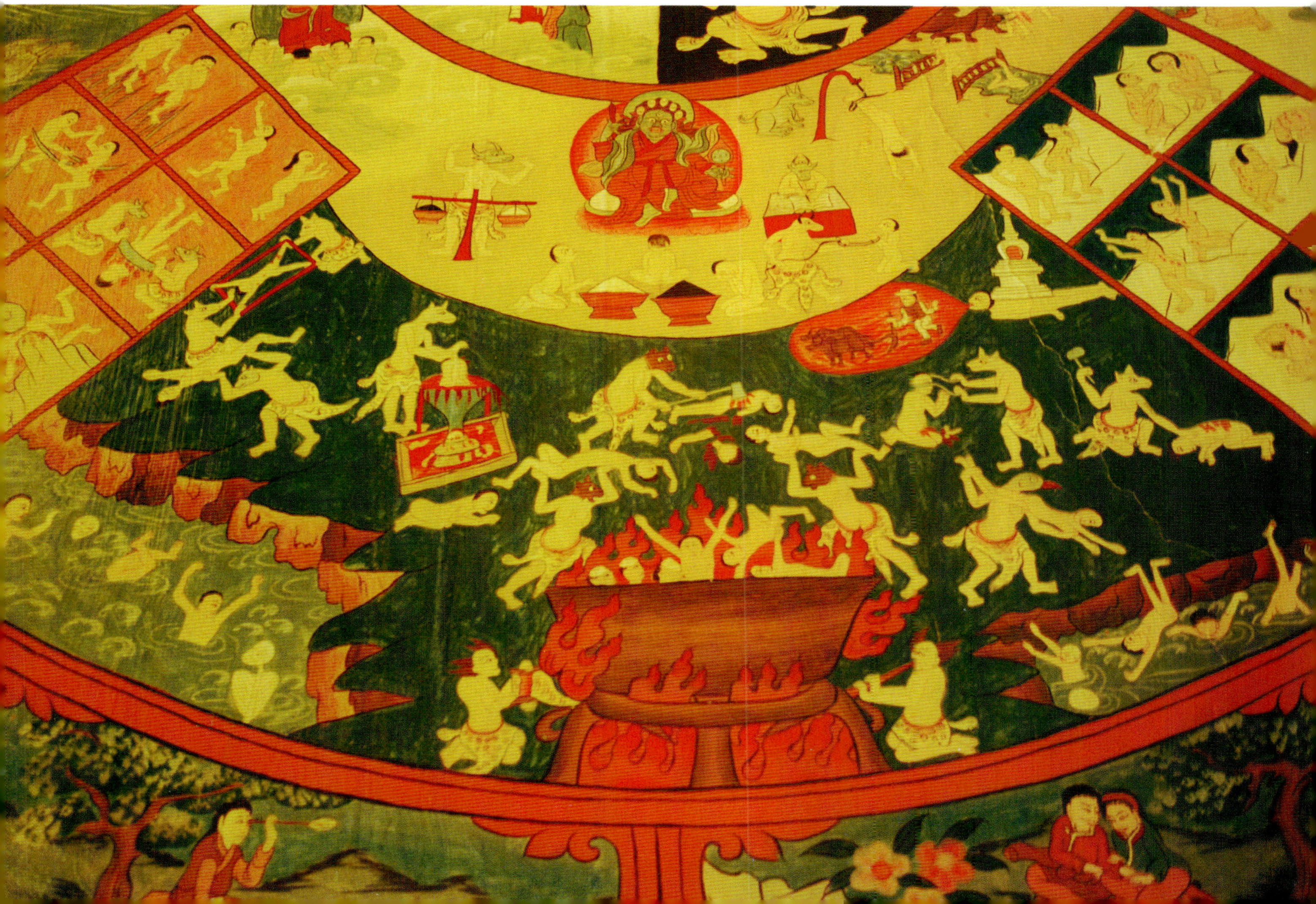

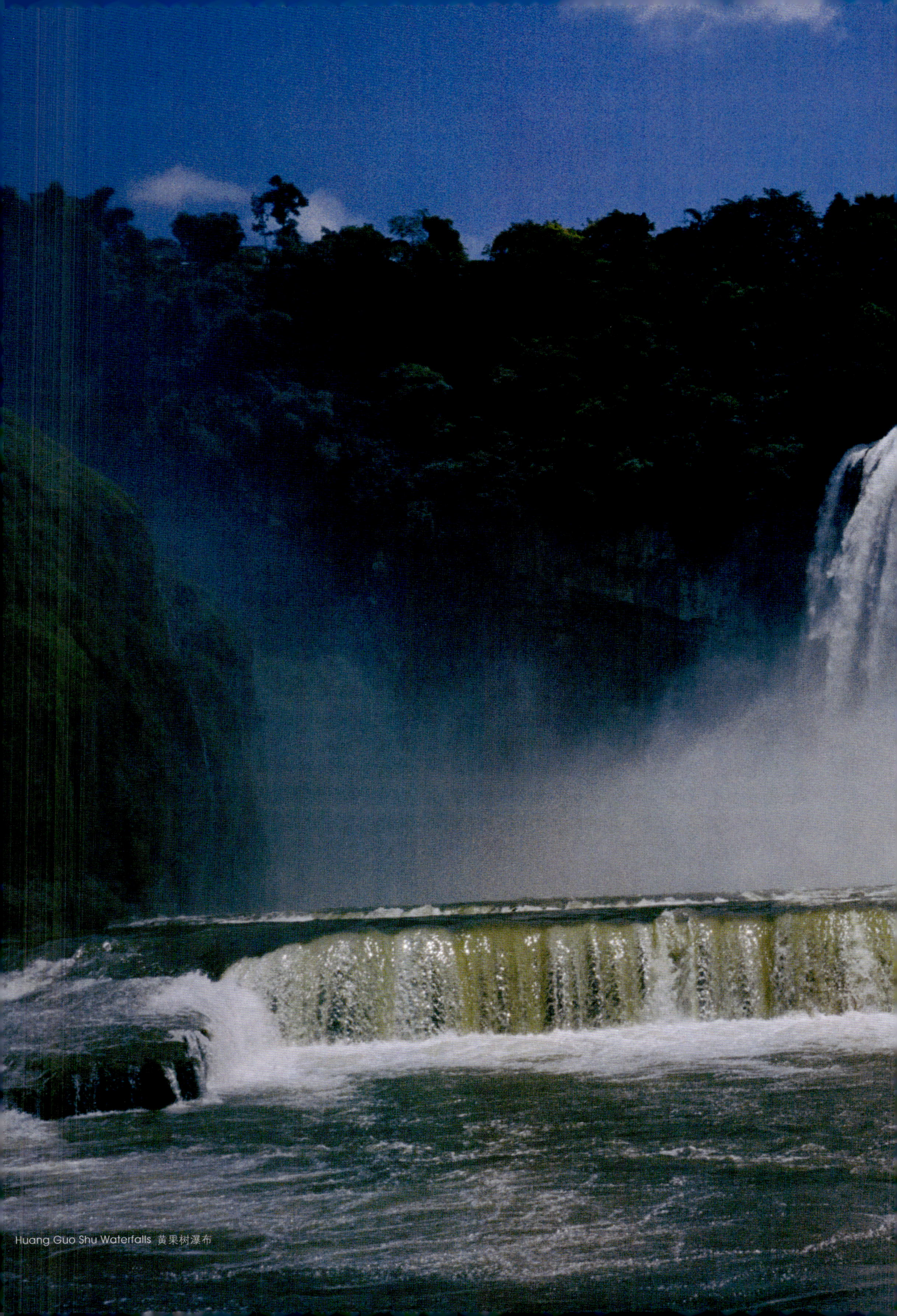

Huang Guo Shu Waterfalls 黄果树瀑布

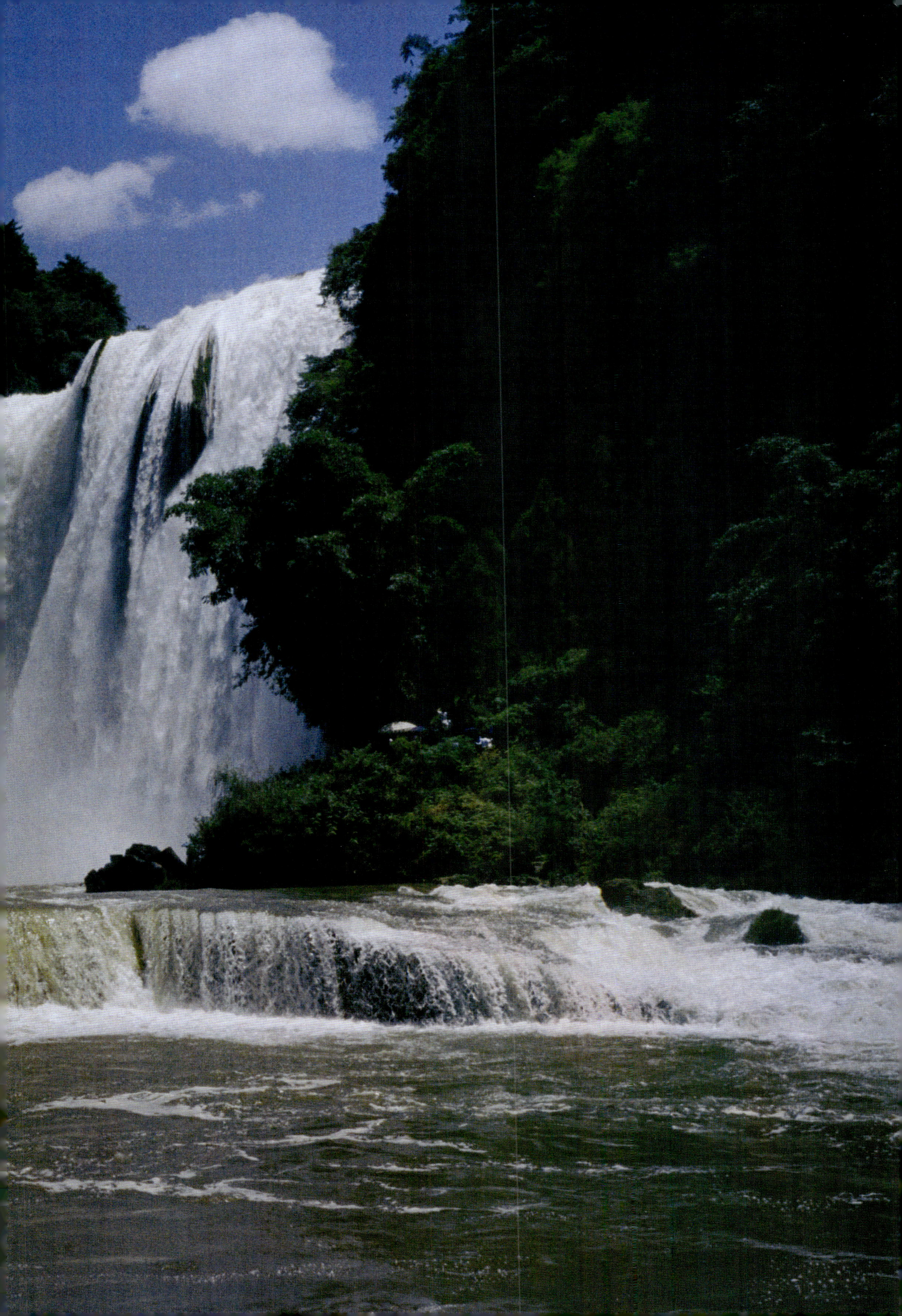

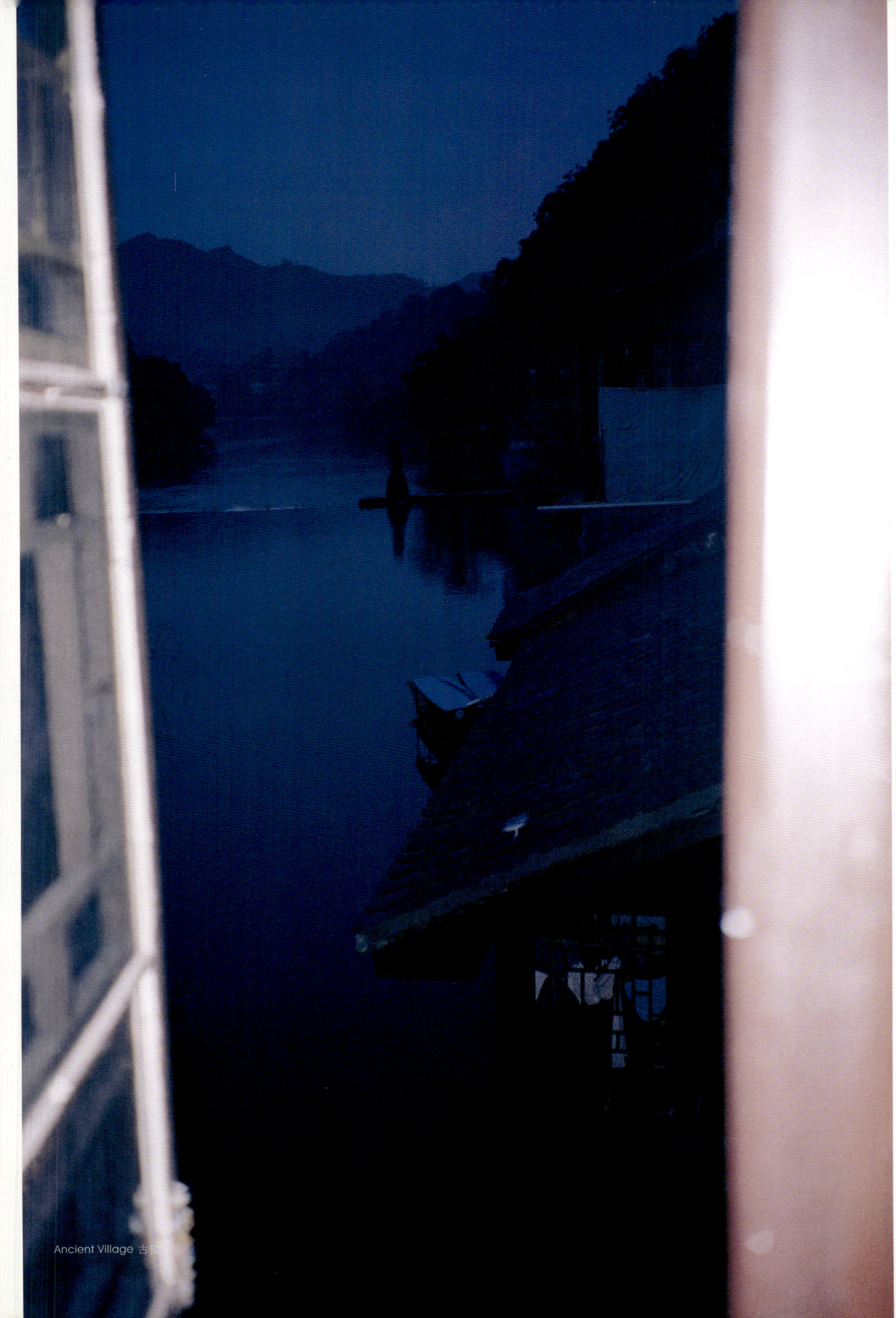
Ancient Village 古镇

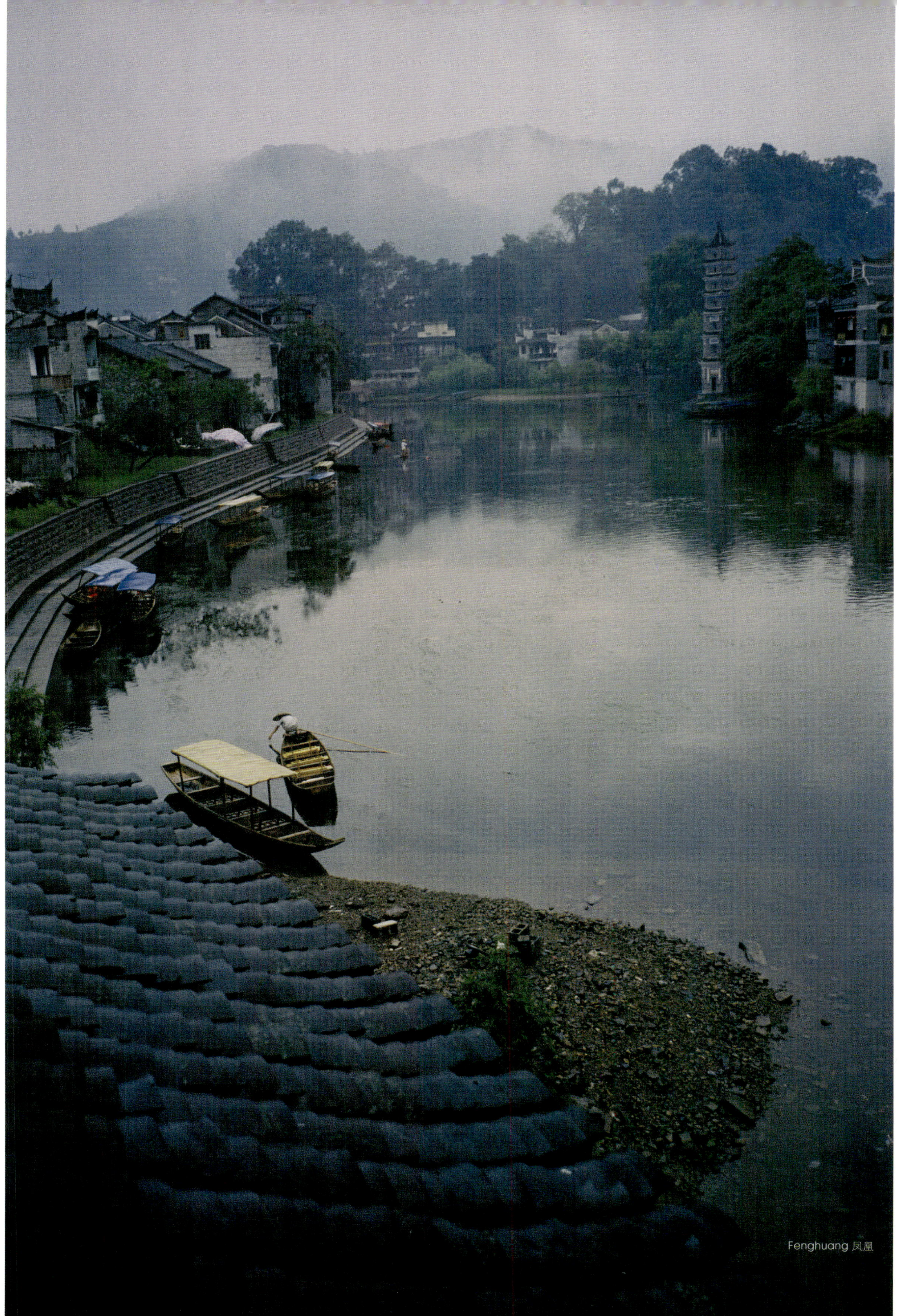

Fenghuang 凤凰

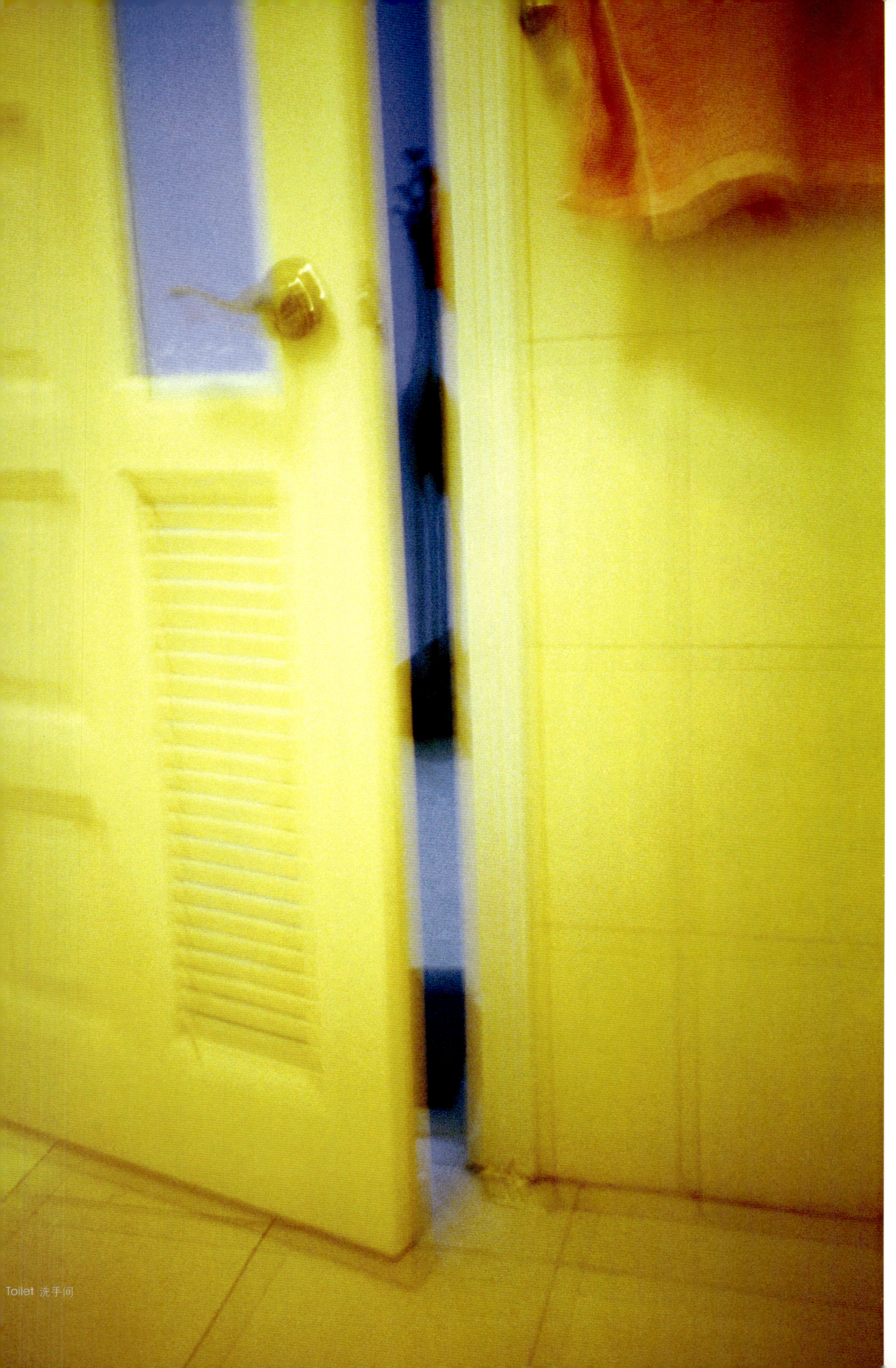

Toilet 洗手间

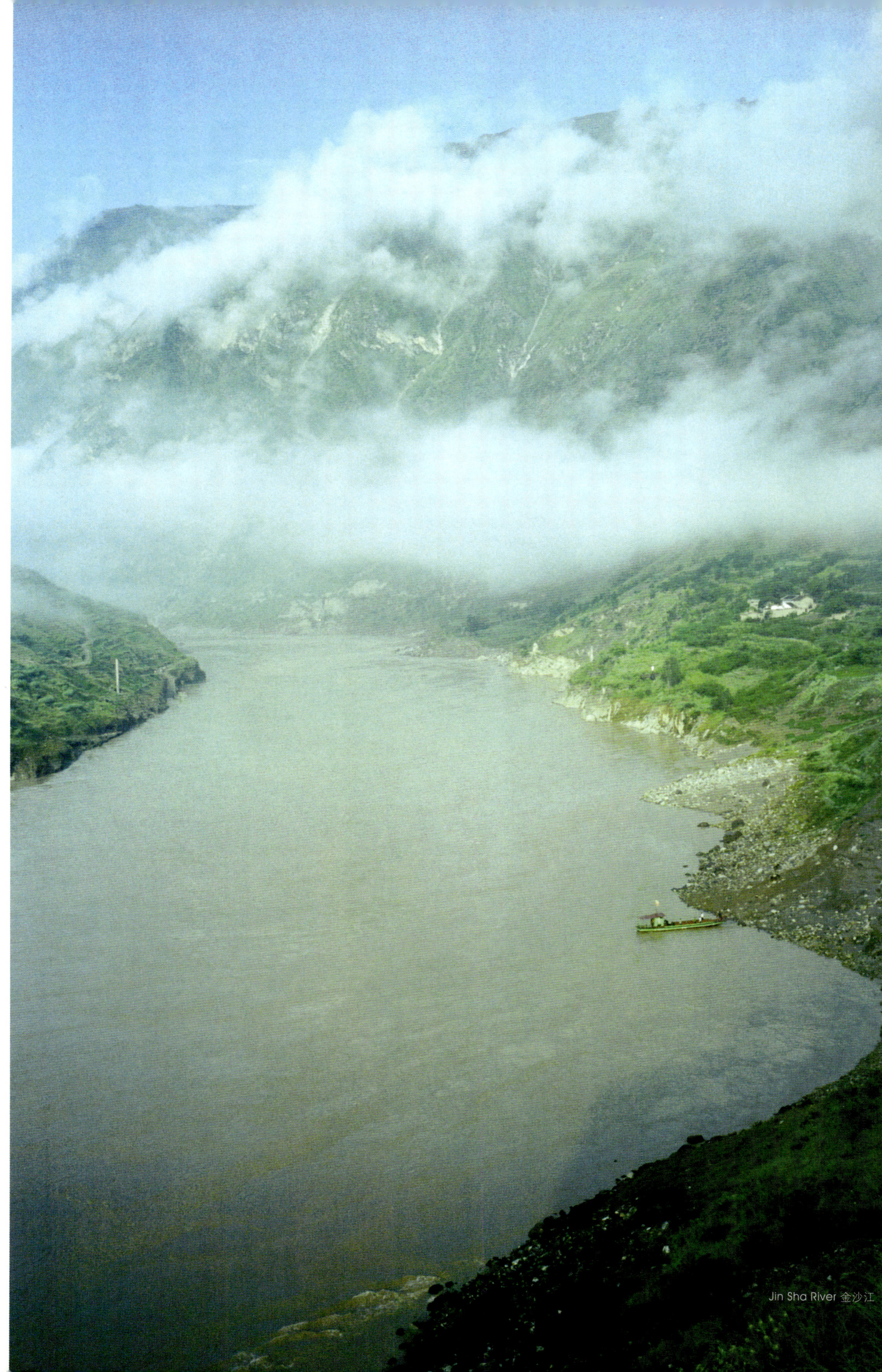

Jin Sha River 金沙江

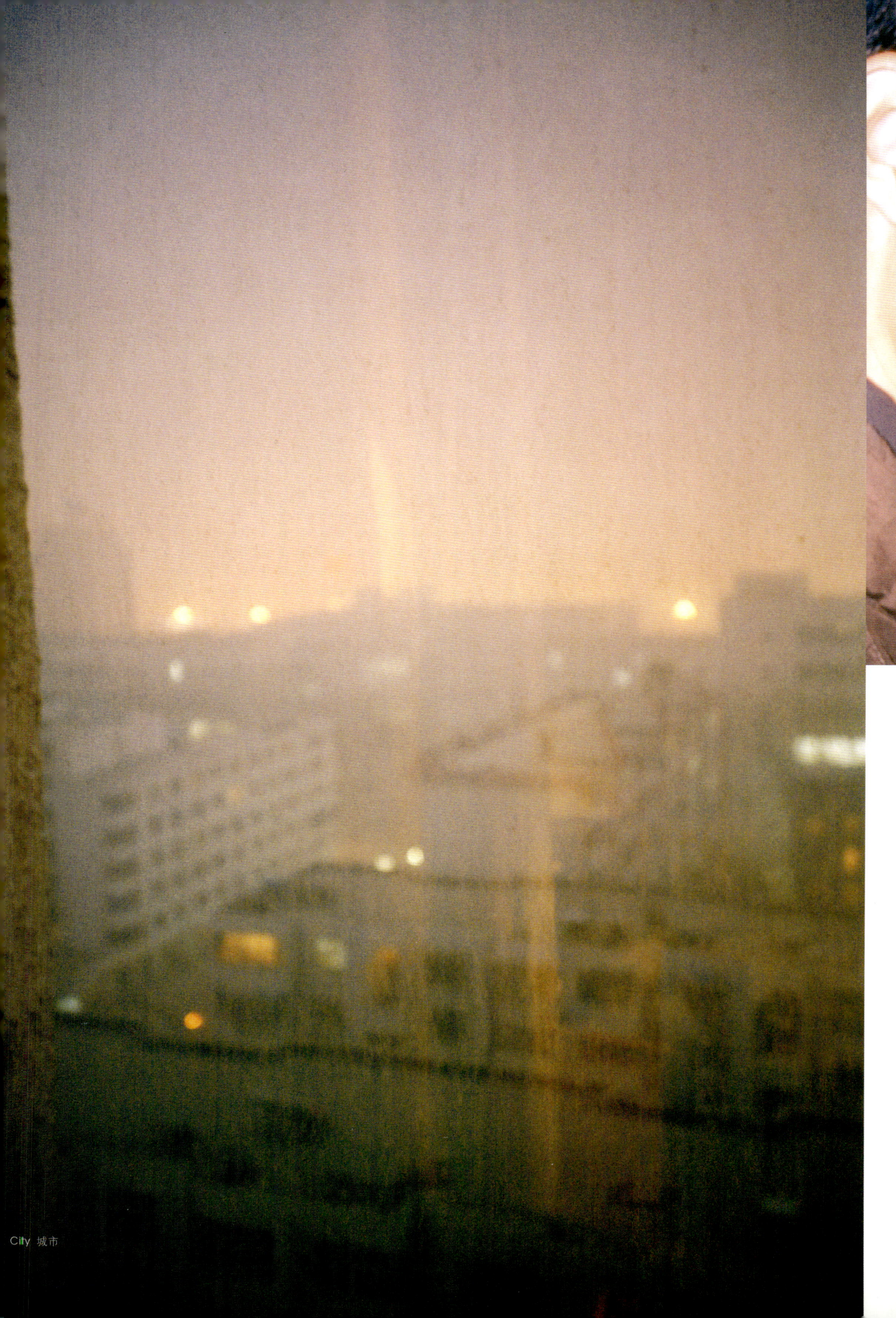

City 城市

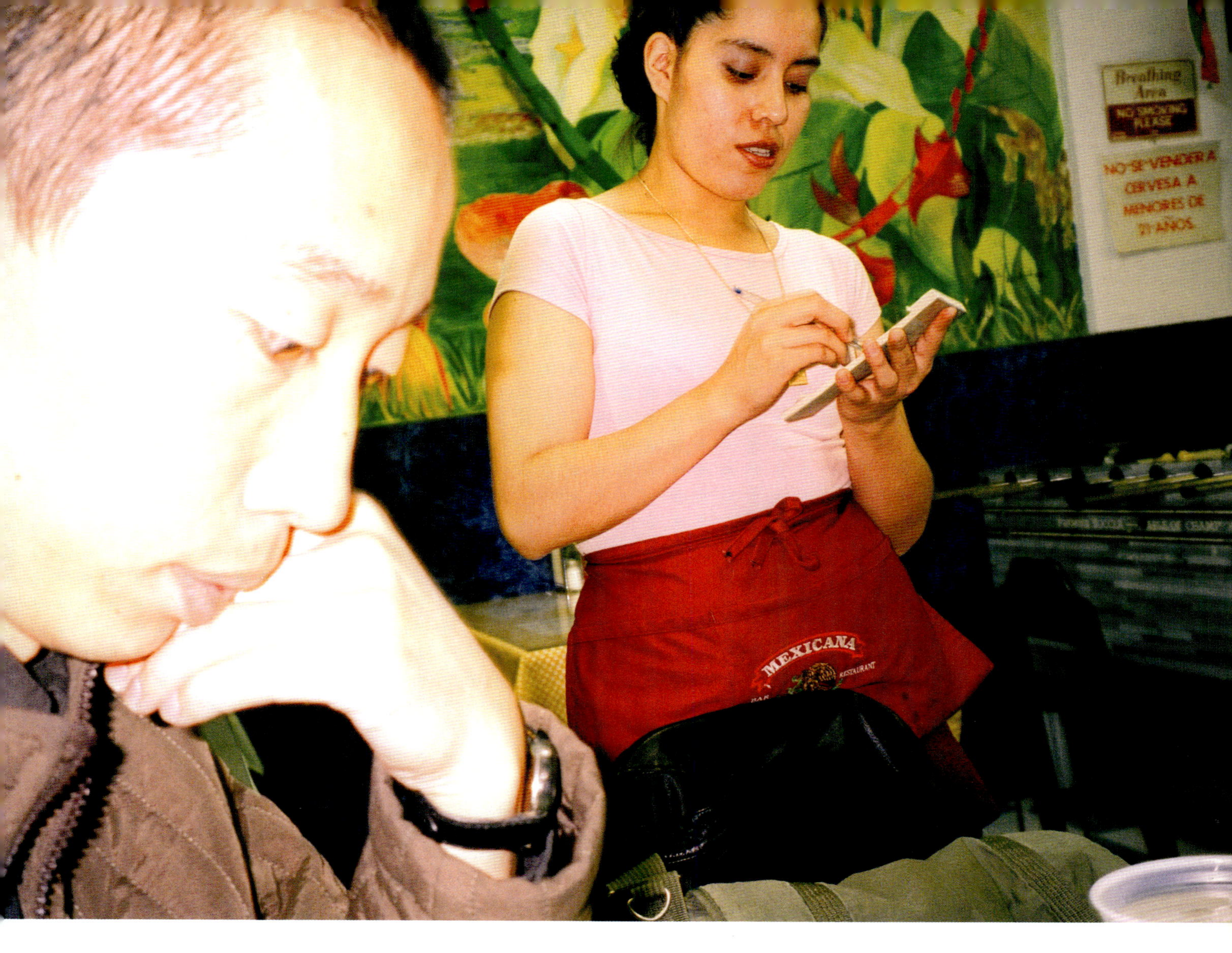

In a Mexican Restaurant, New York　在墨西哥餐厅

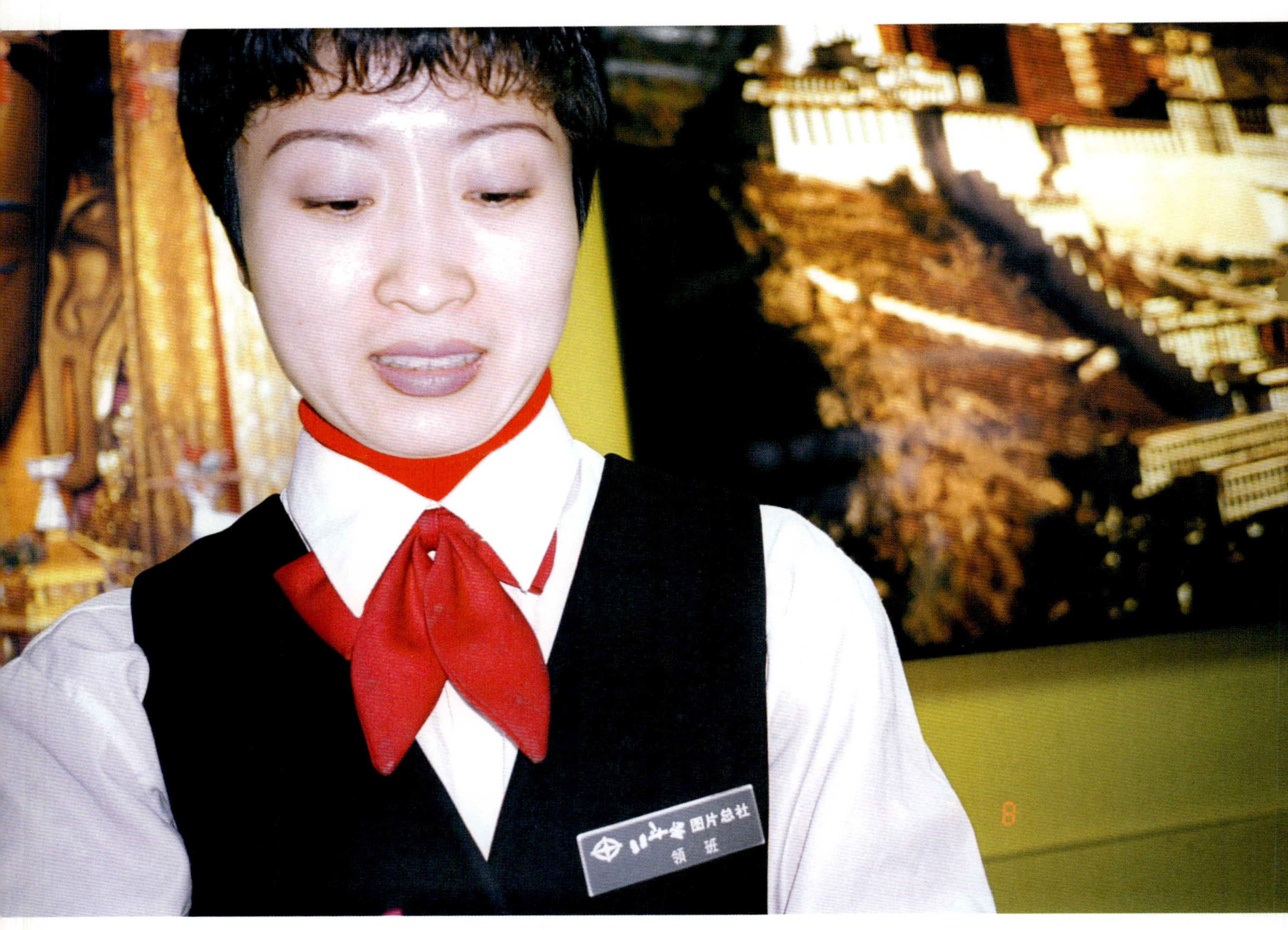

Photo Developing Store 冲印店

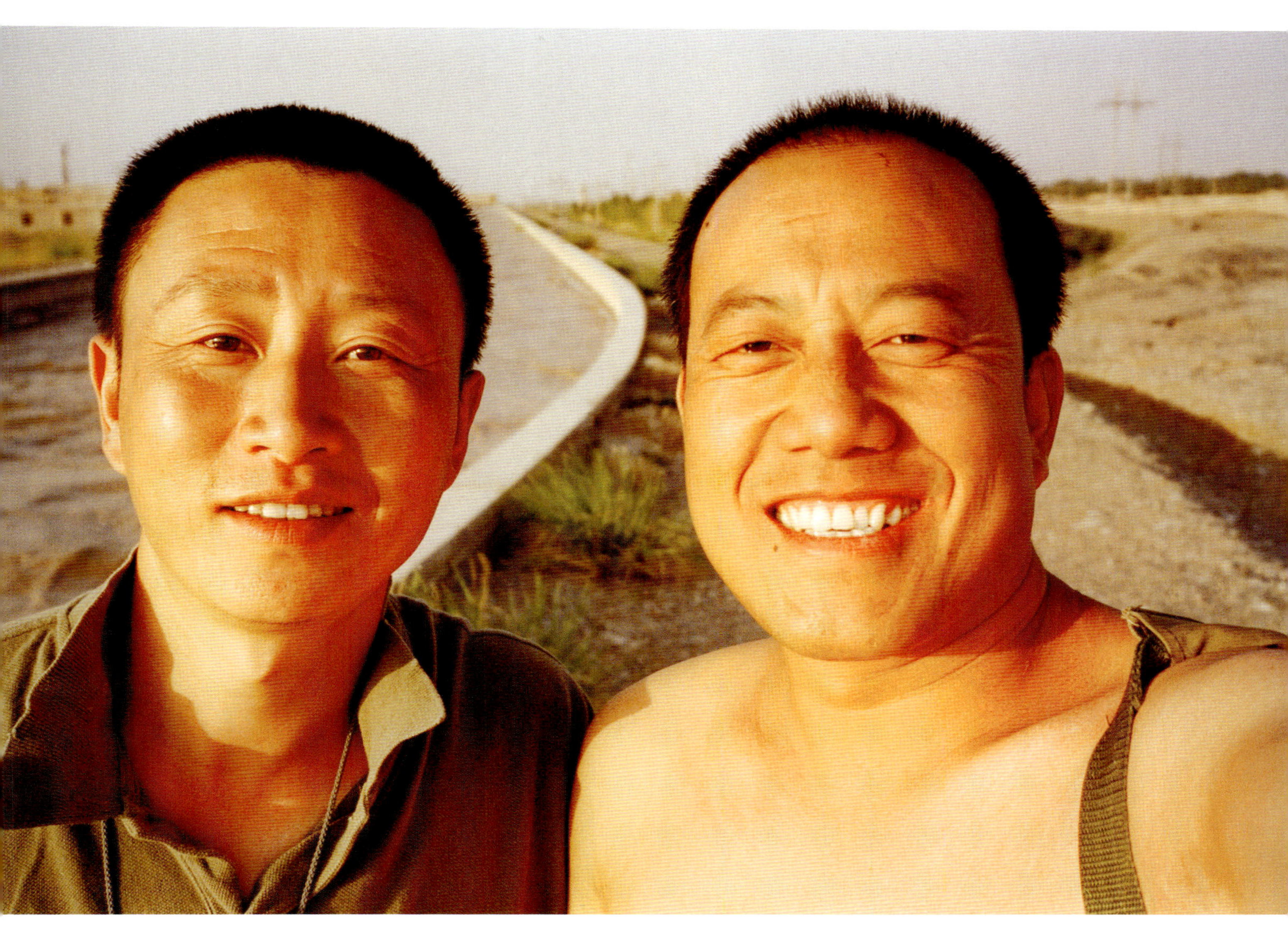

Two Youths 两个年青人

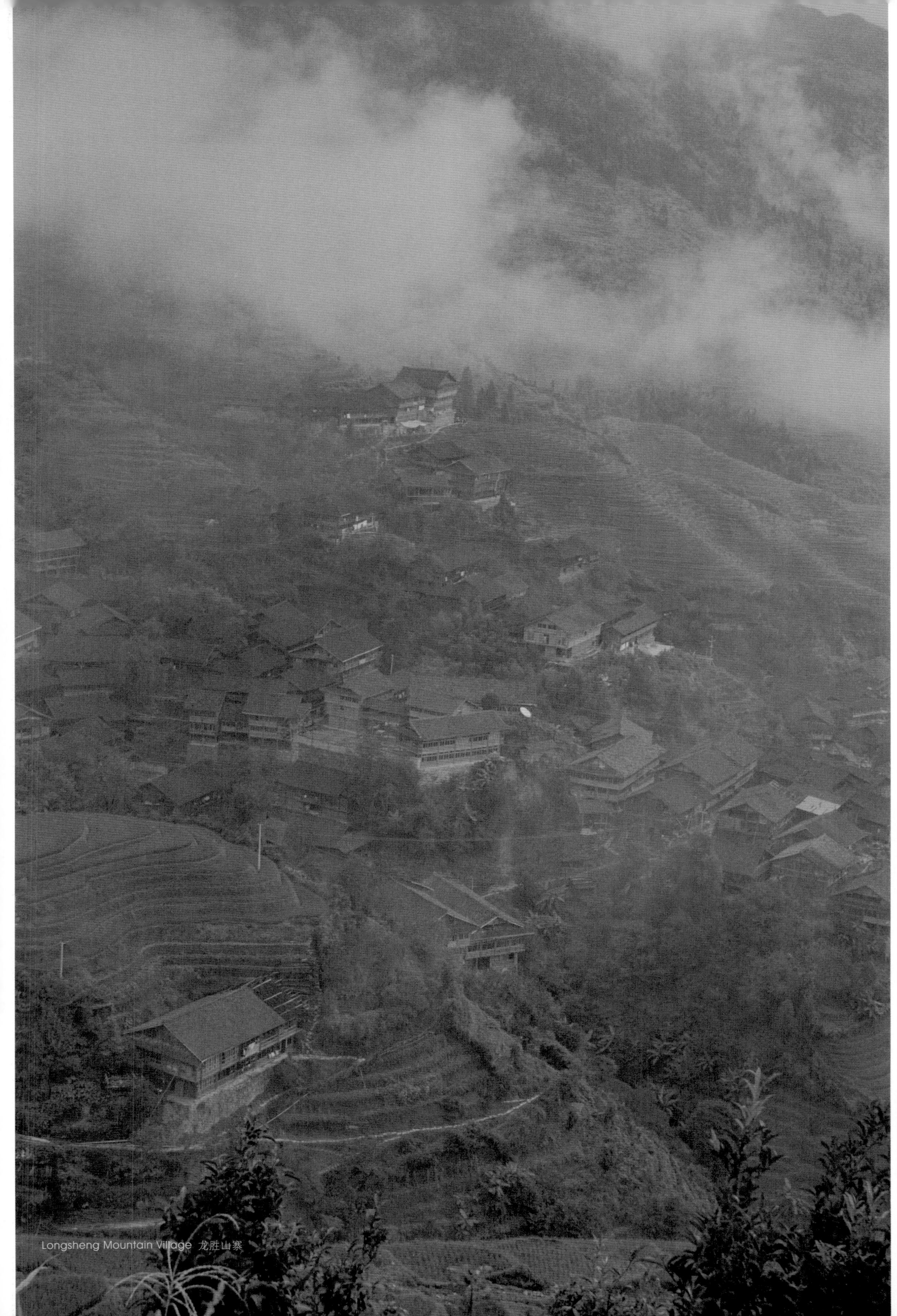

Longsheng Mountain Village 龙胜山寨

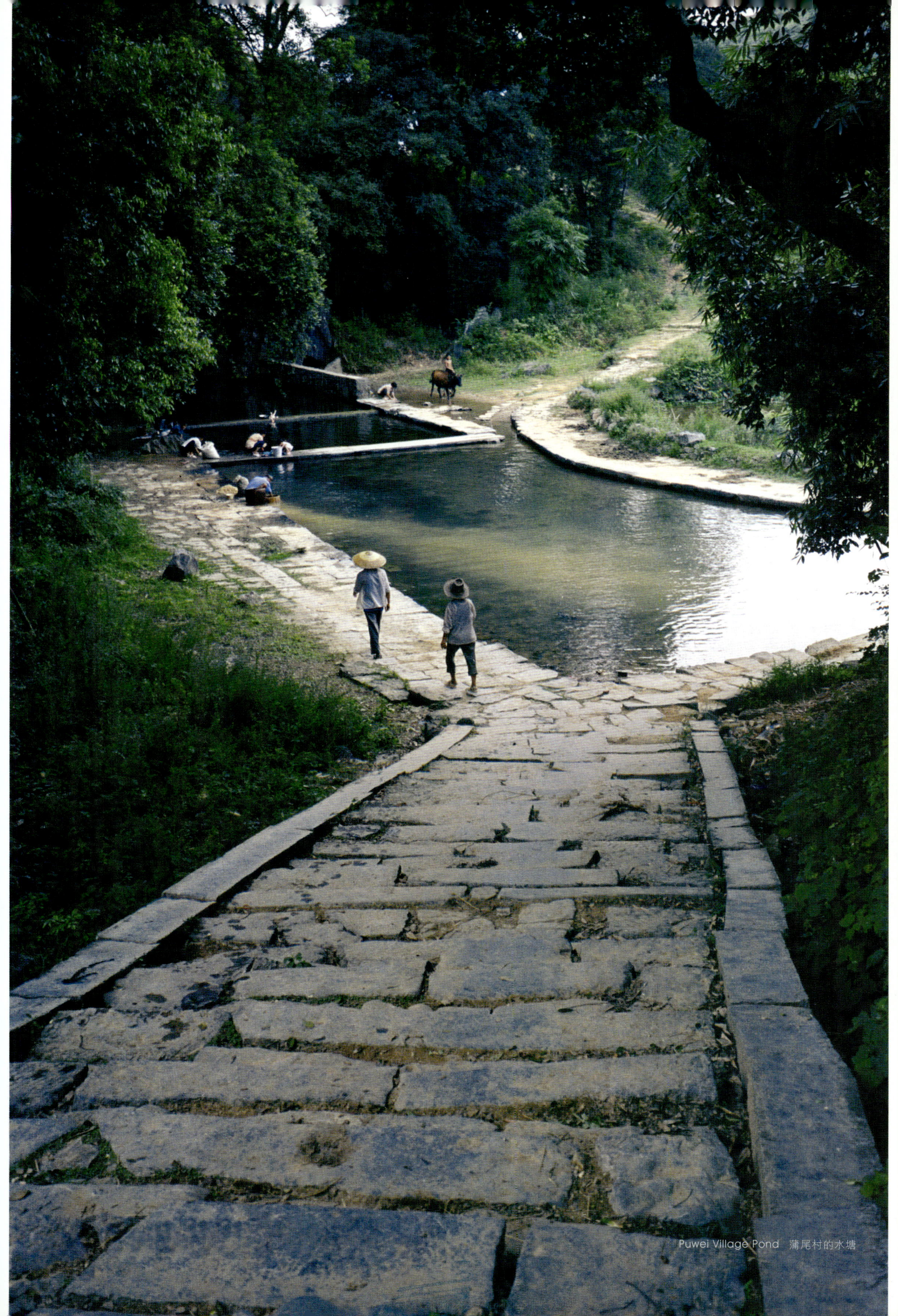

Puwei Village Pond 蒲尾村的水塘

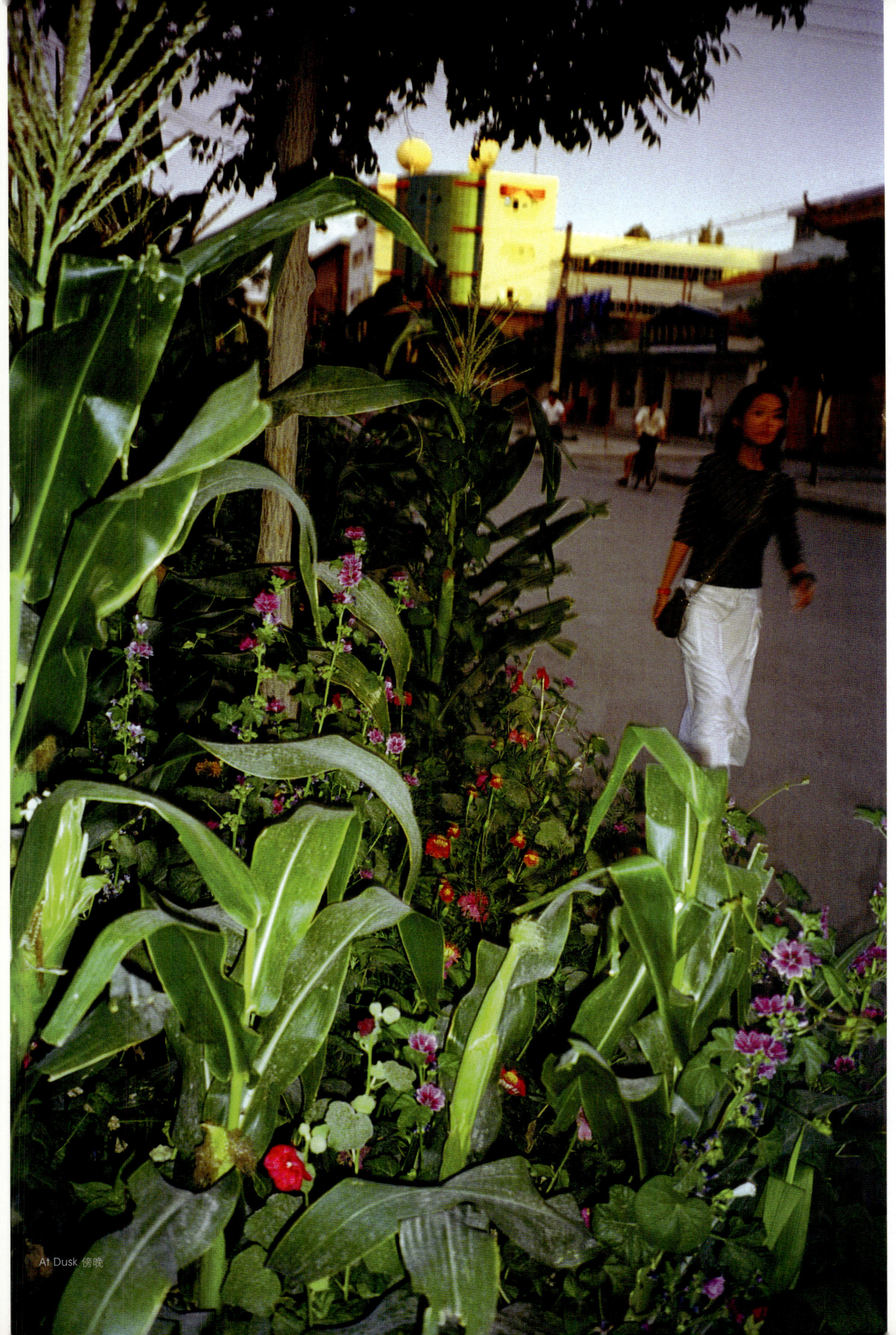
At Dusk 傍晚

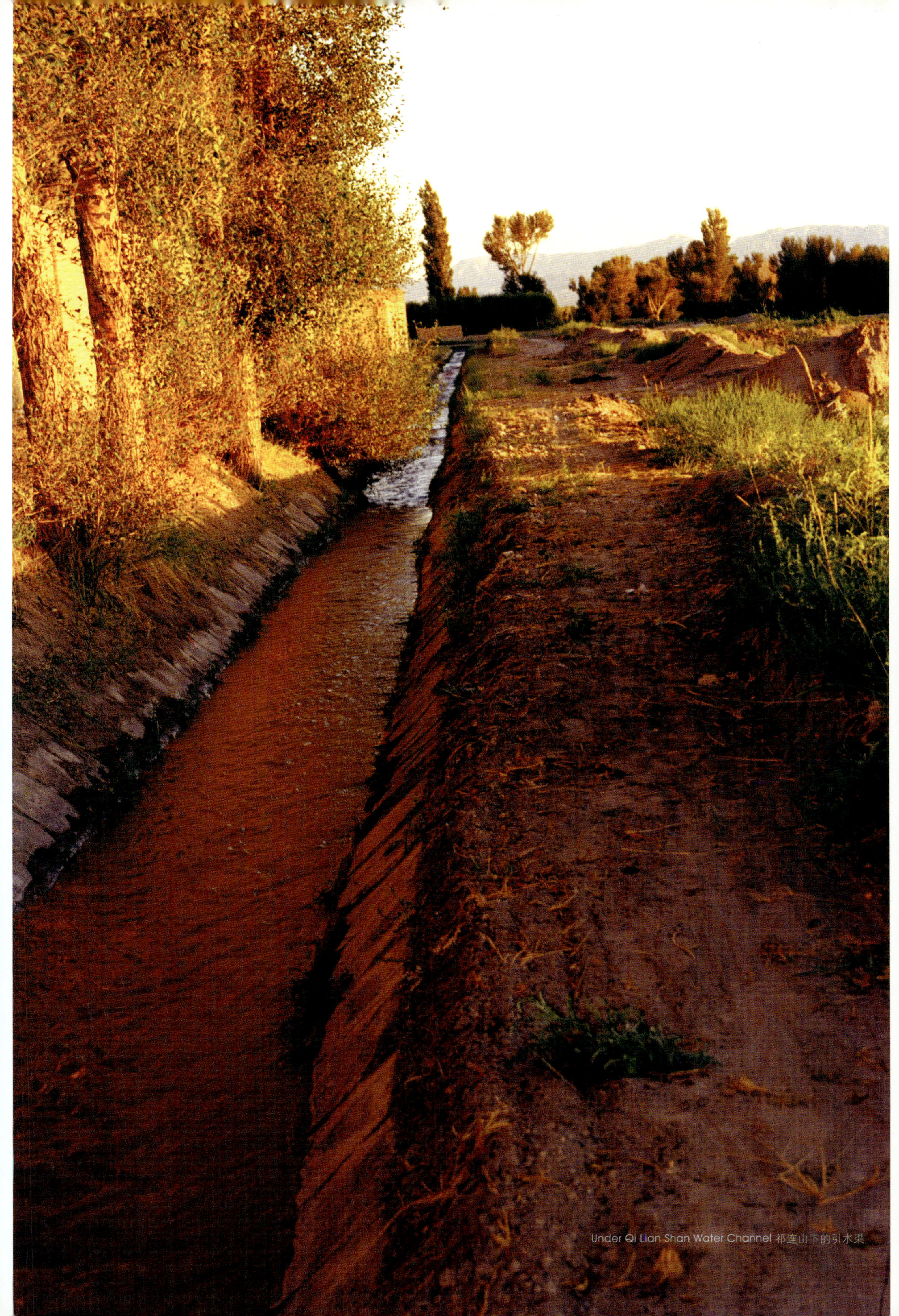

Under Qi Lian Shan Water Channel 祁连山下的引水渠

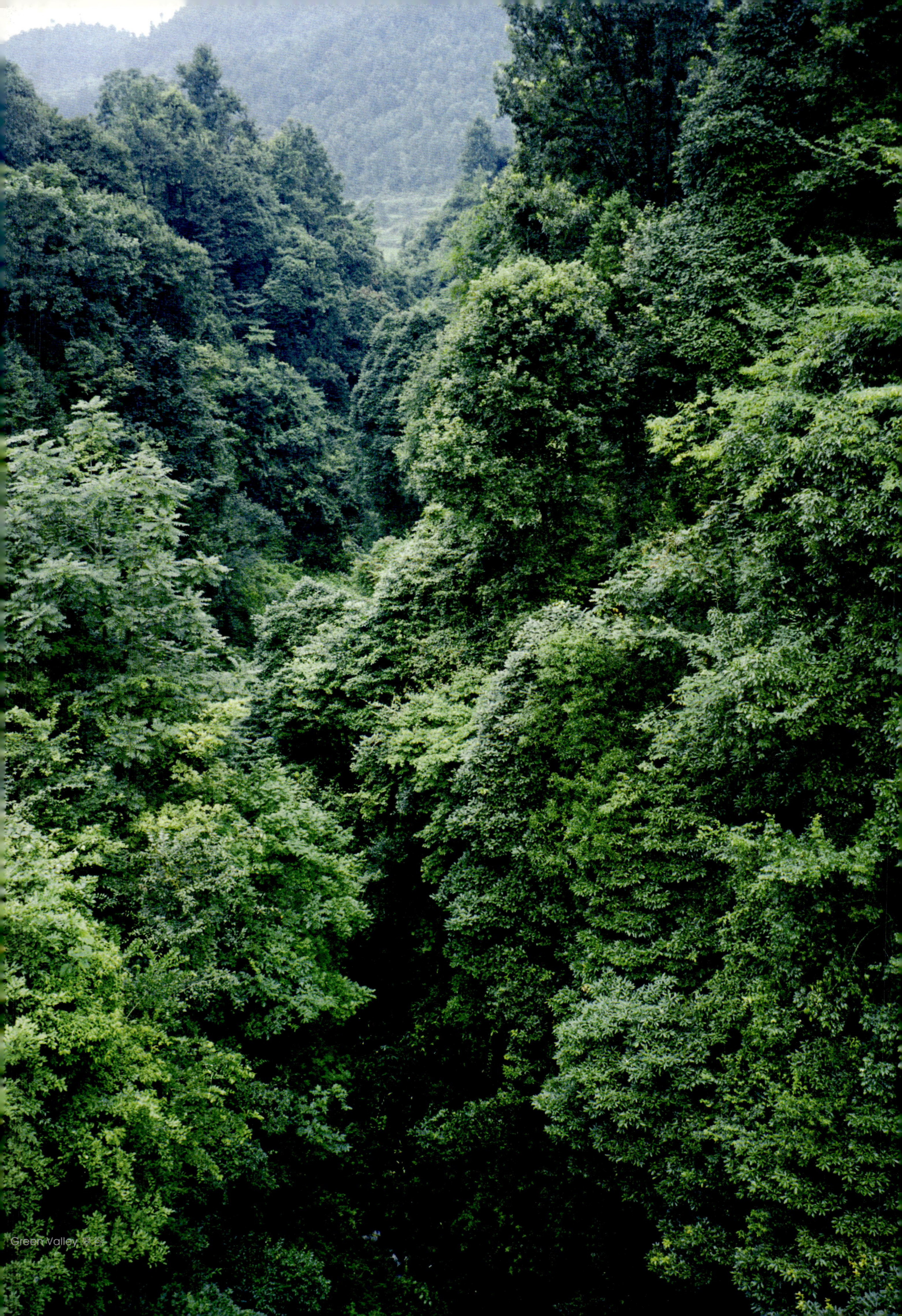
Green Valley 翠谷

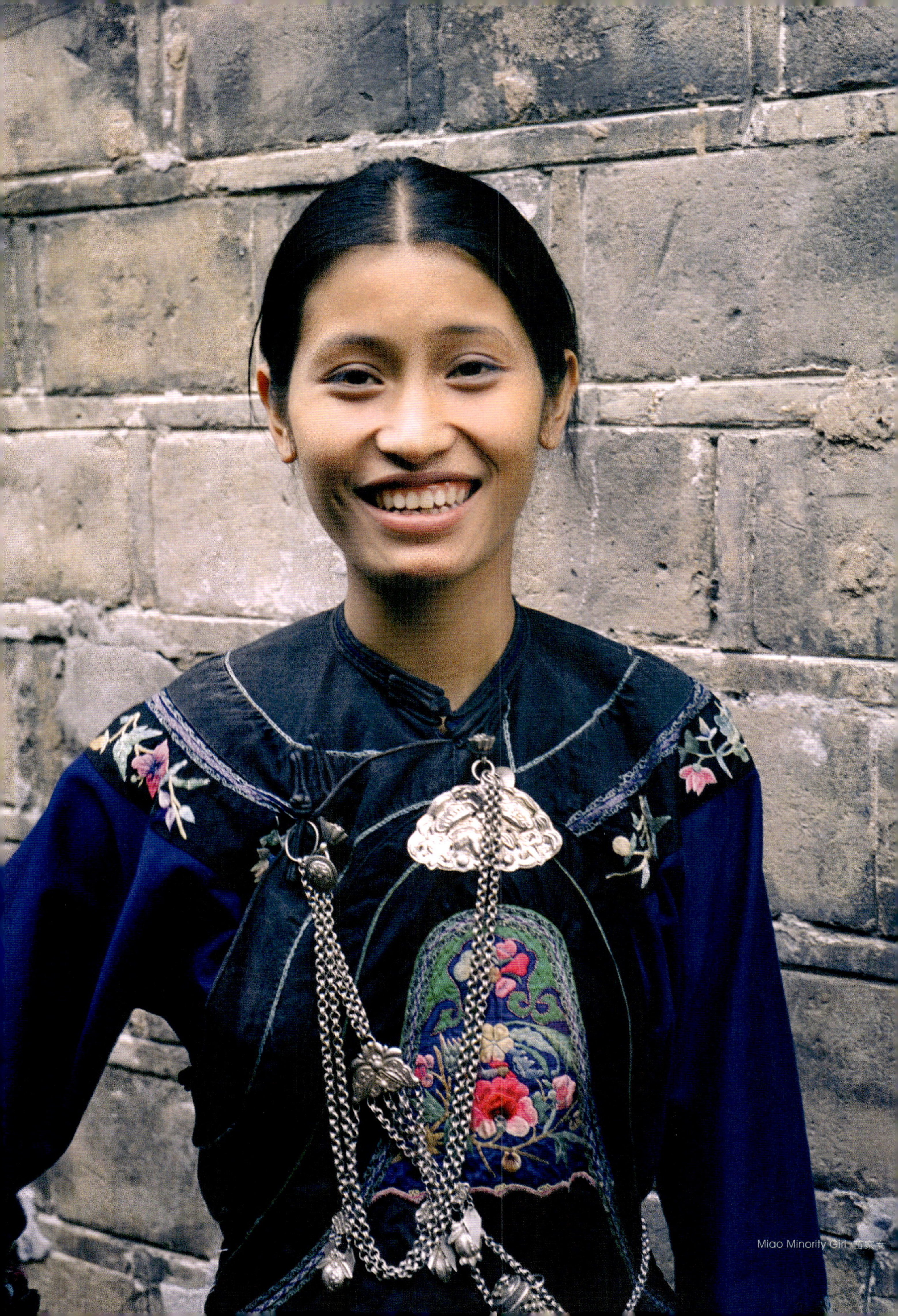

Miao Minority Girl 苗家女

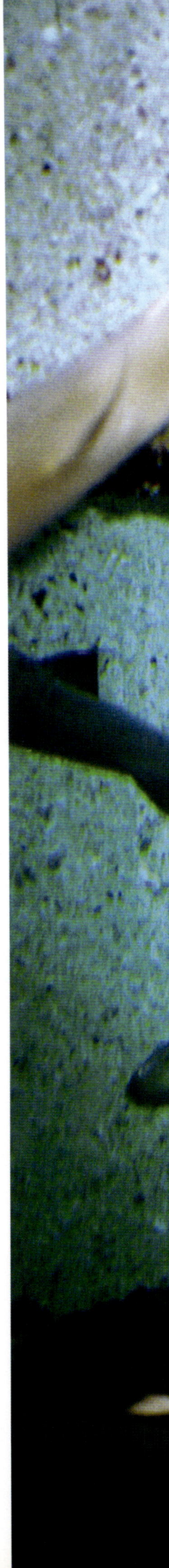

Dive　跳水

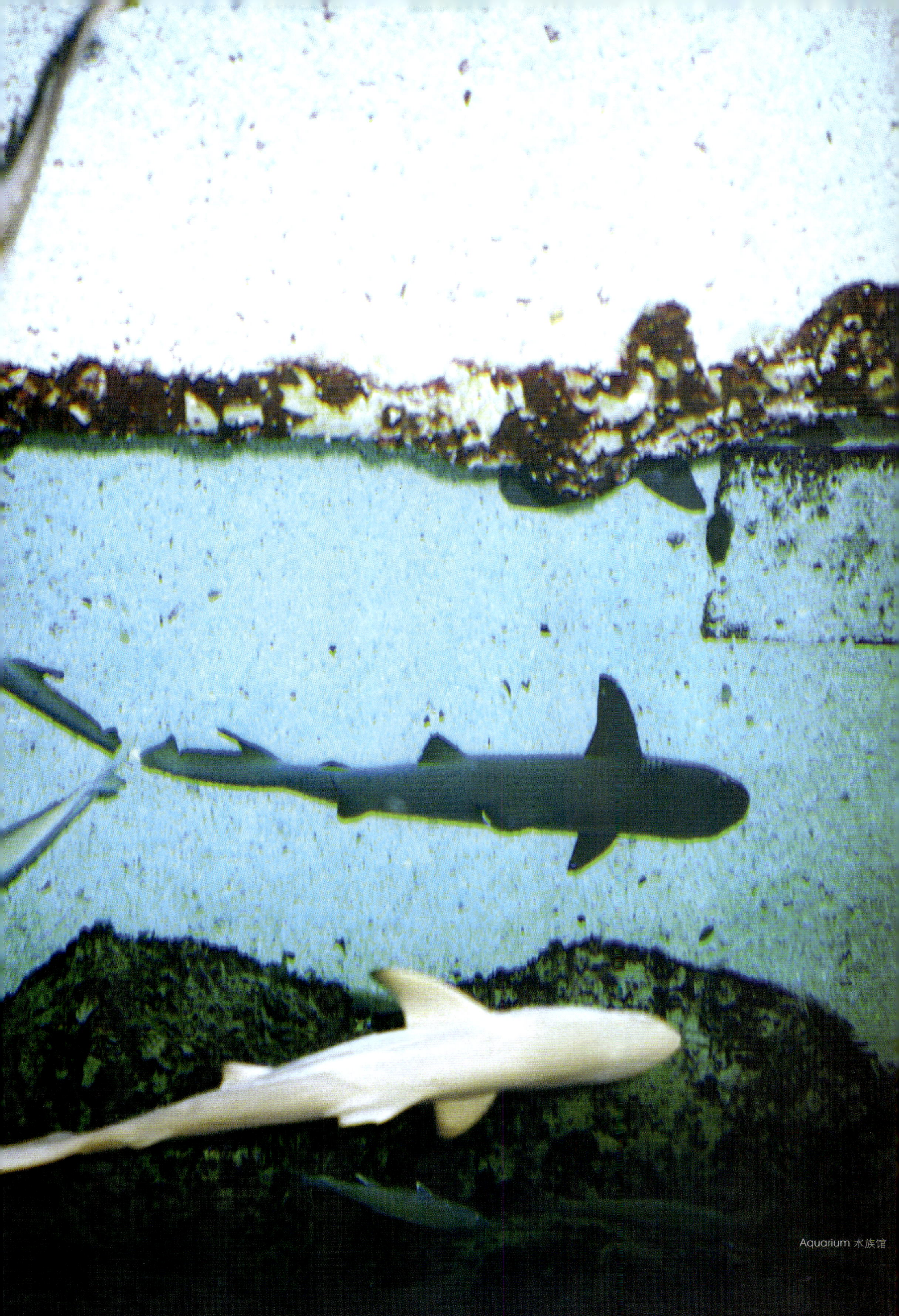
Aquarium 水族馆

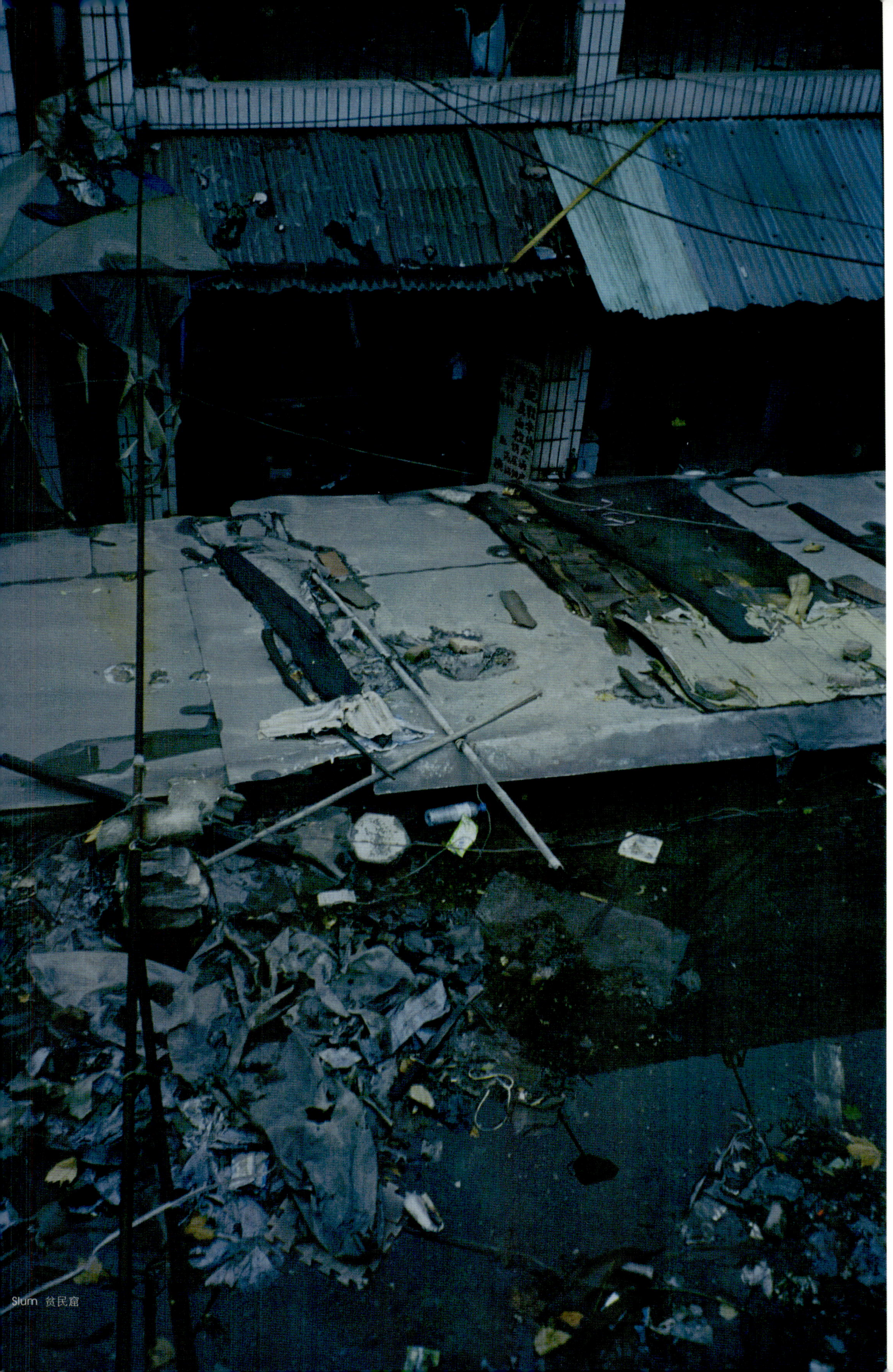

Slum 贫民窟

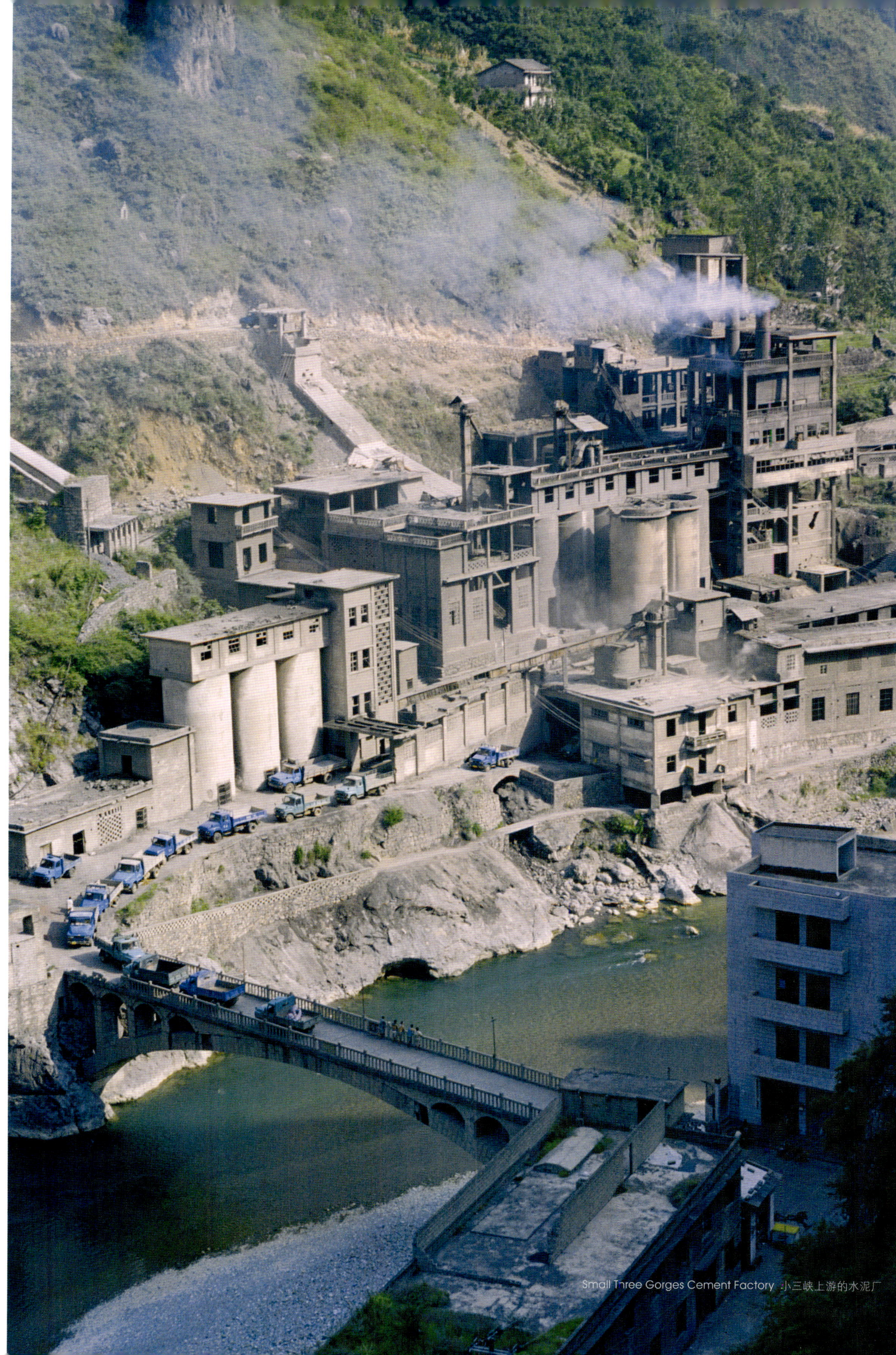

Small Three Gorges Cement Factory 小三峡上游的水泥厂

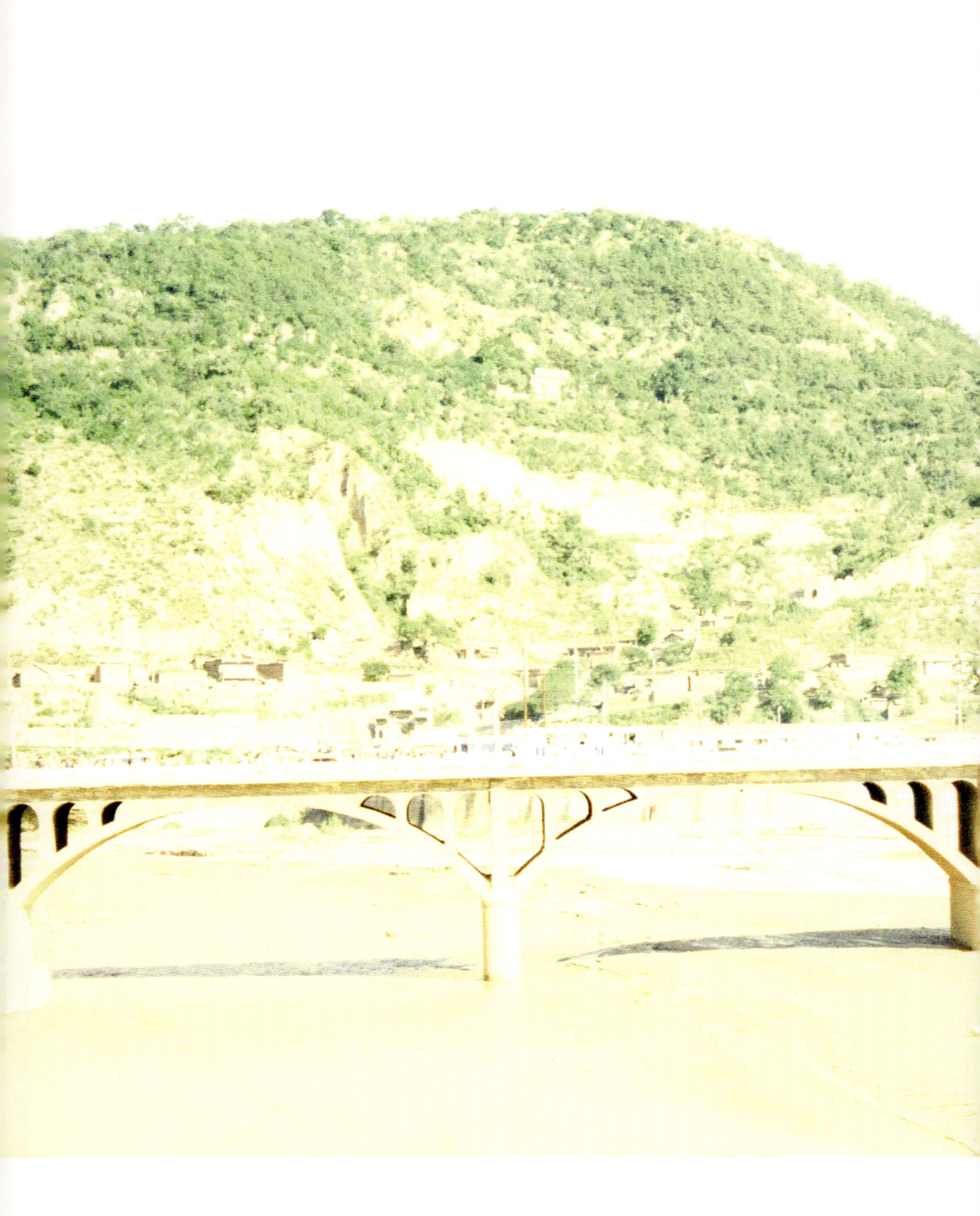

Bao Ta Mountain 宝塔山

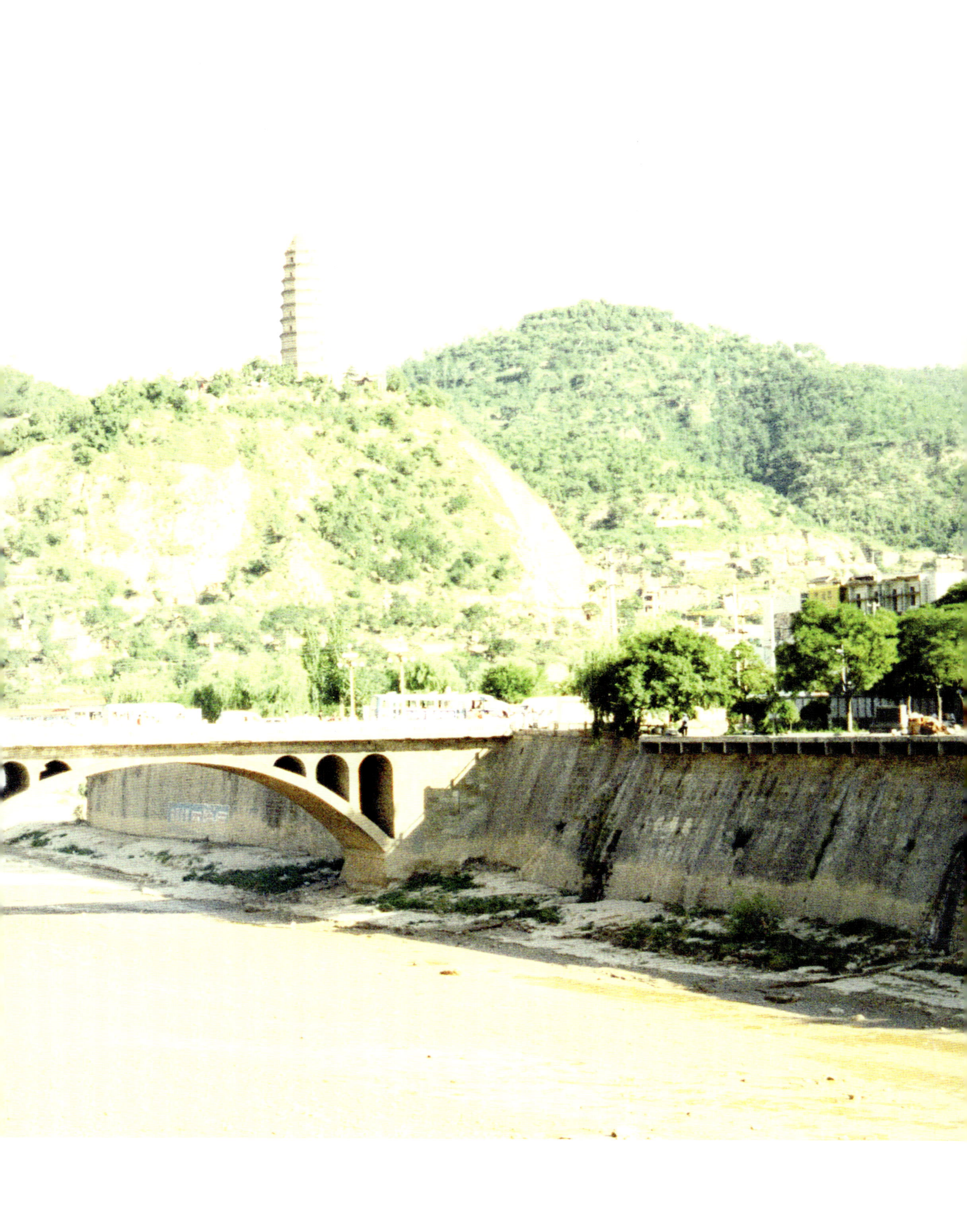

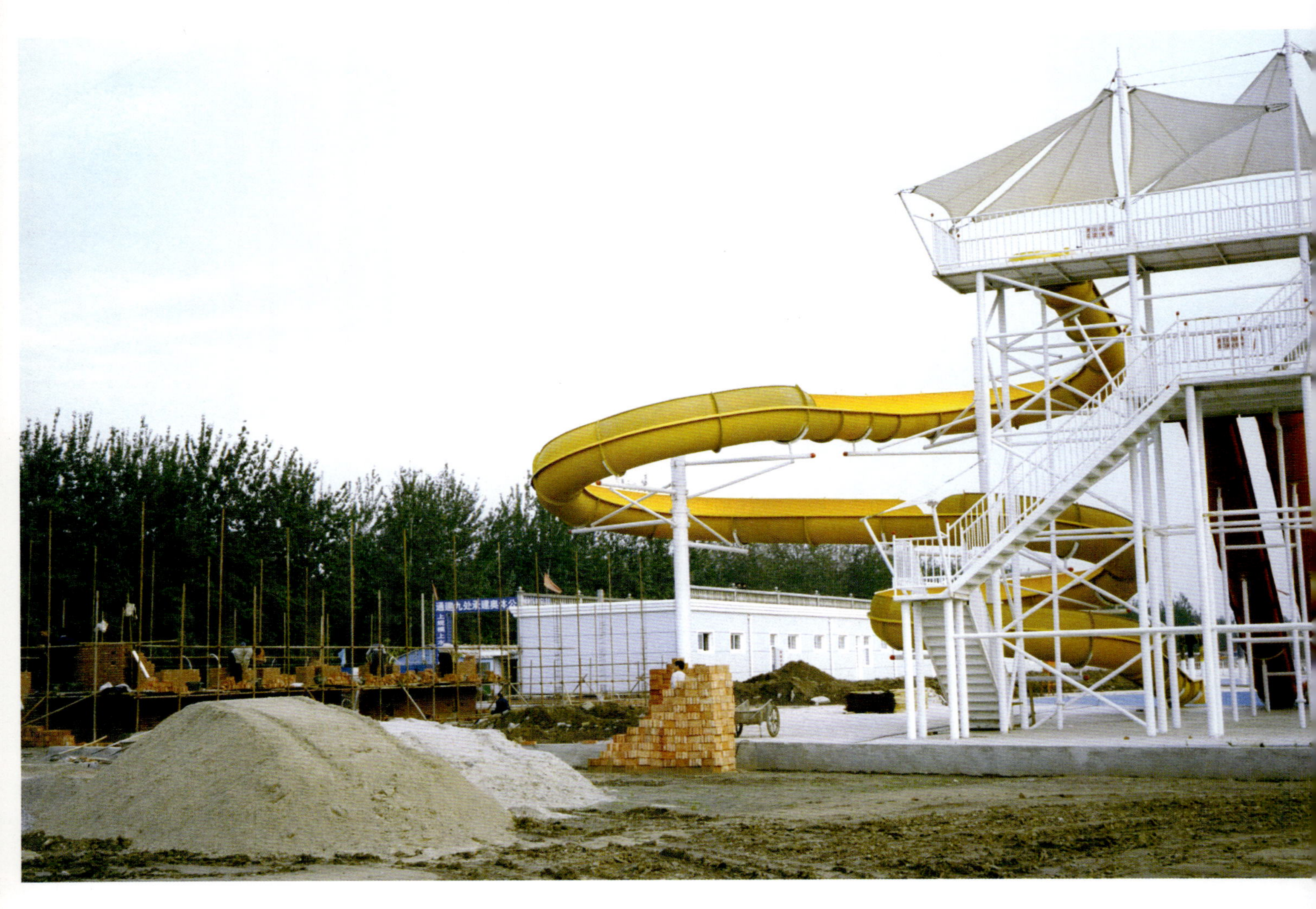

Toy 玩具

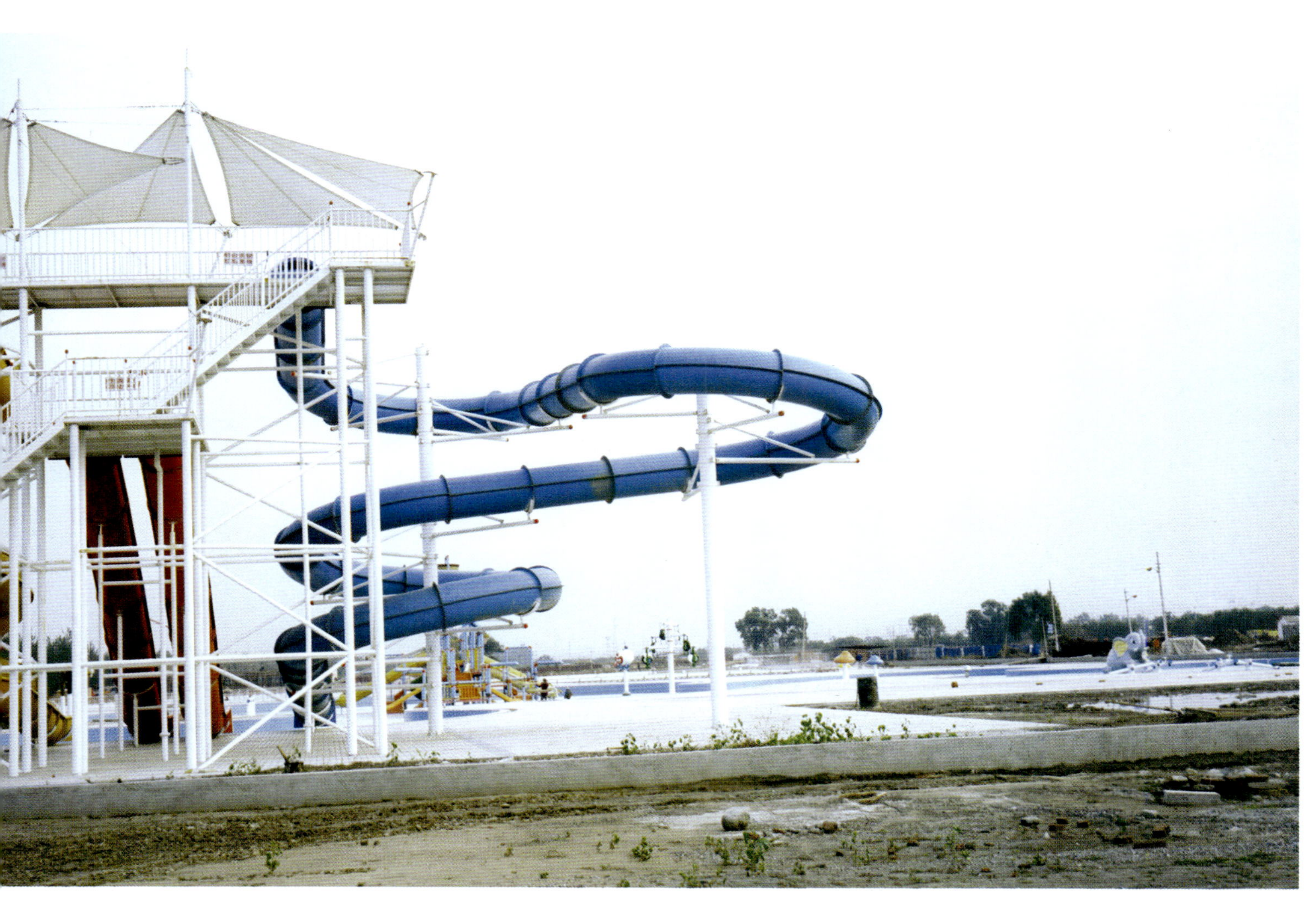

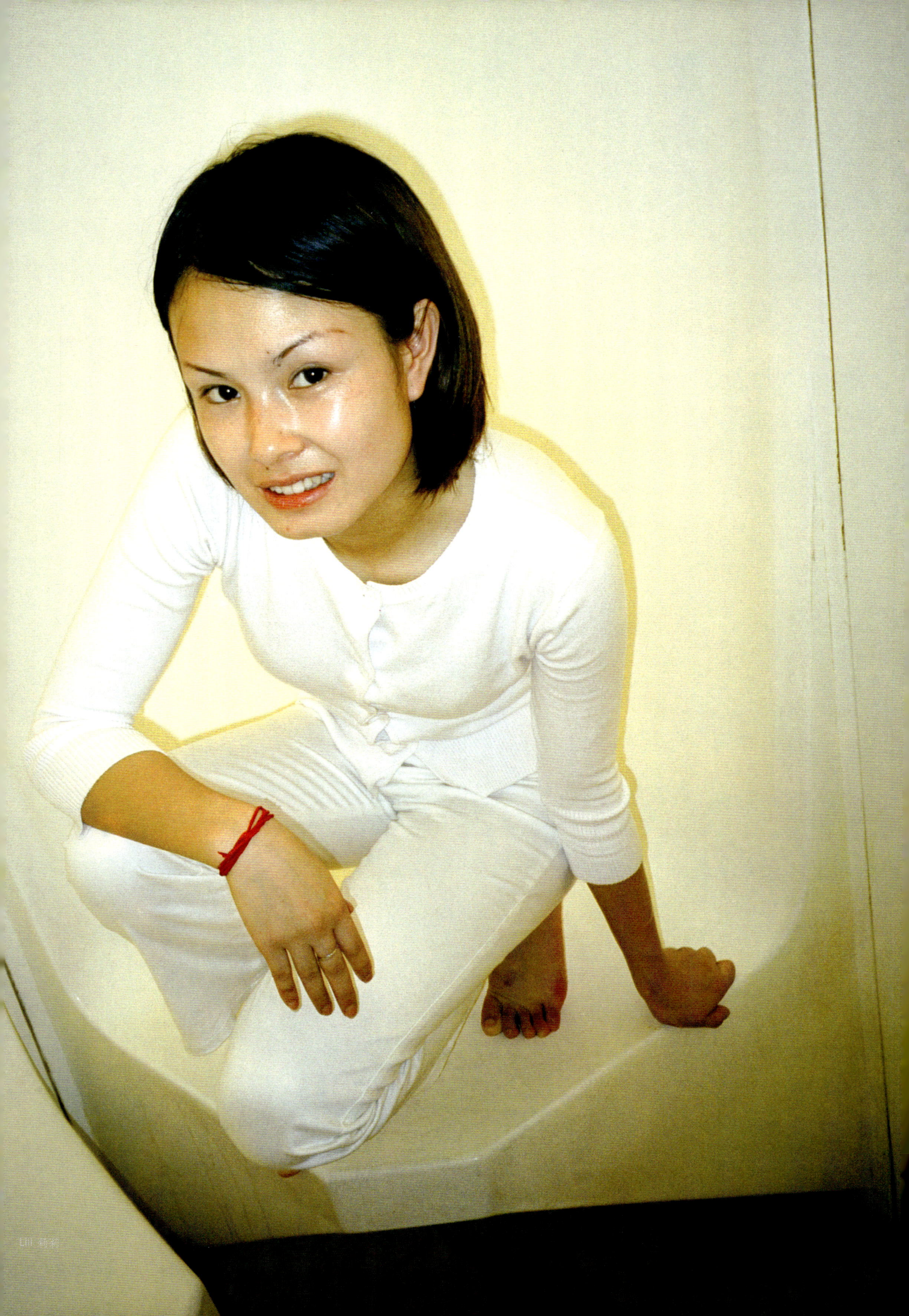
Lili 莉莉

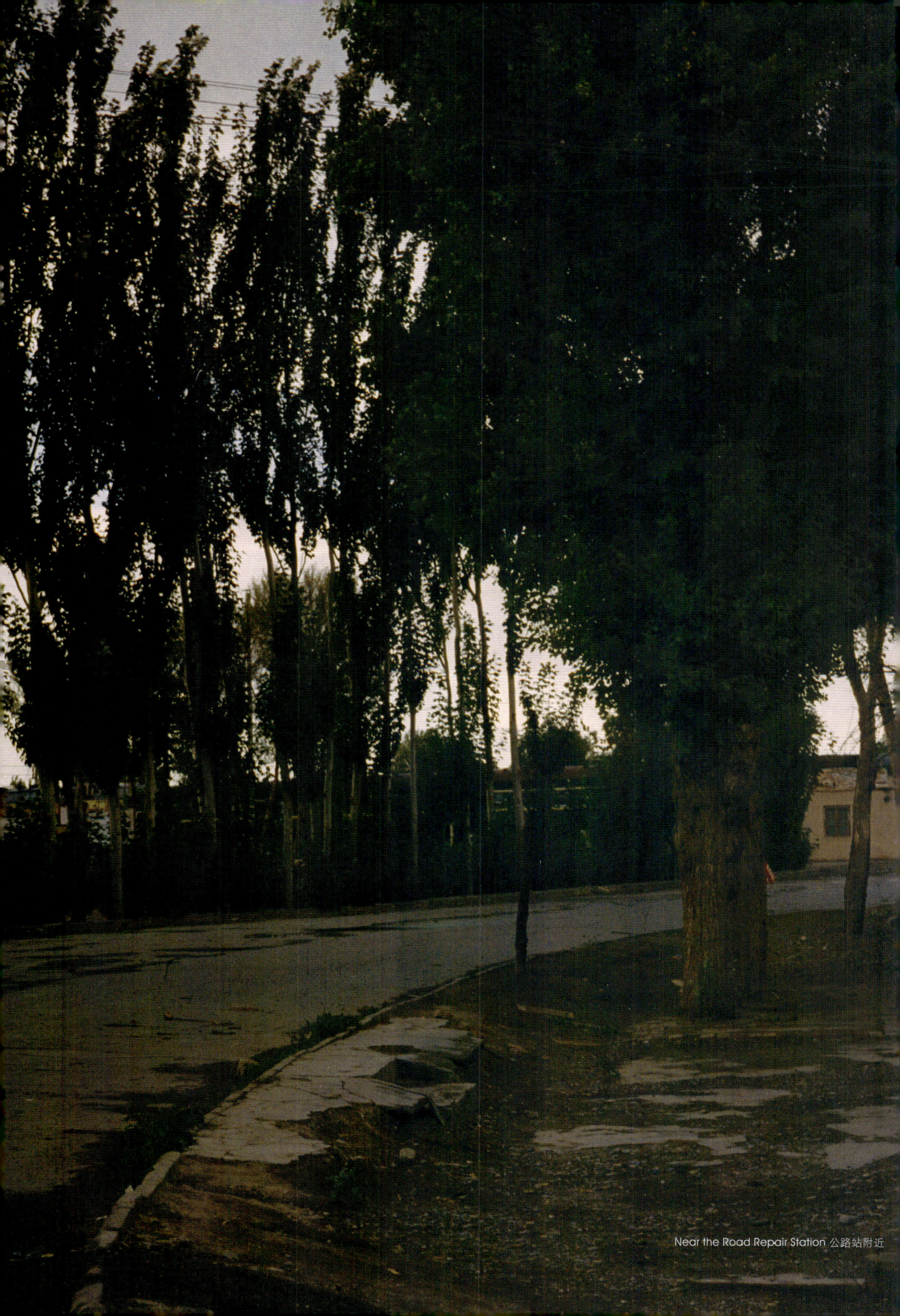
Near the Road Repair Station 公路站附近

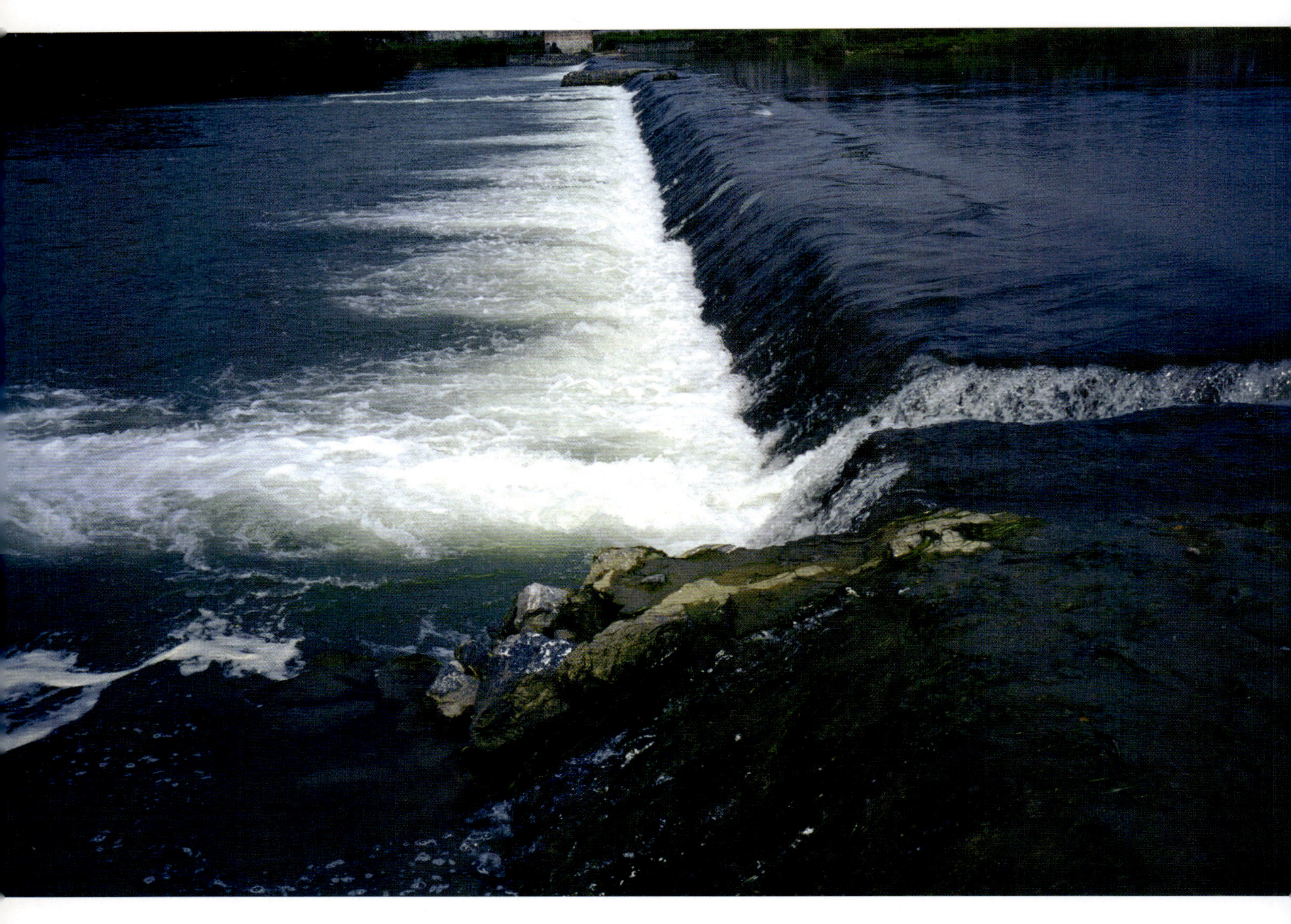

Dam 水坝

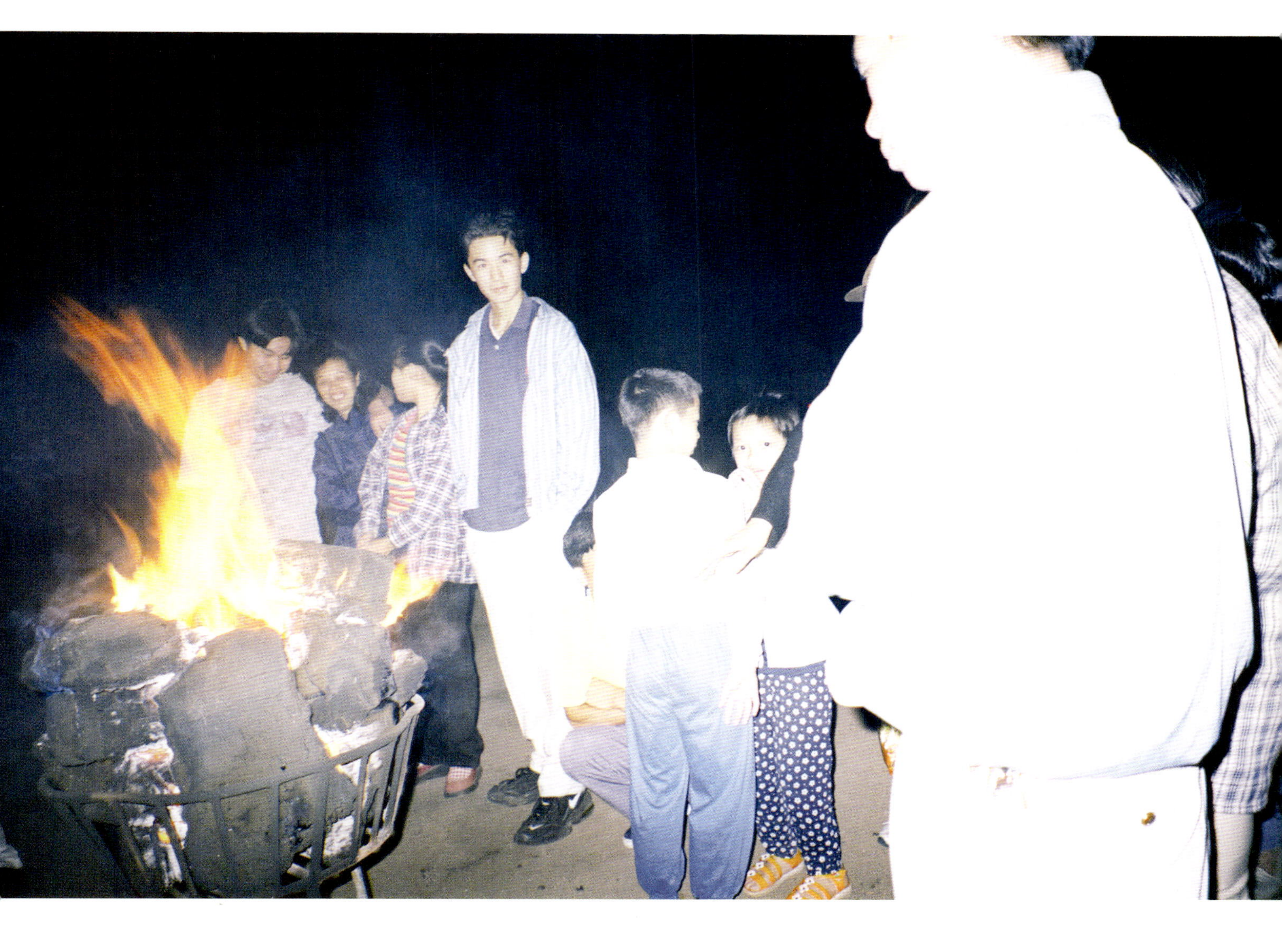

Bonfire 篝火

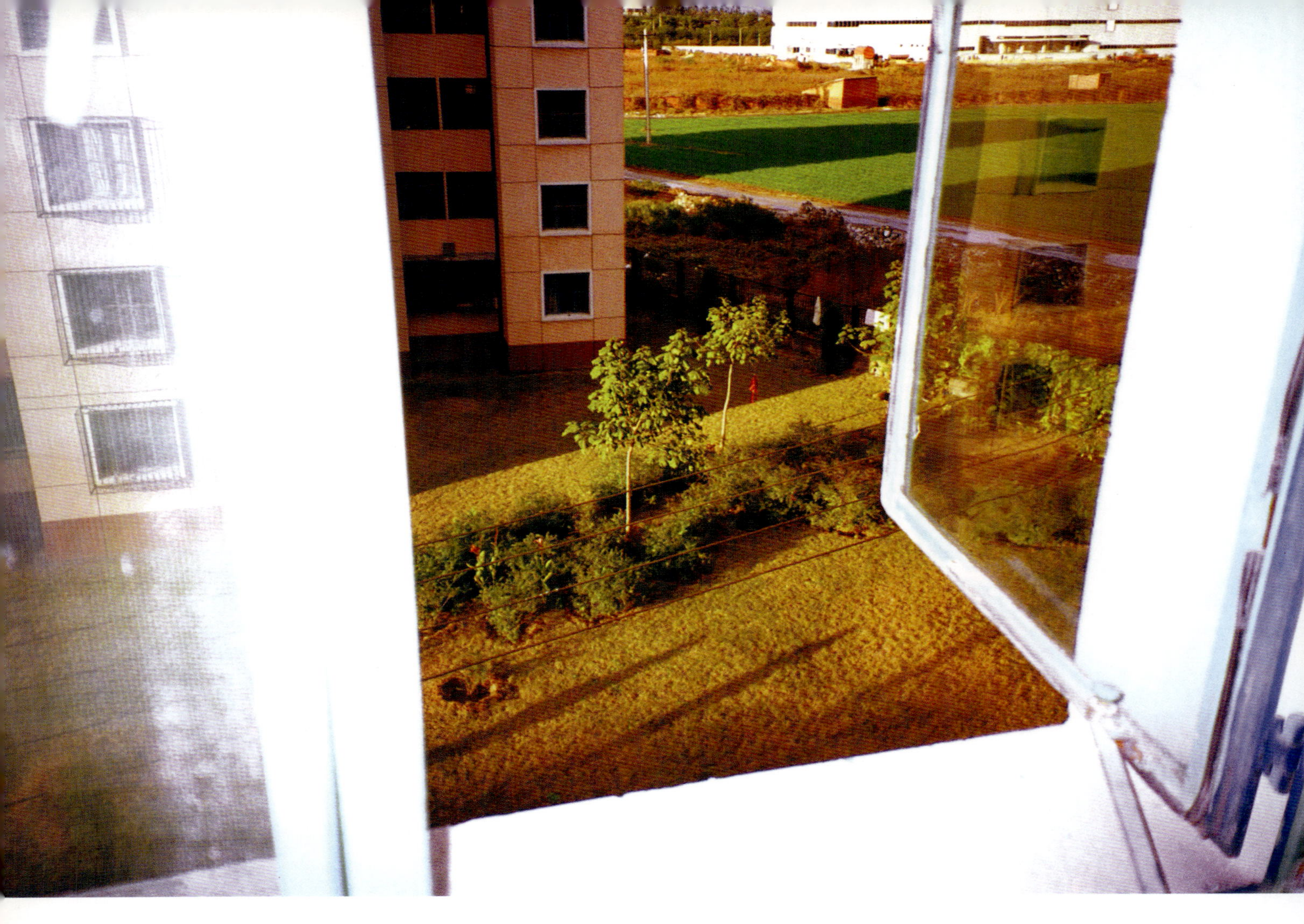

South Street of Yu Bridge 玉桥南里

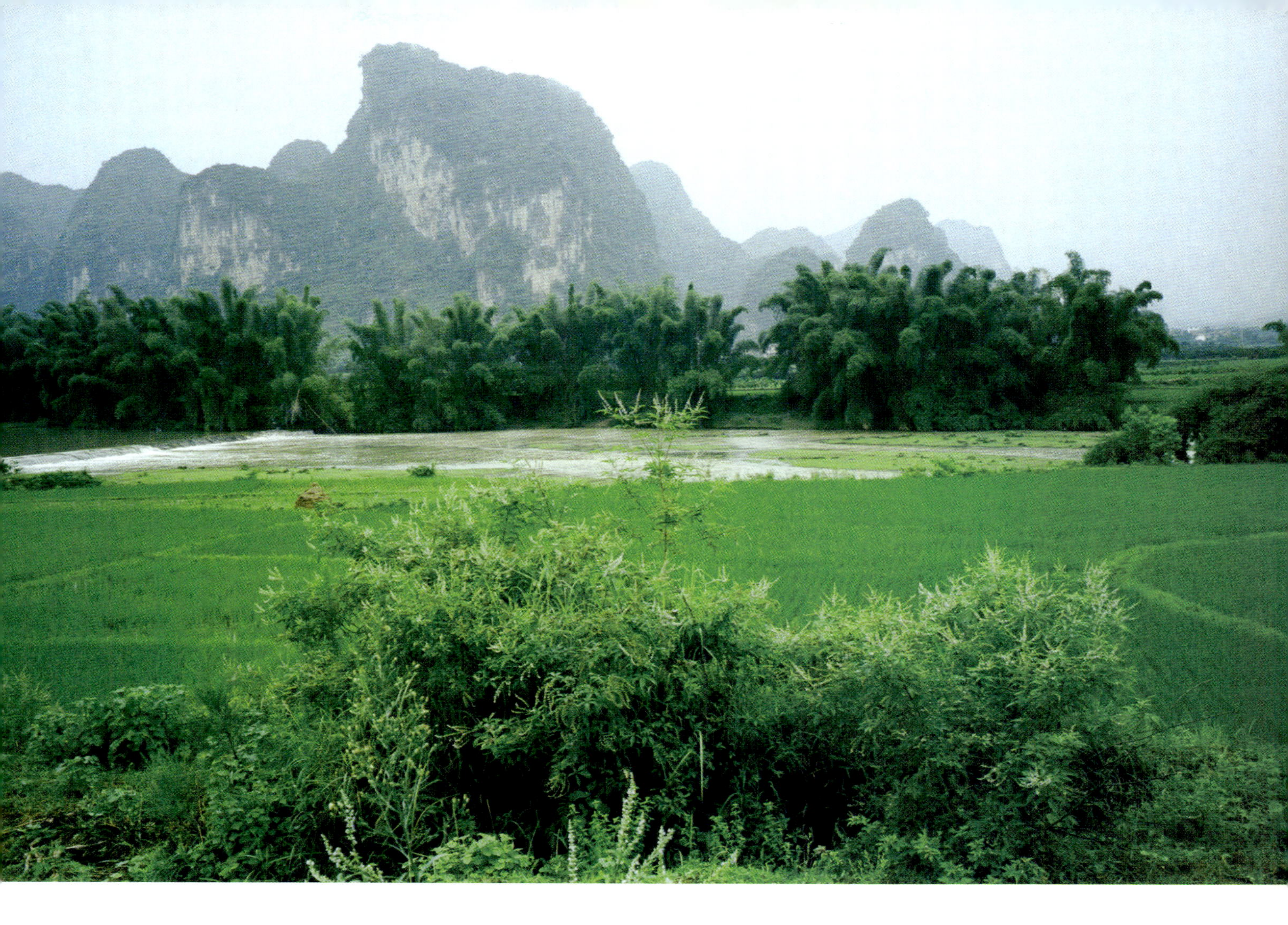

Yangshuo 阳朔

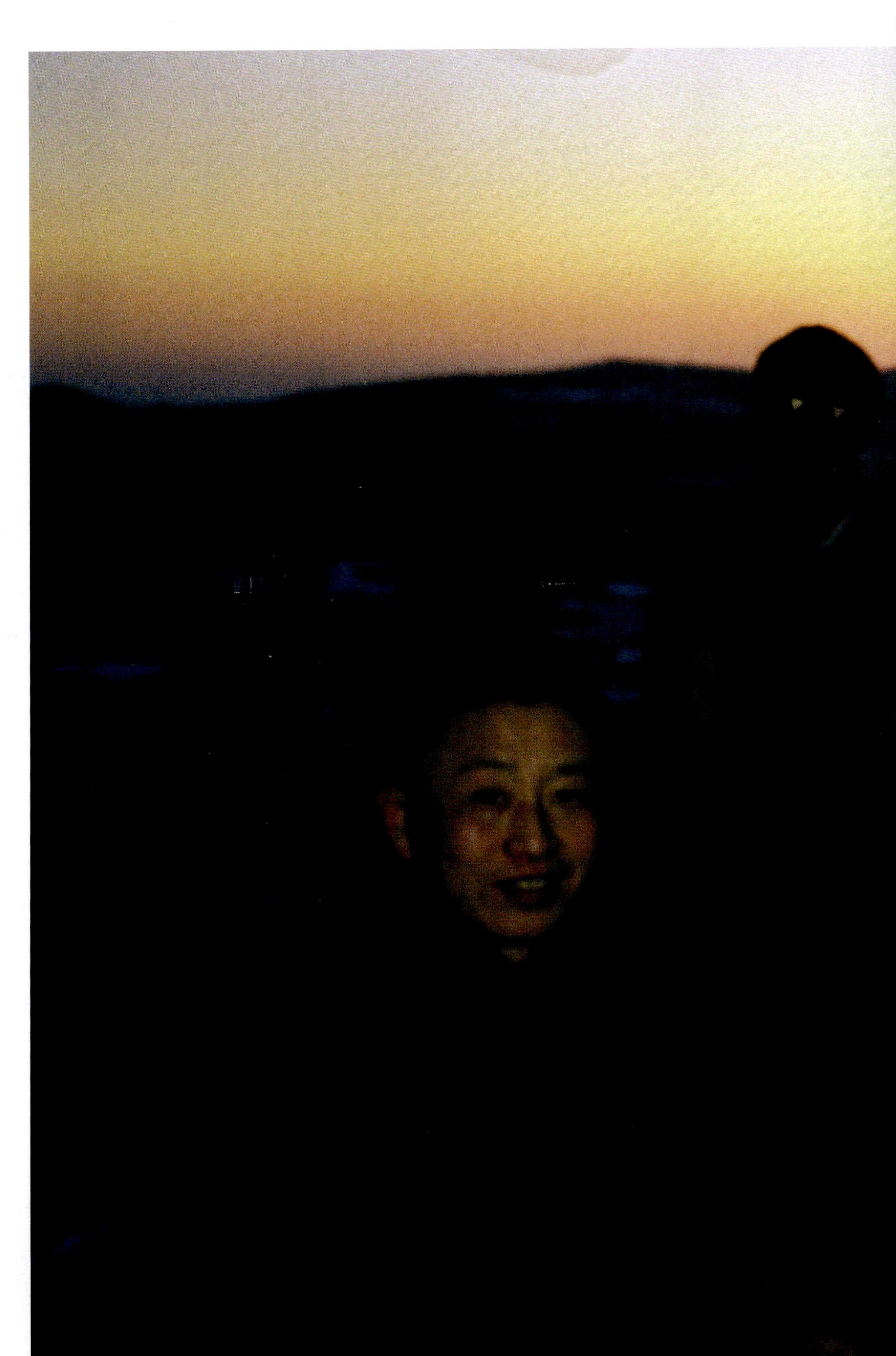

On a Mountain Peak 在山顶

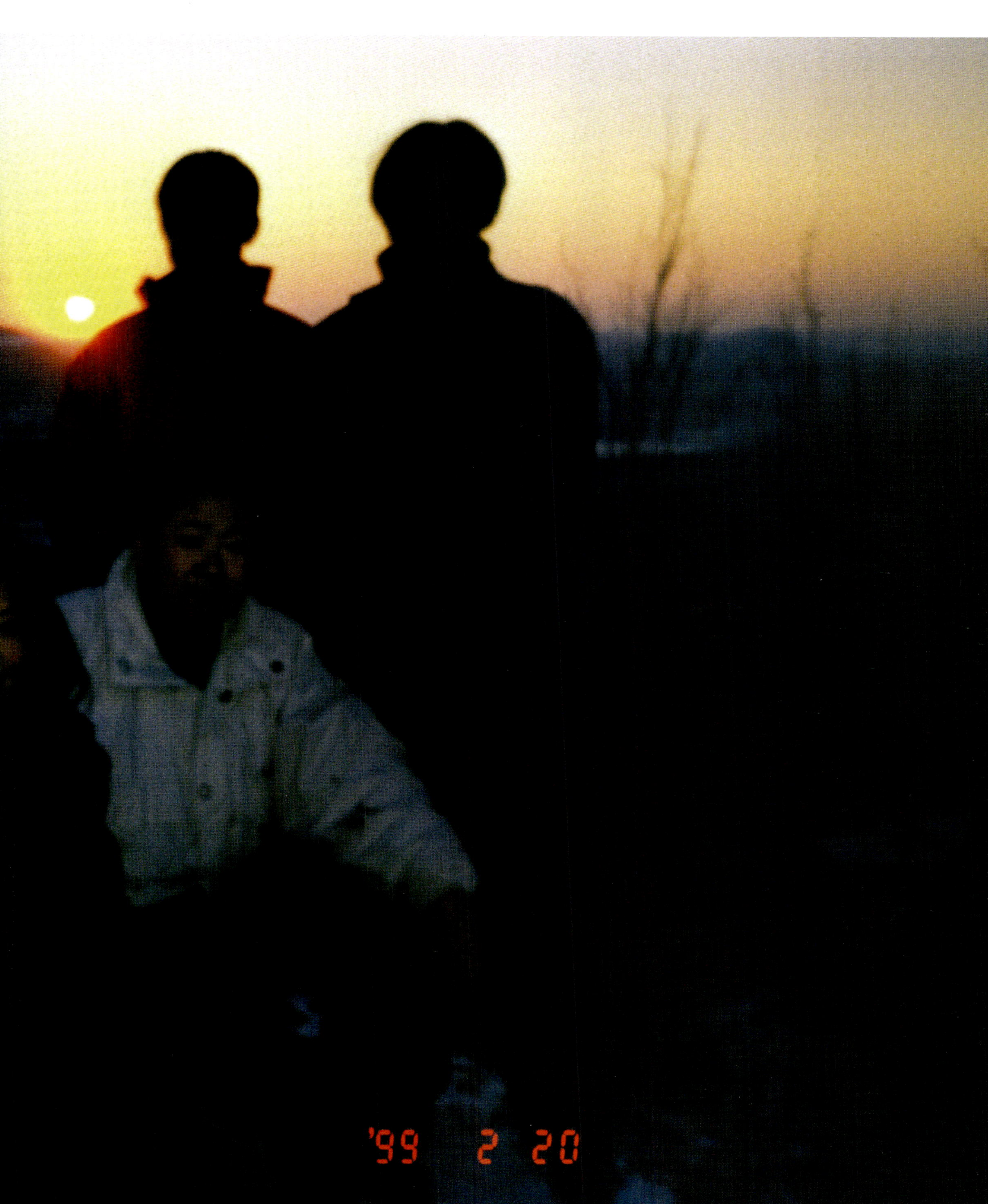

'99 2 20

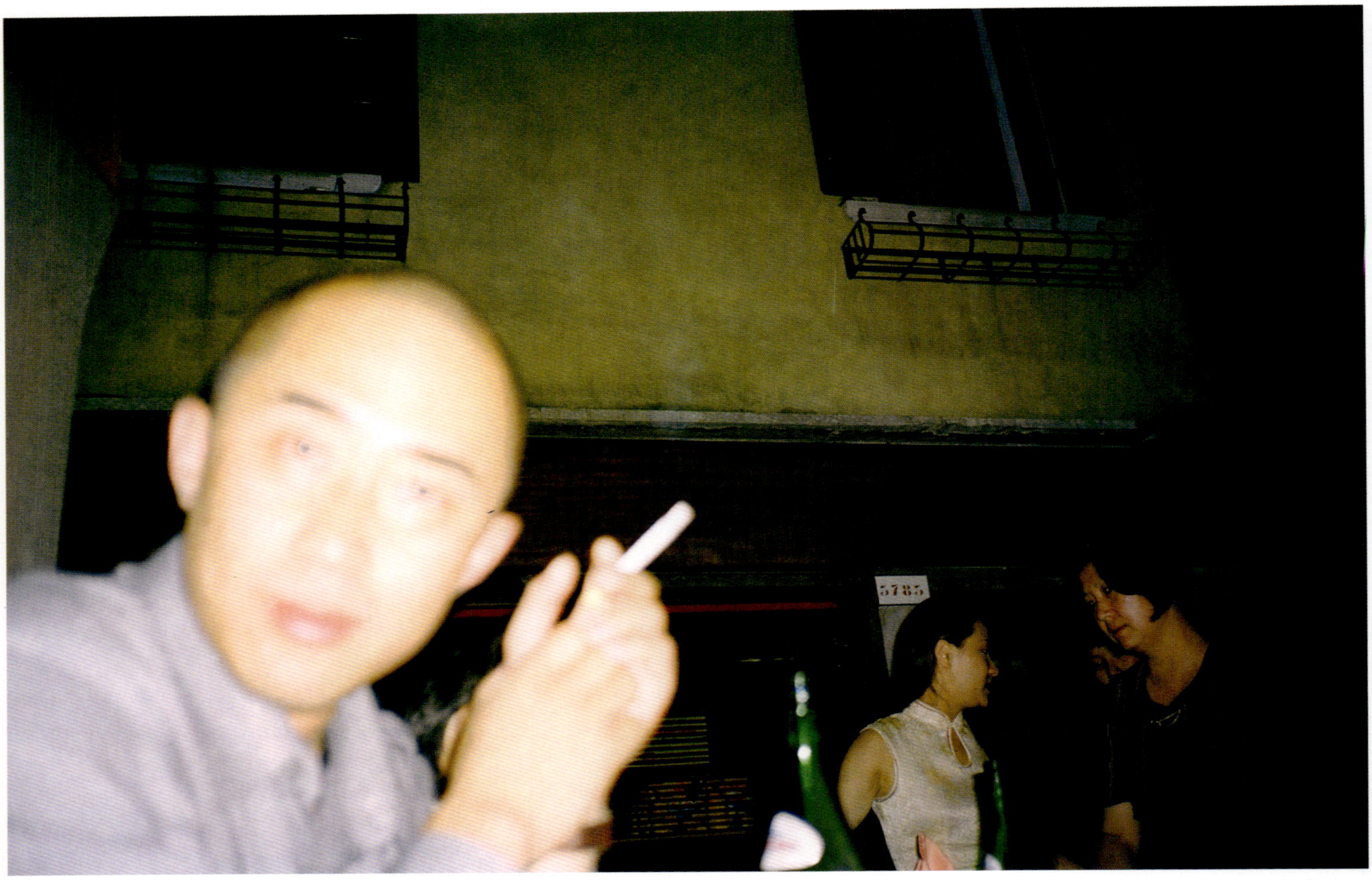

Artist 画家

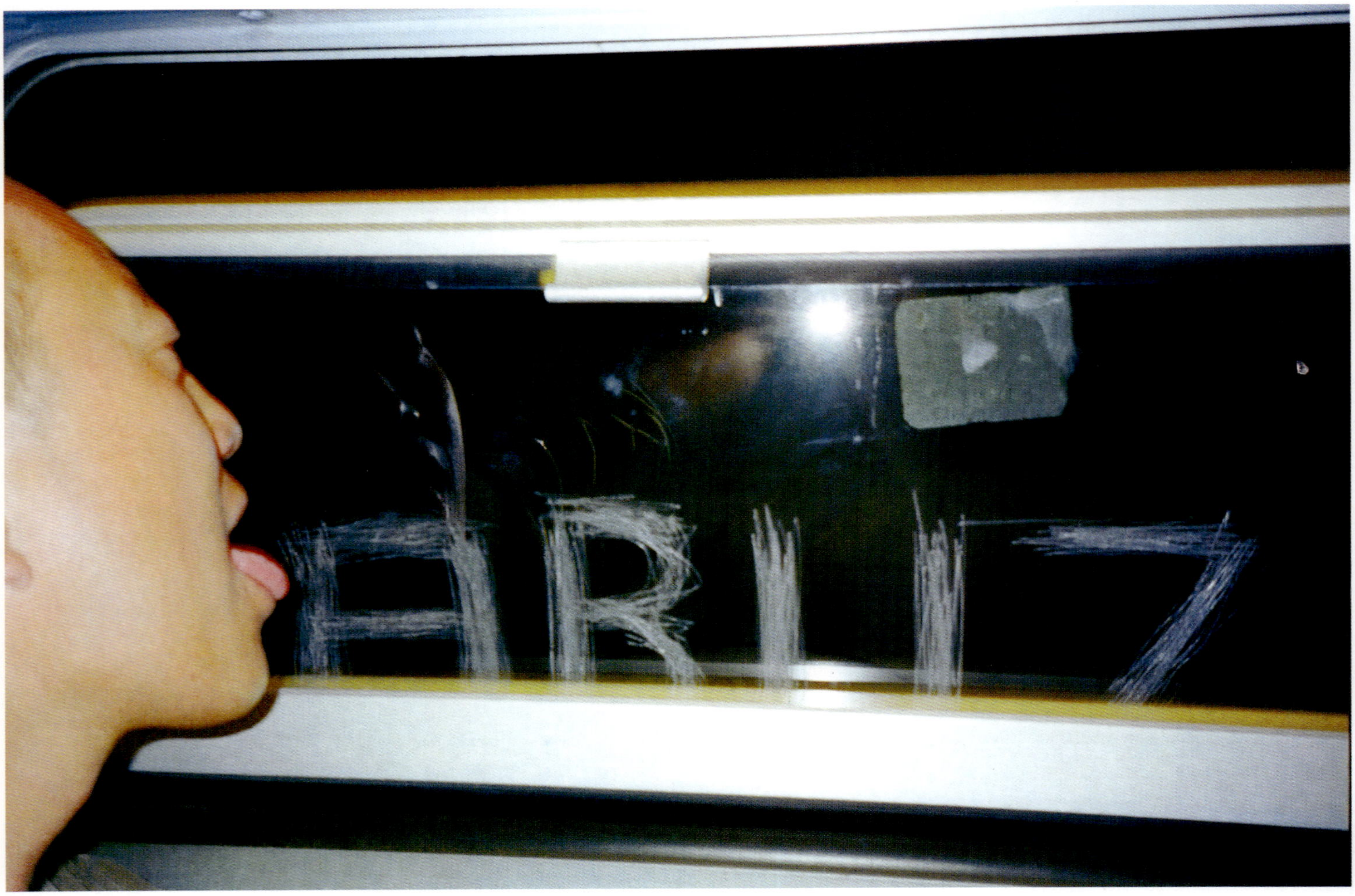

On the Paris Subway 在巴黎地铁上

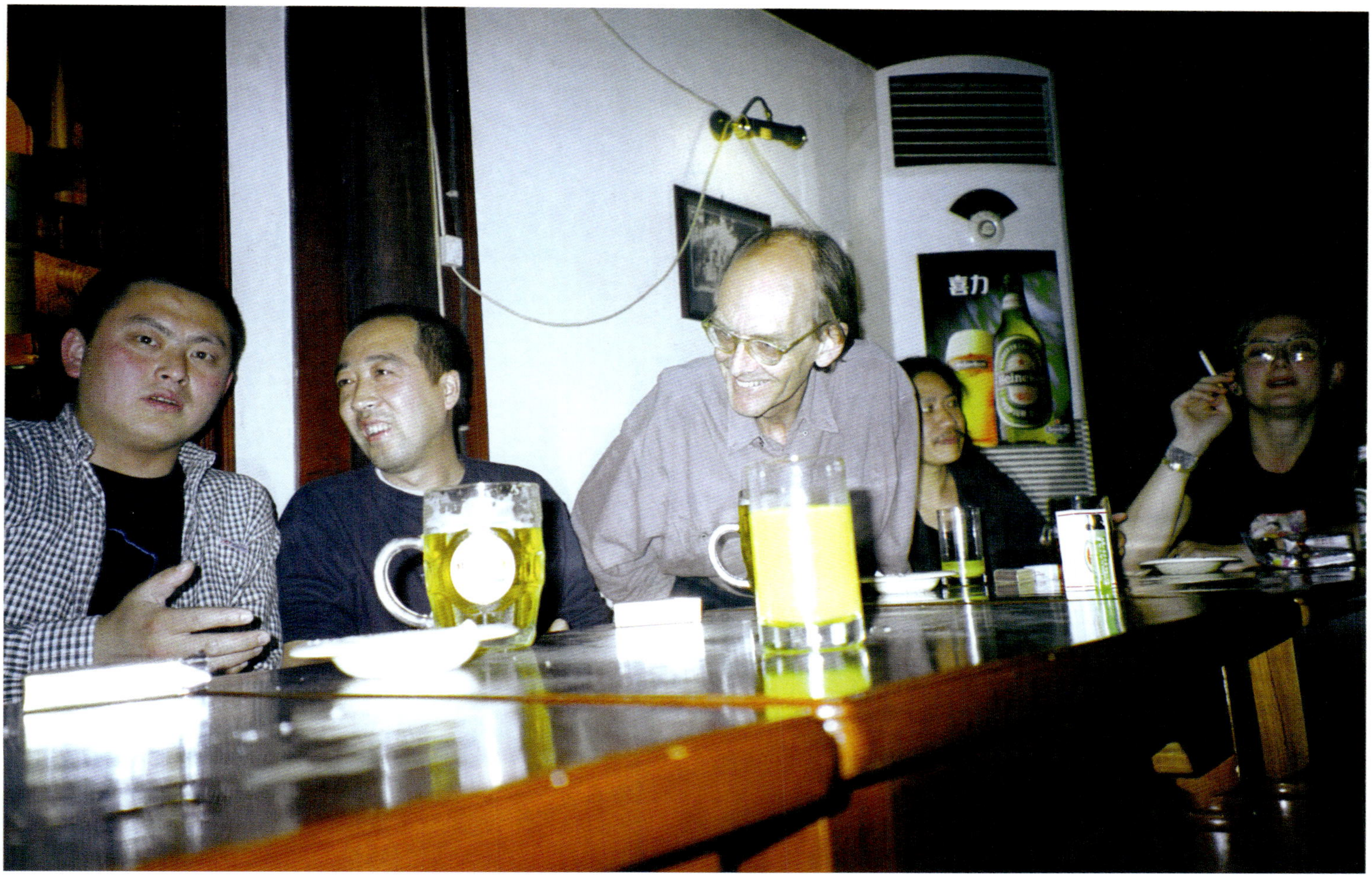

Hans, October 1998 1998年的汉斯

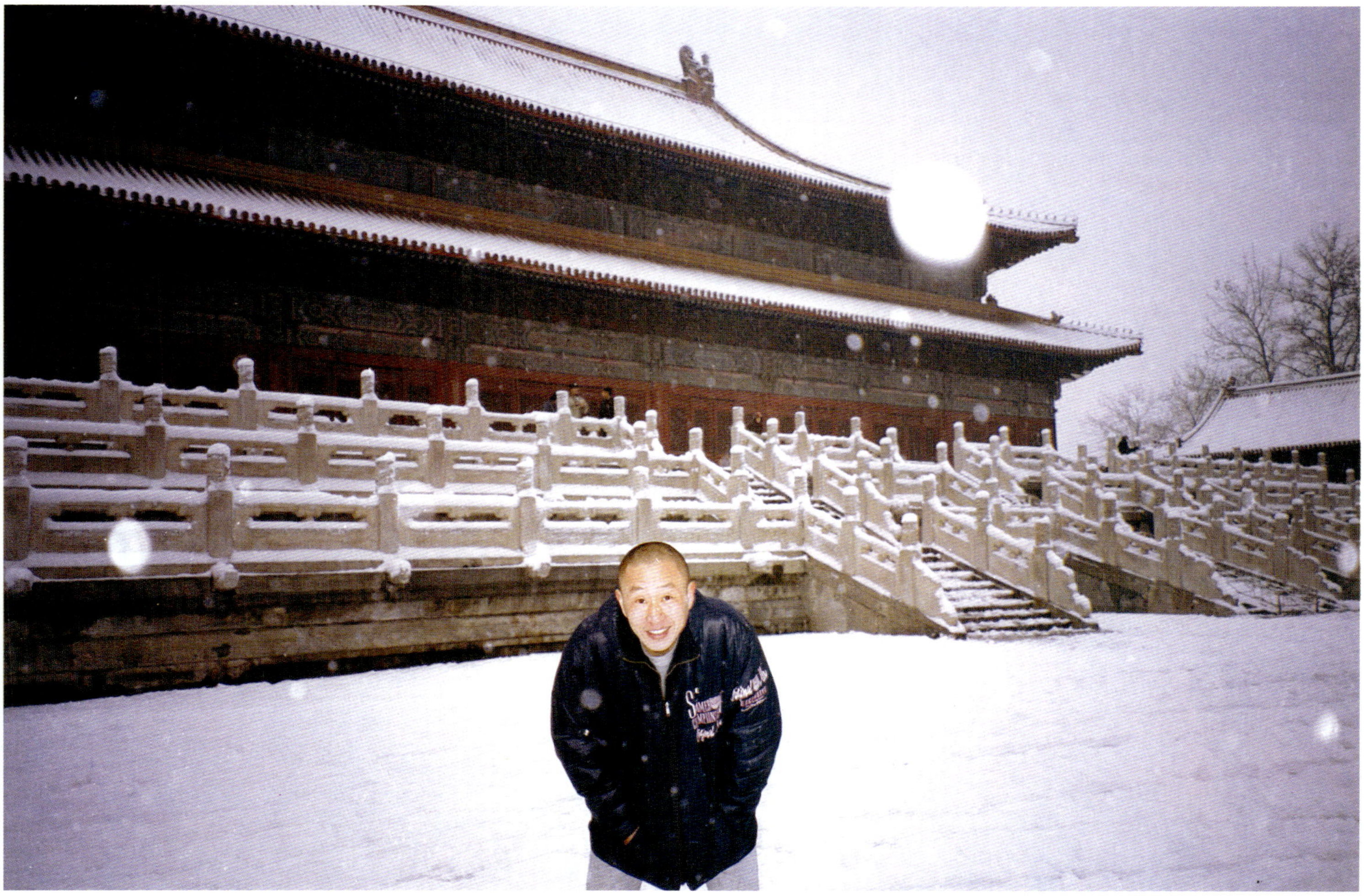

Ma Yunfei at the Forbidden City 马云飞在太庙

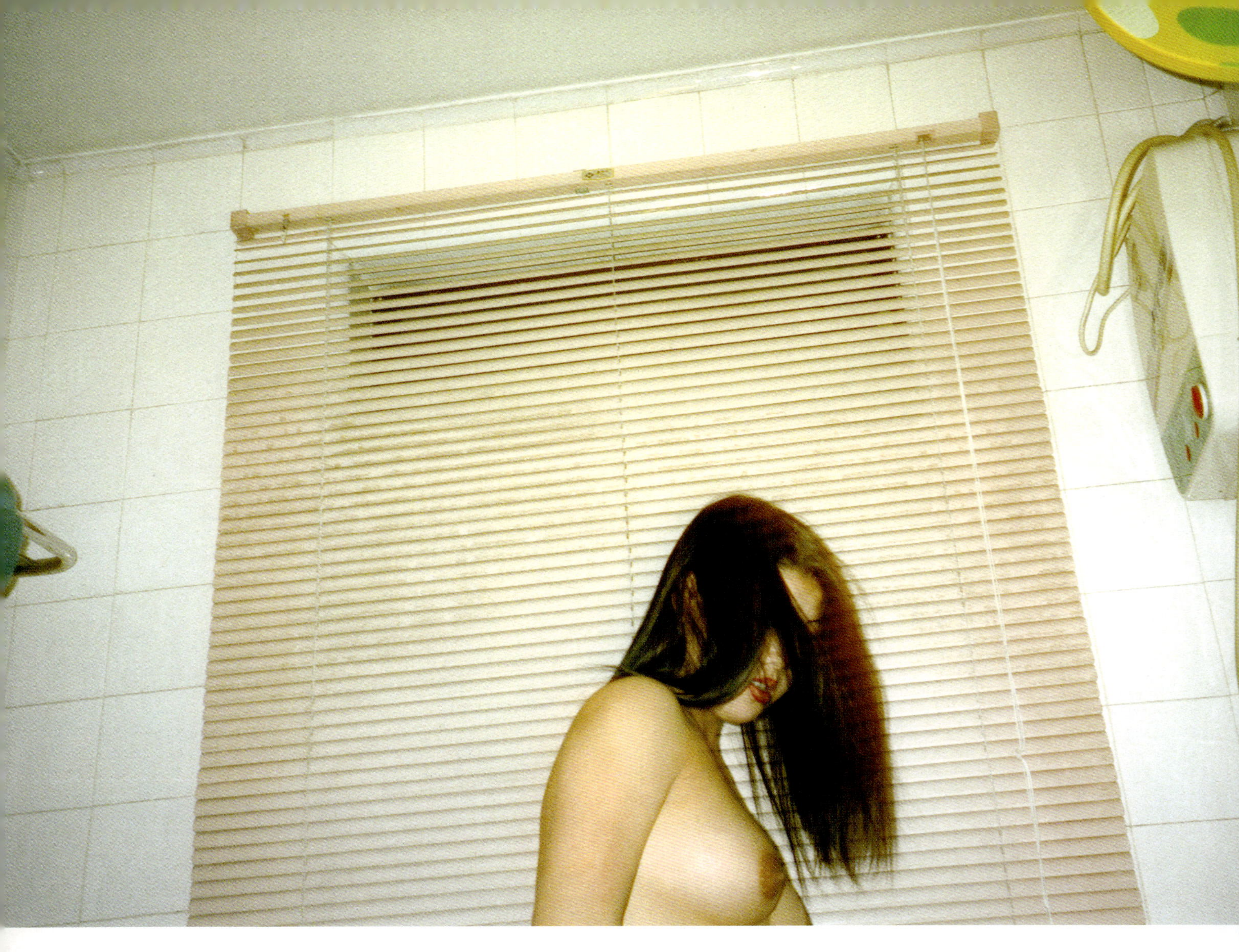

Shower 冲澡间

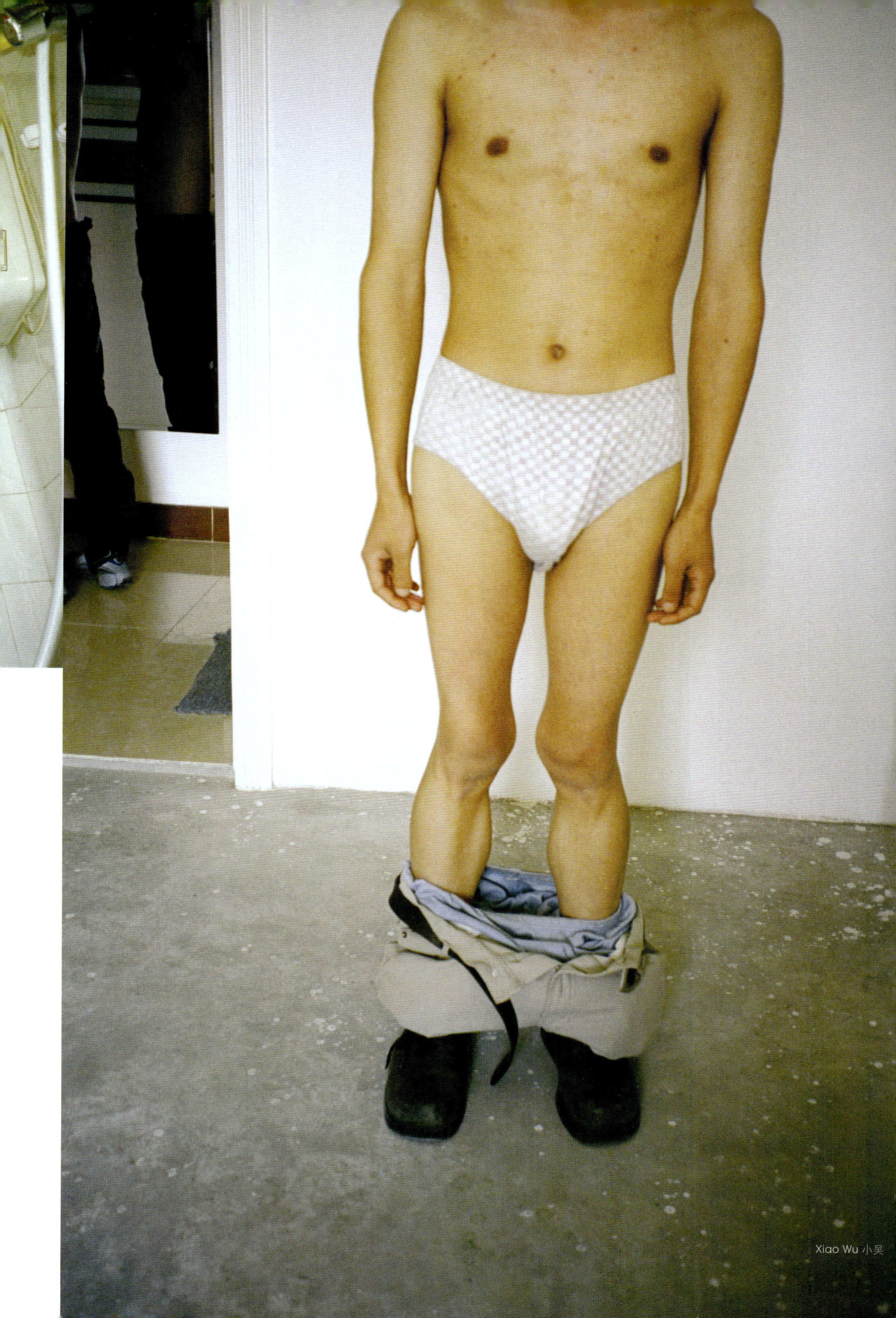

Xiao Wu 小吴

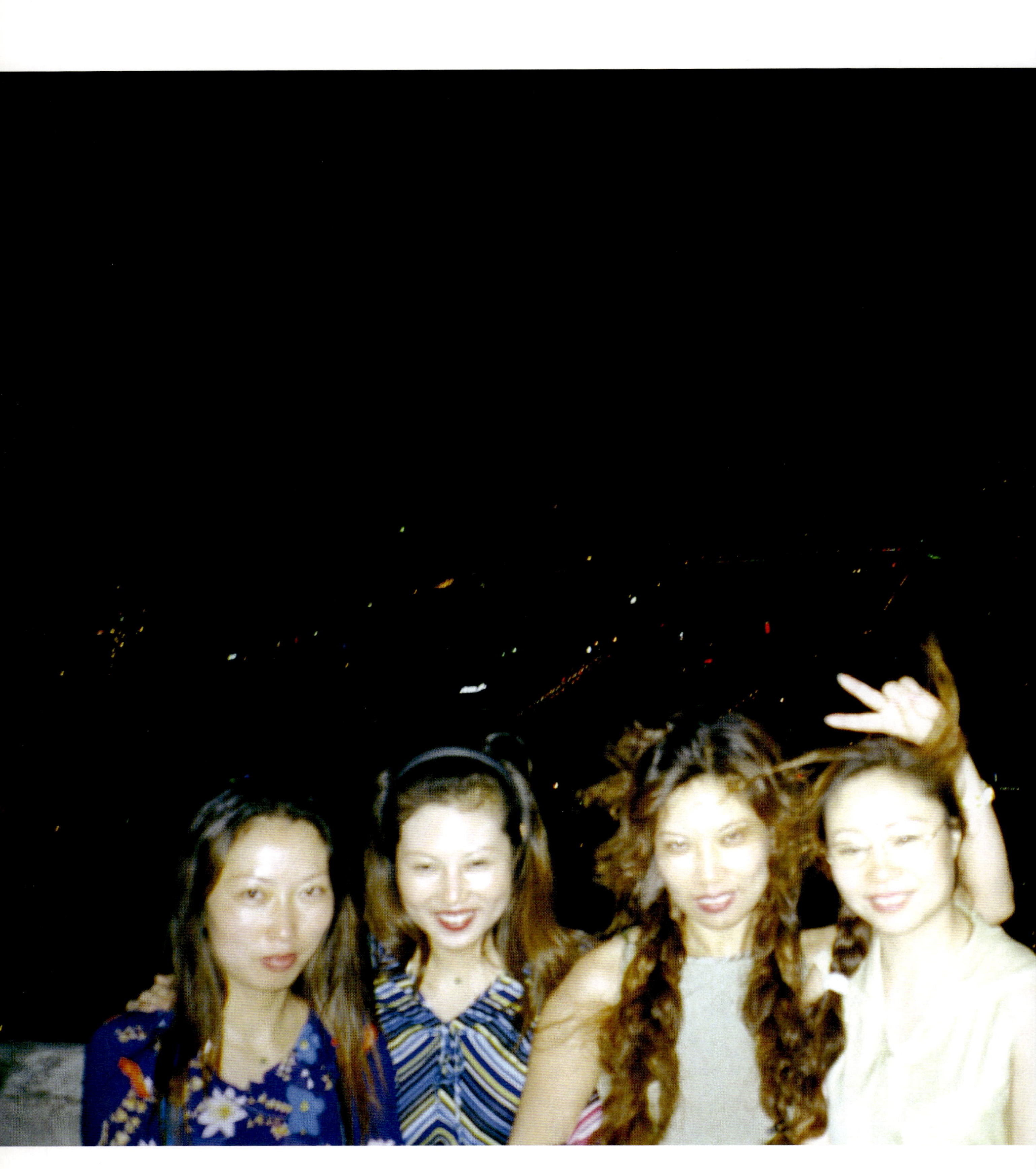

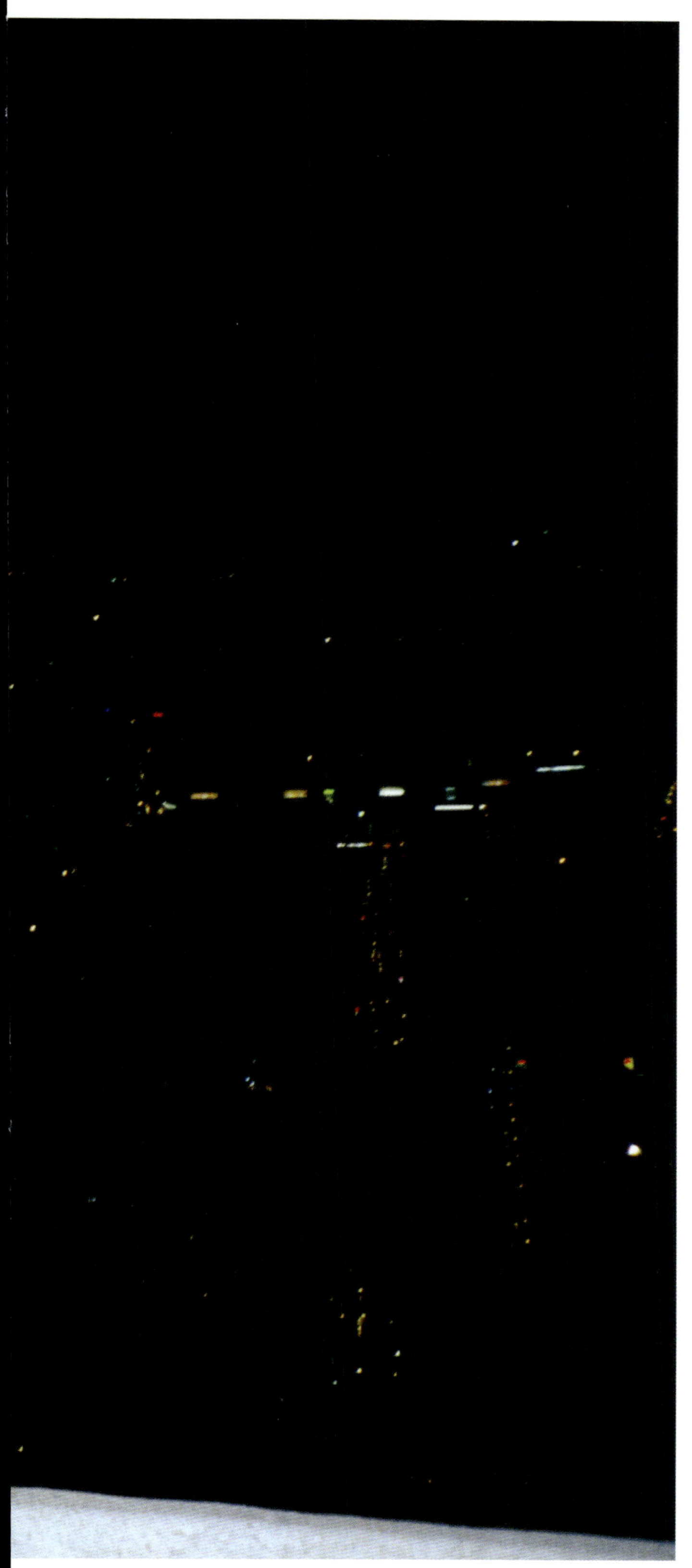

Four Girls from Lanzhou 四个兰州姑娘

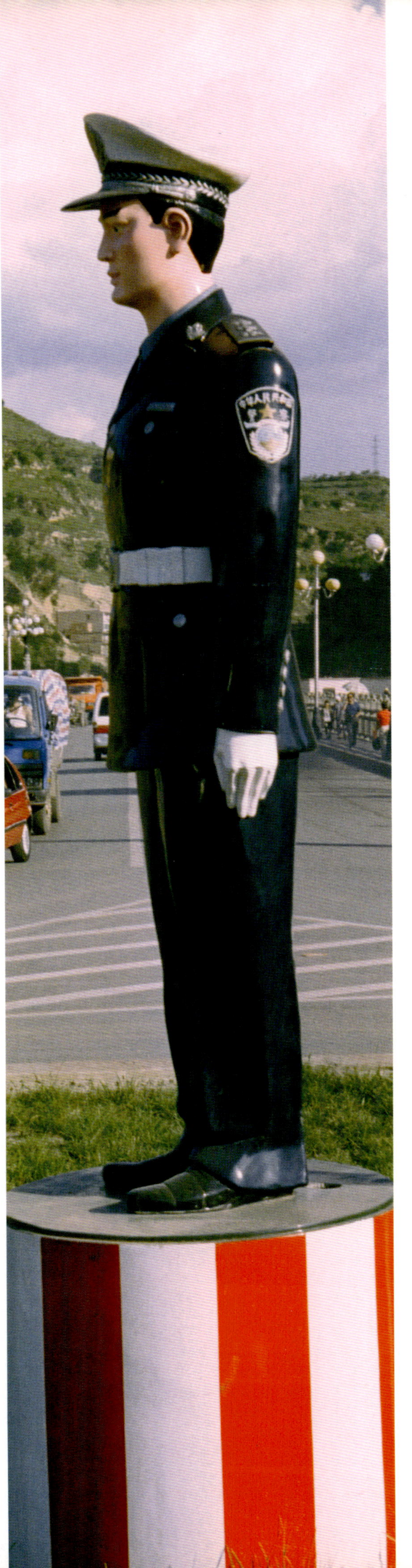

Policeman Statue 假警察

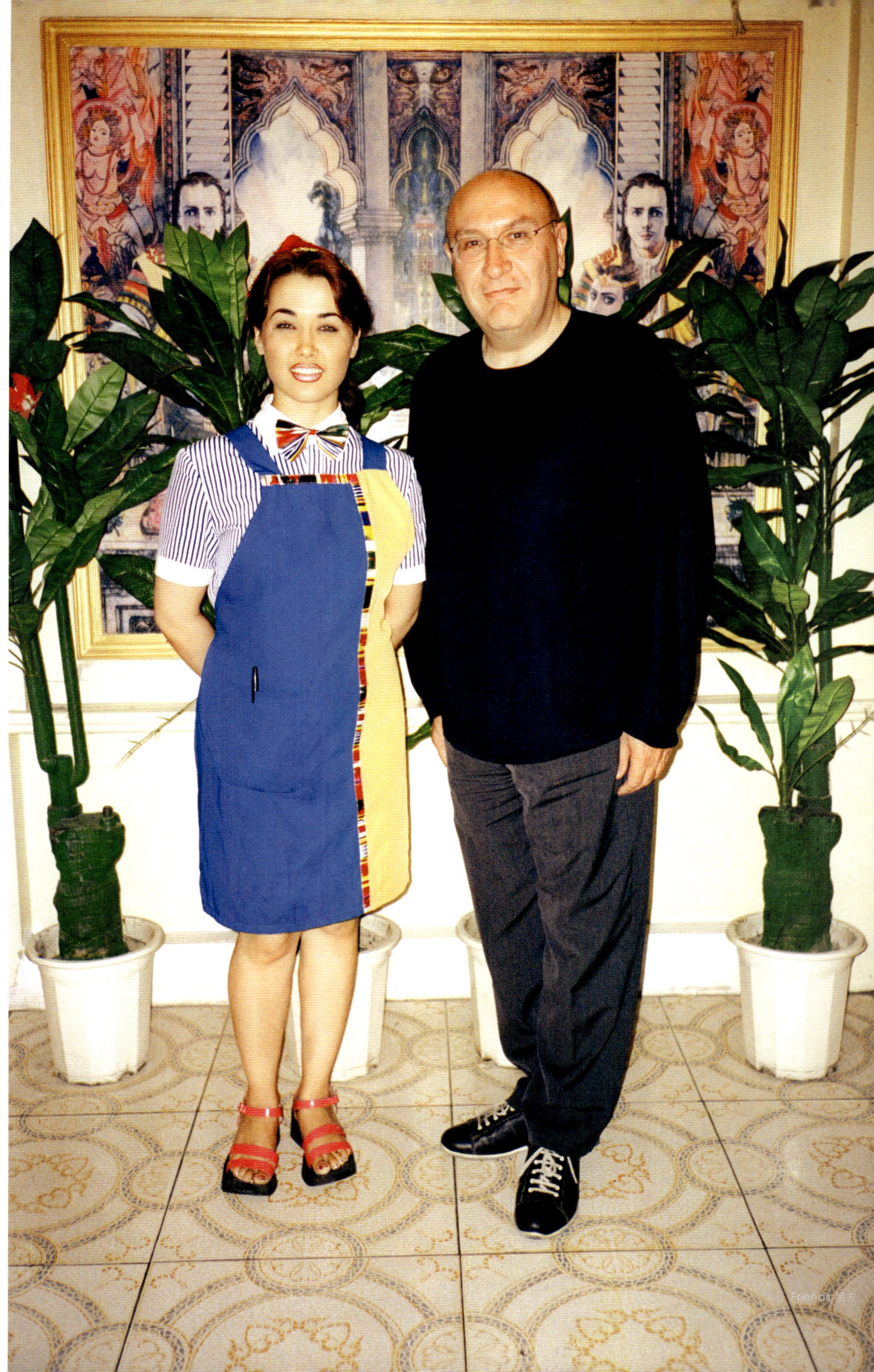
Friends 朋友

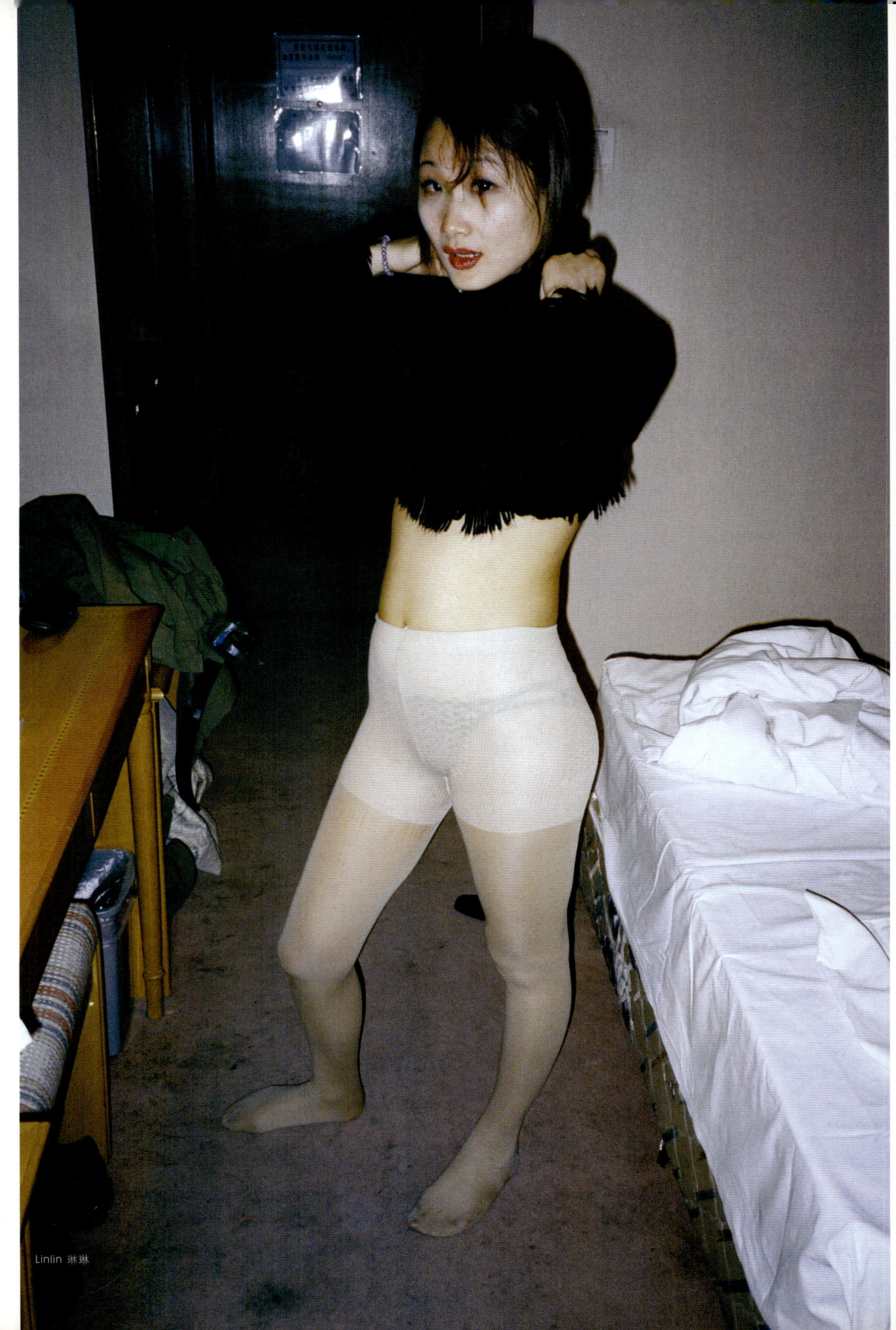

Linlin 琳琳

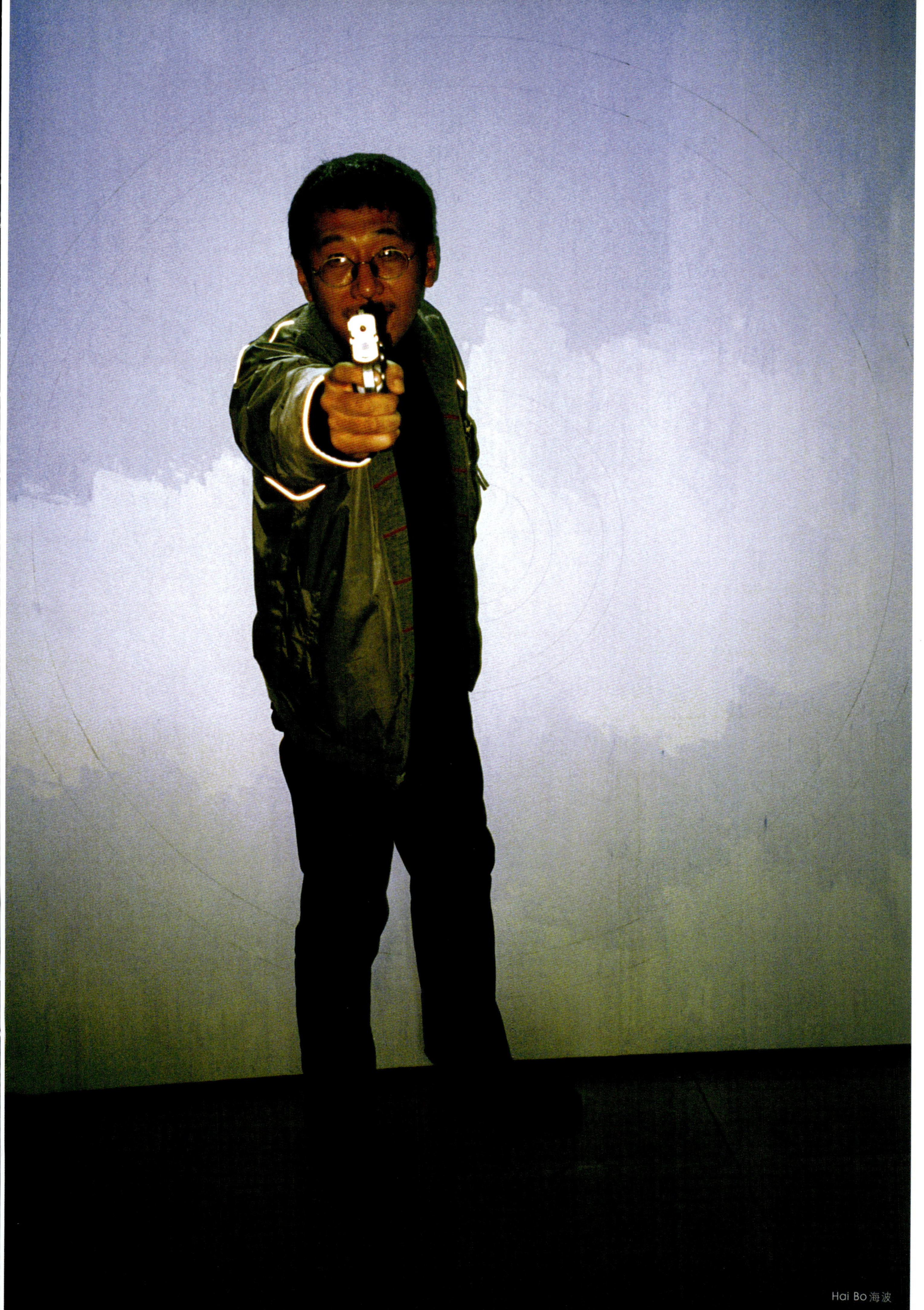

Hai Bo 海波

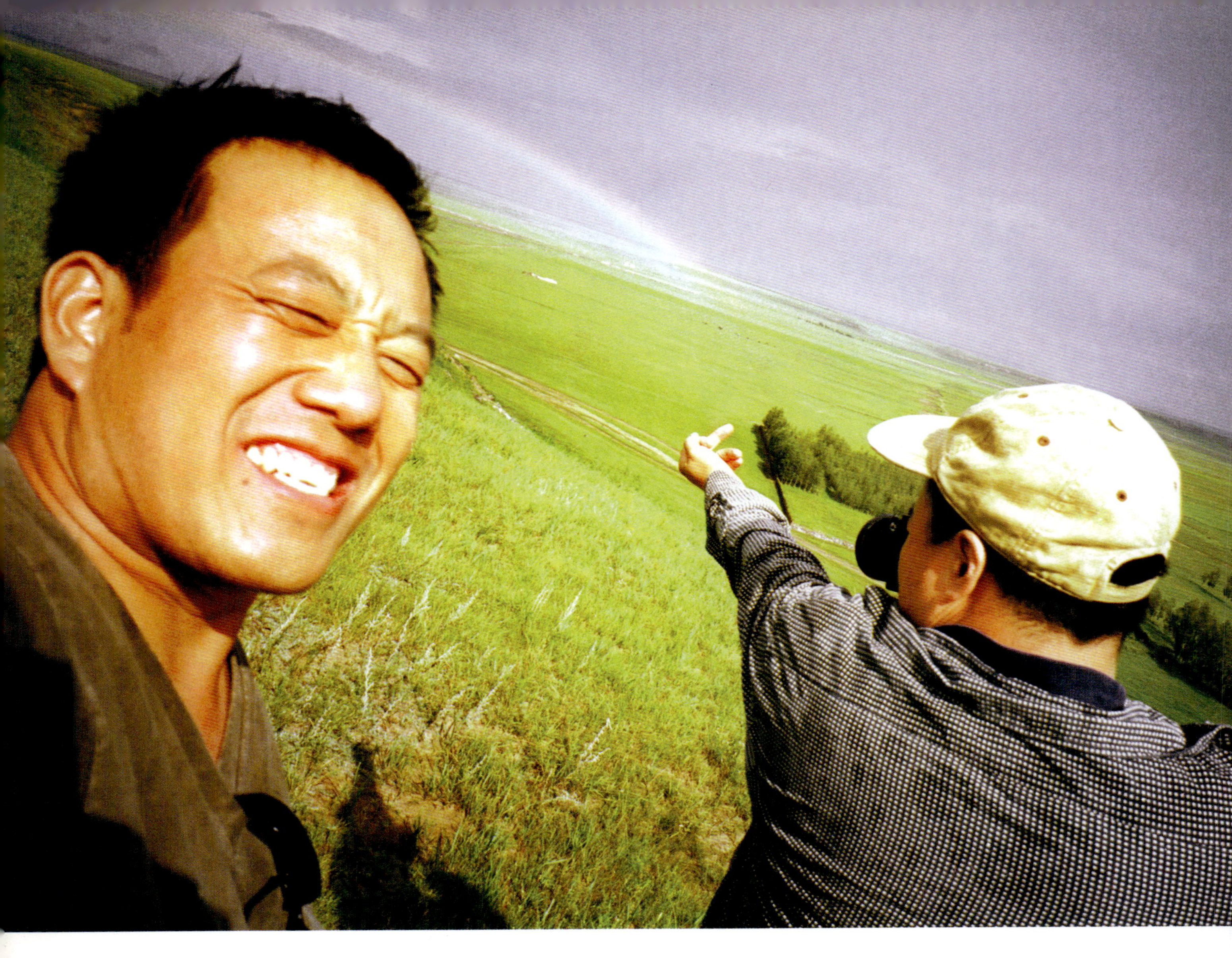

Taking a Photo 拍照

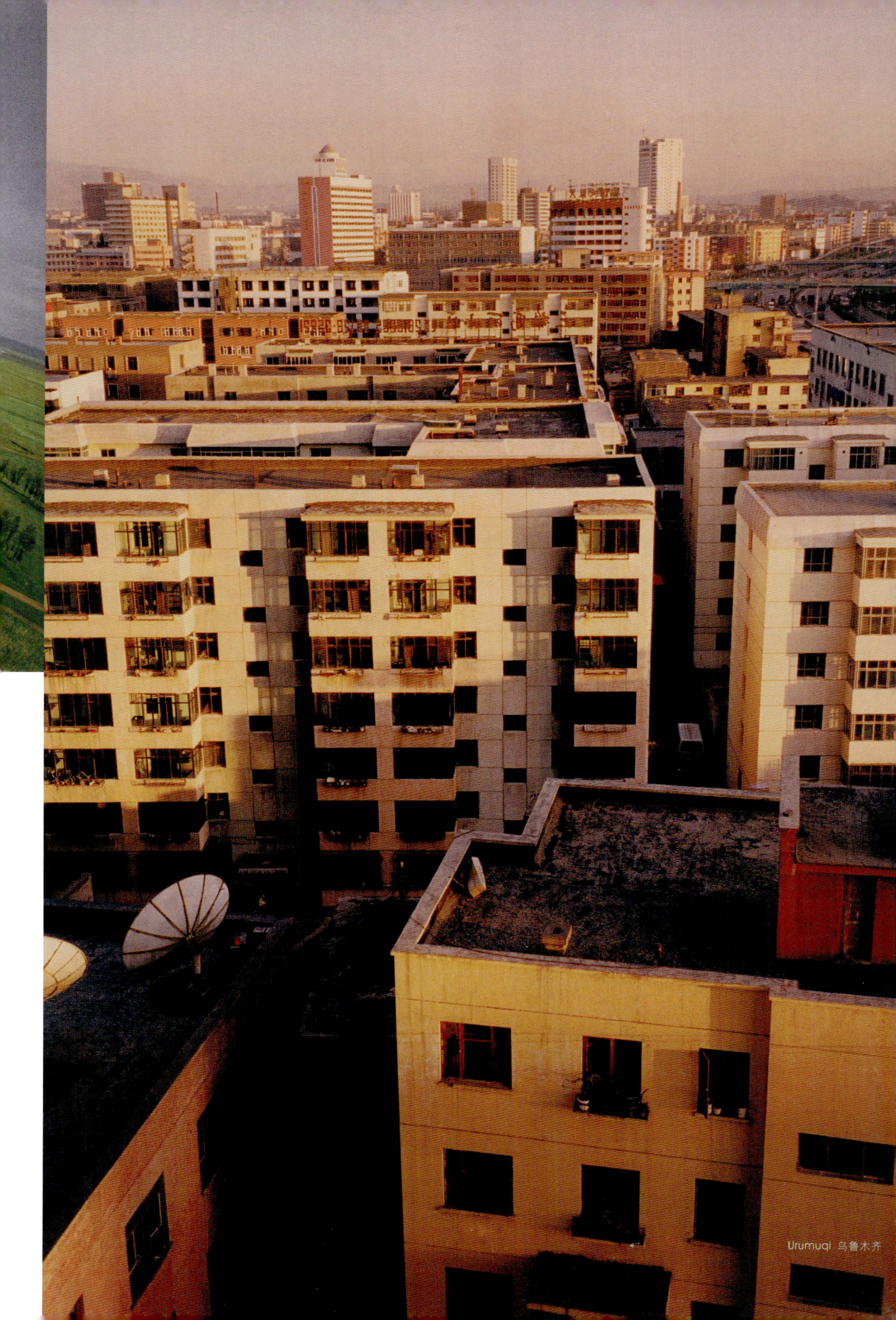
Urumuqi 乌鲁木齐

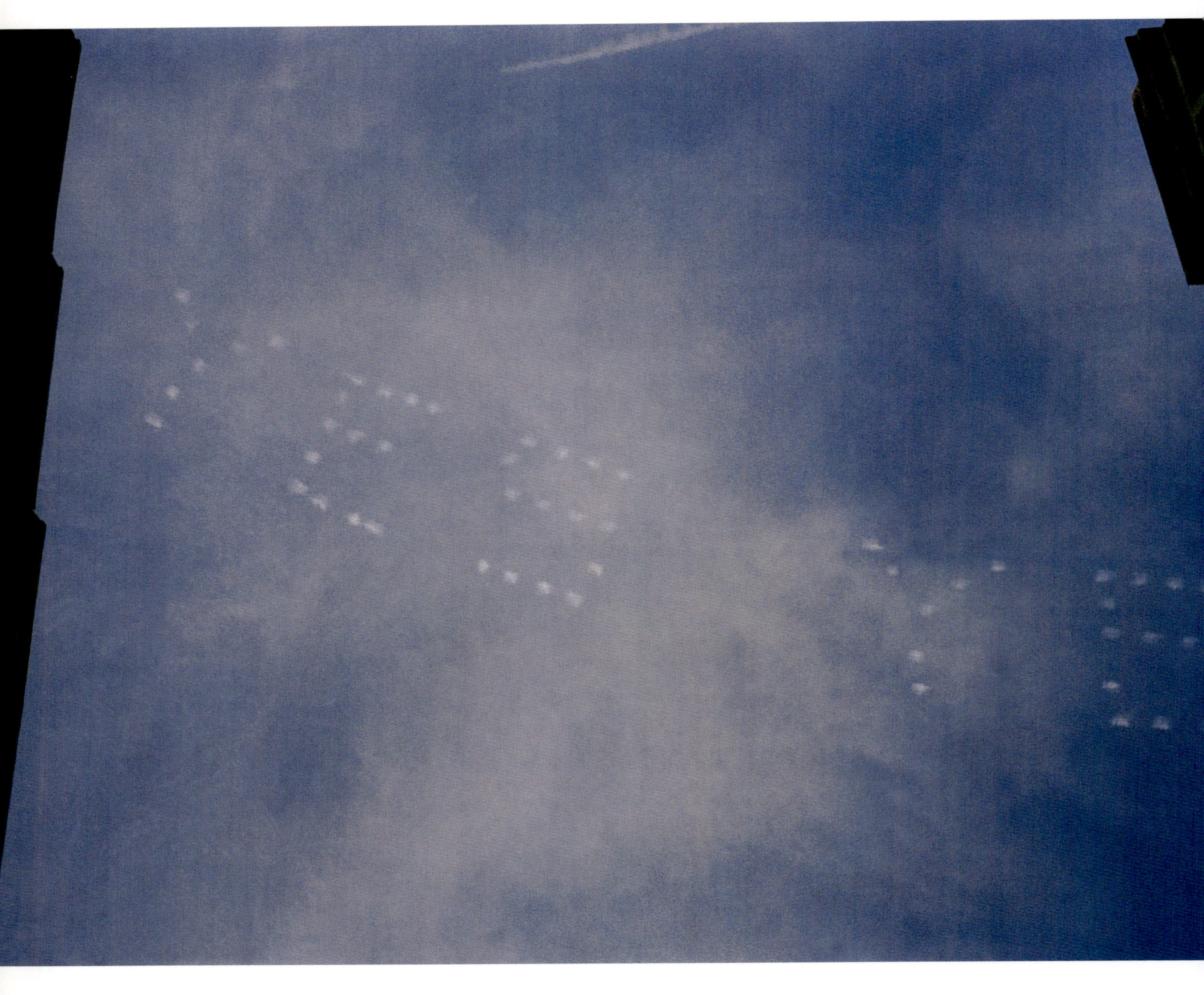

New York Sky 纽约上空

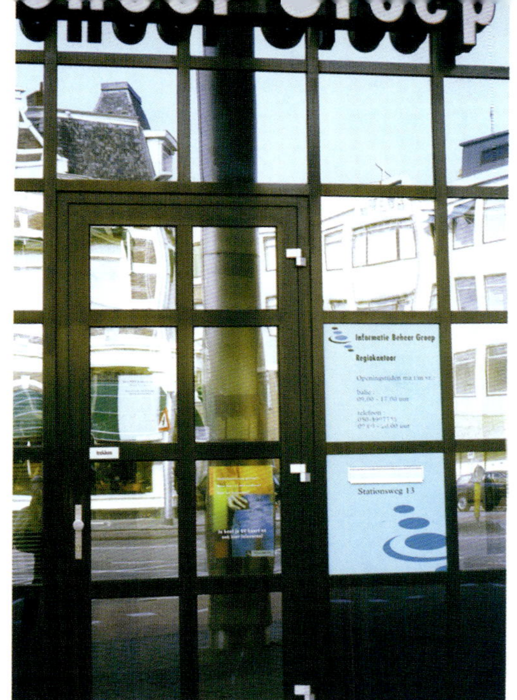
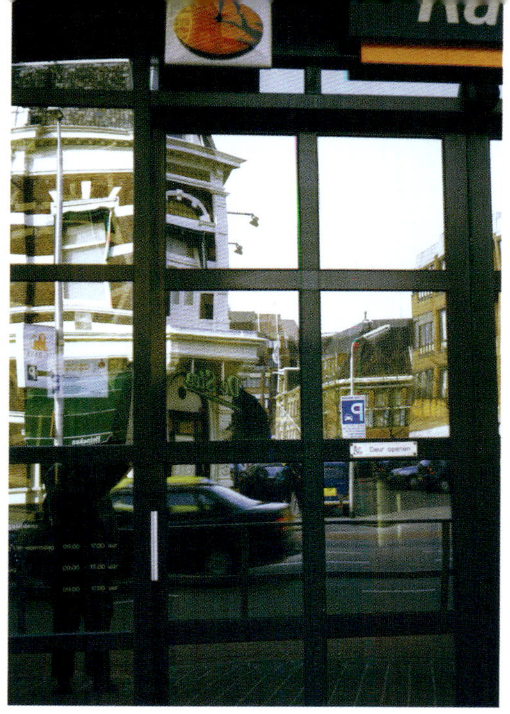
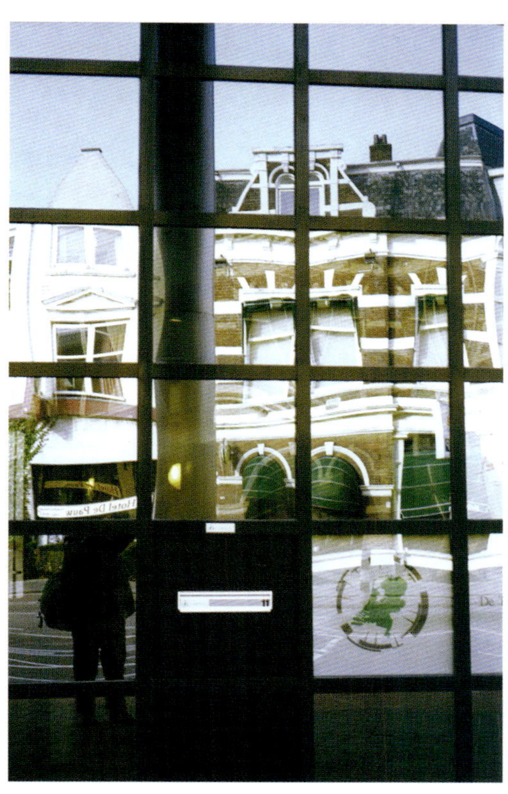
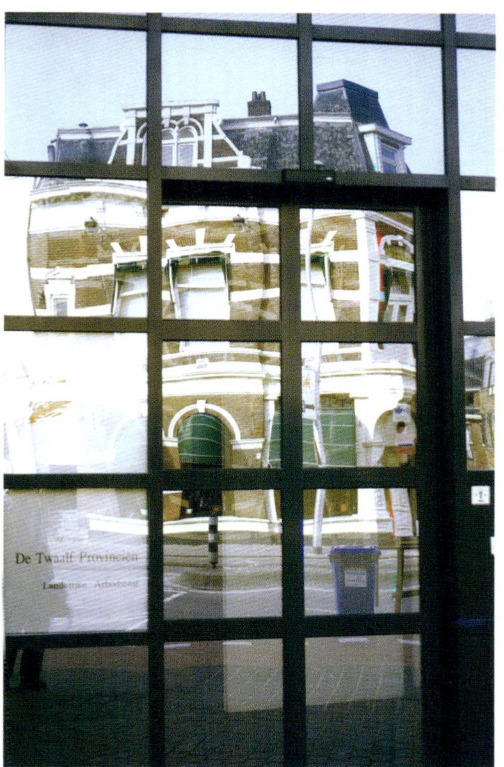
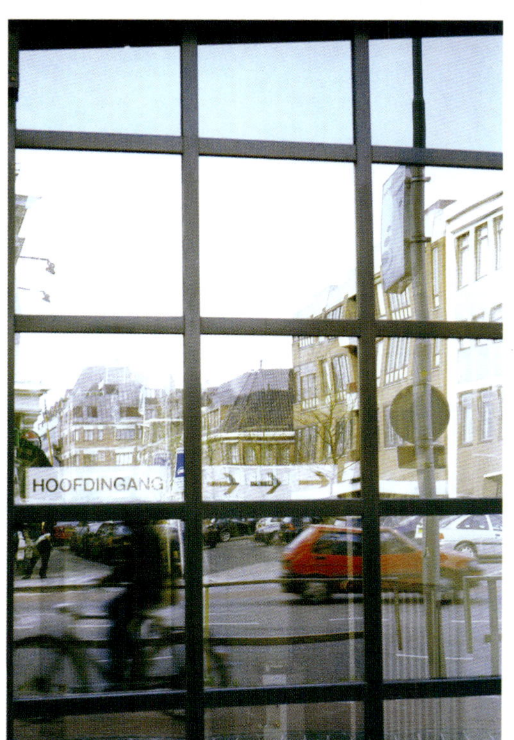
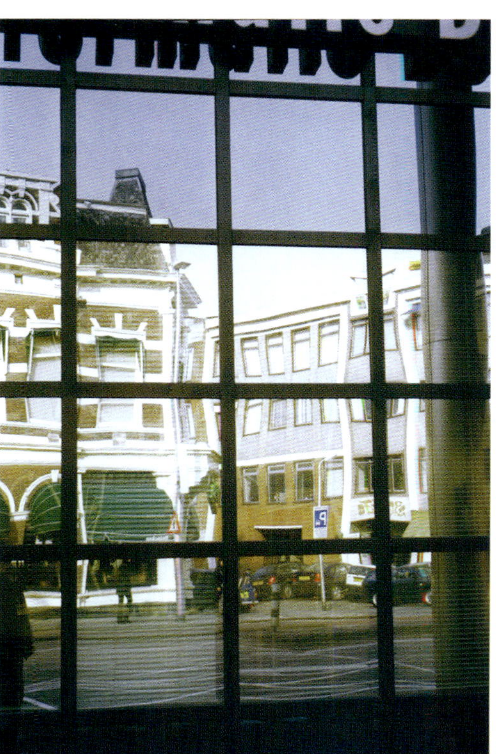

Leeuwarden 利沃尔顿市

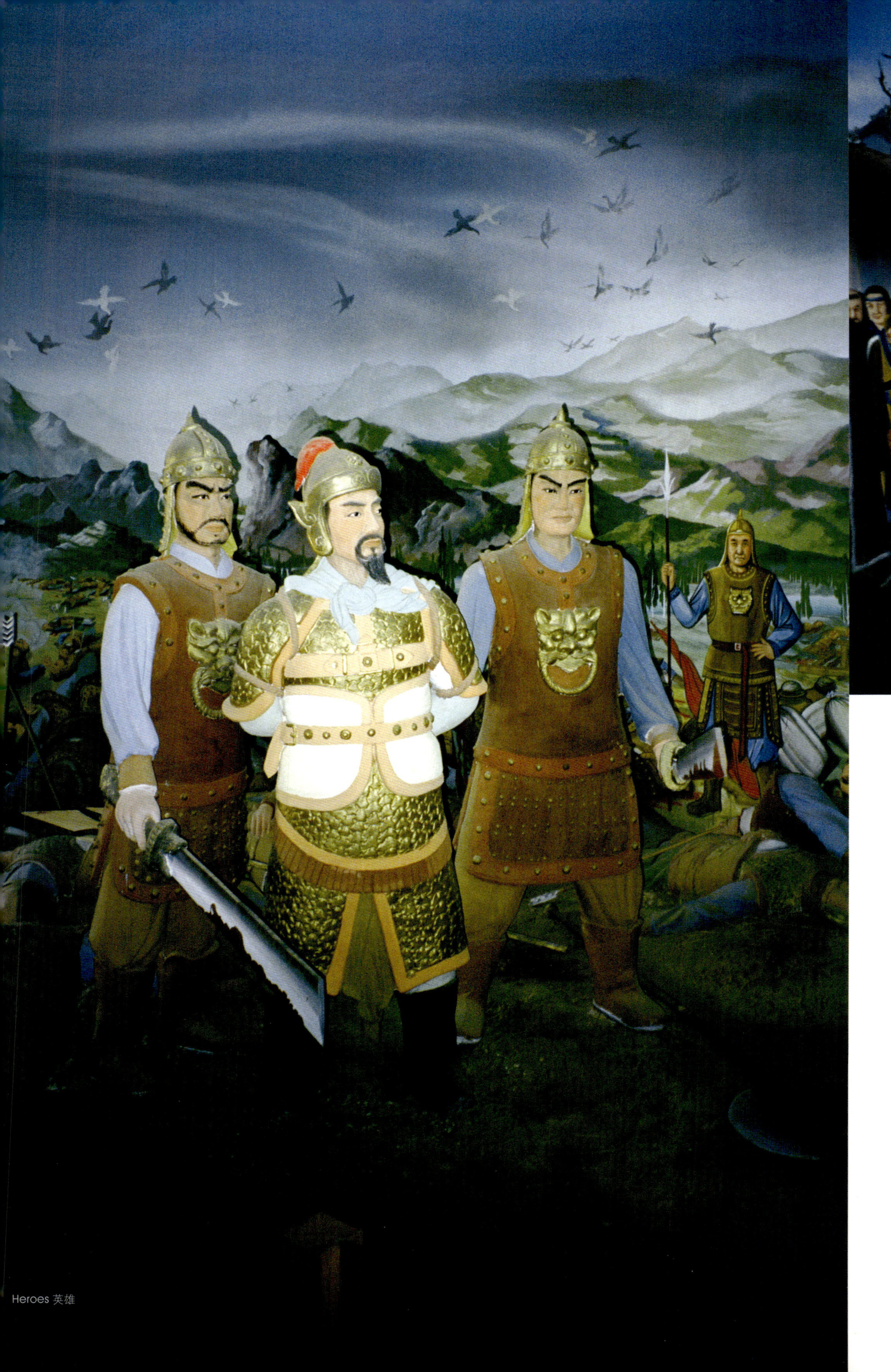
Heroes 英雄

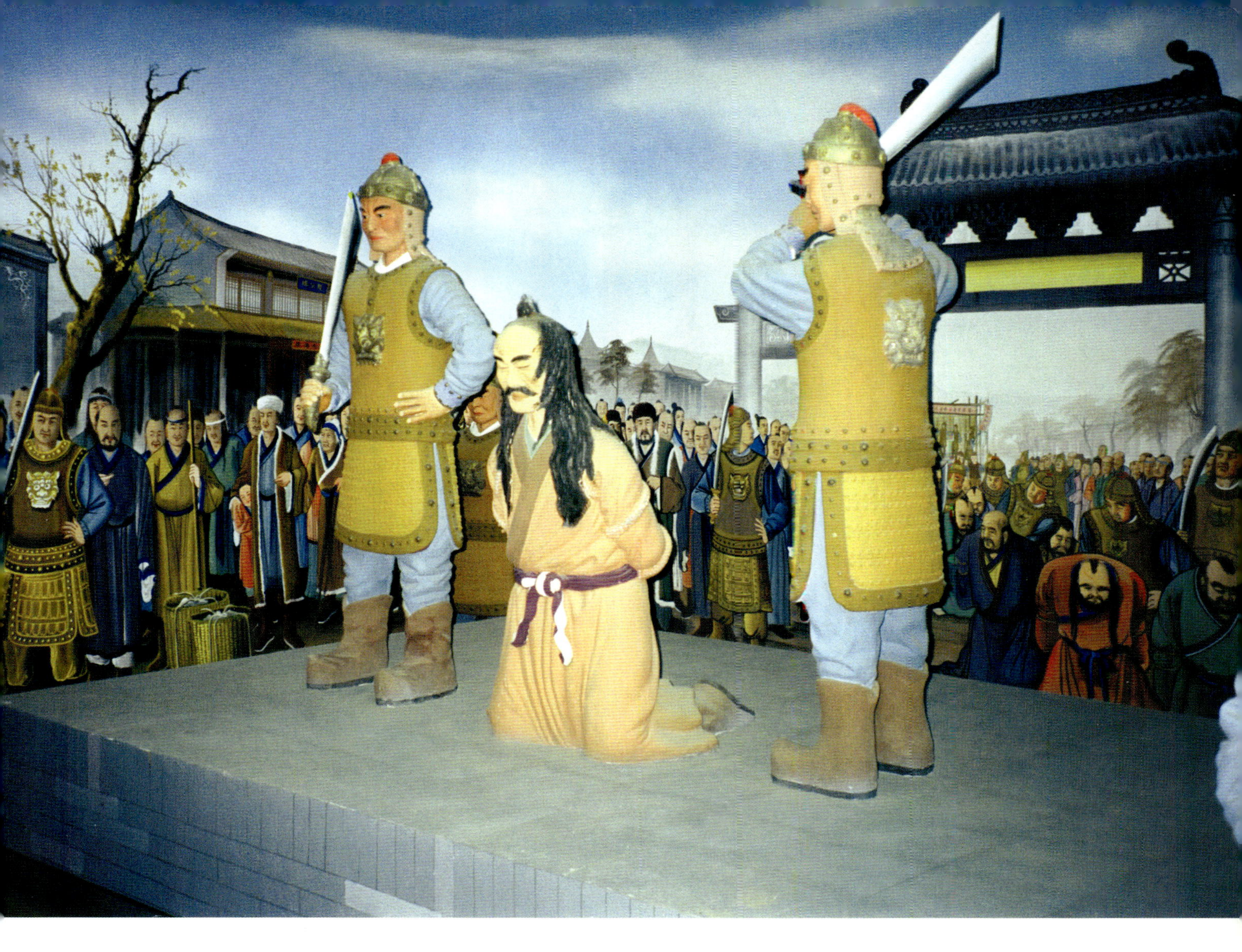

Criminal Execution 囚陡

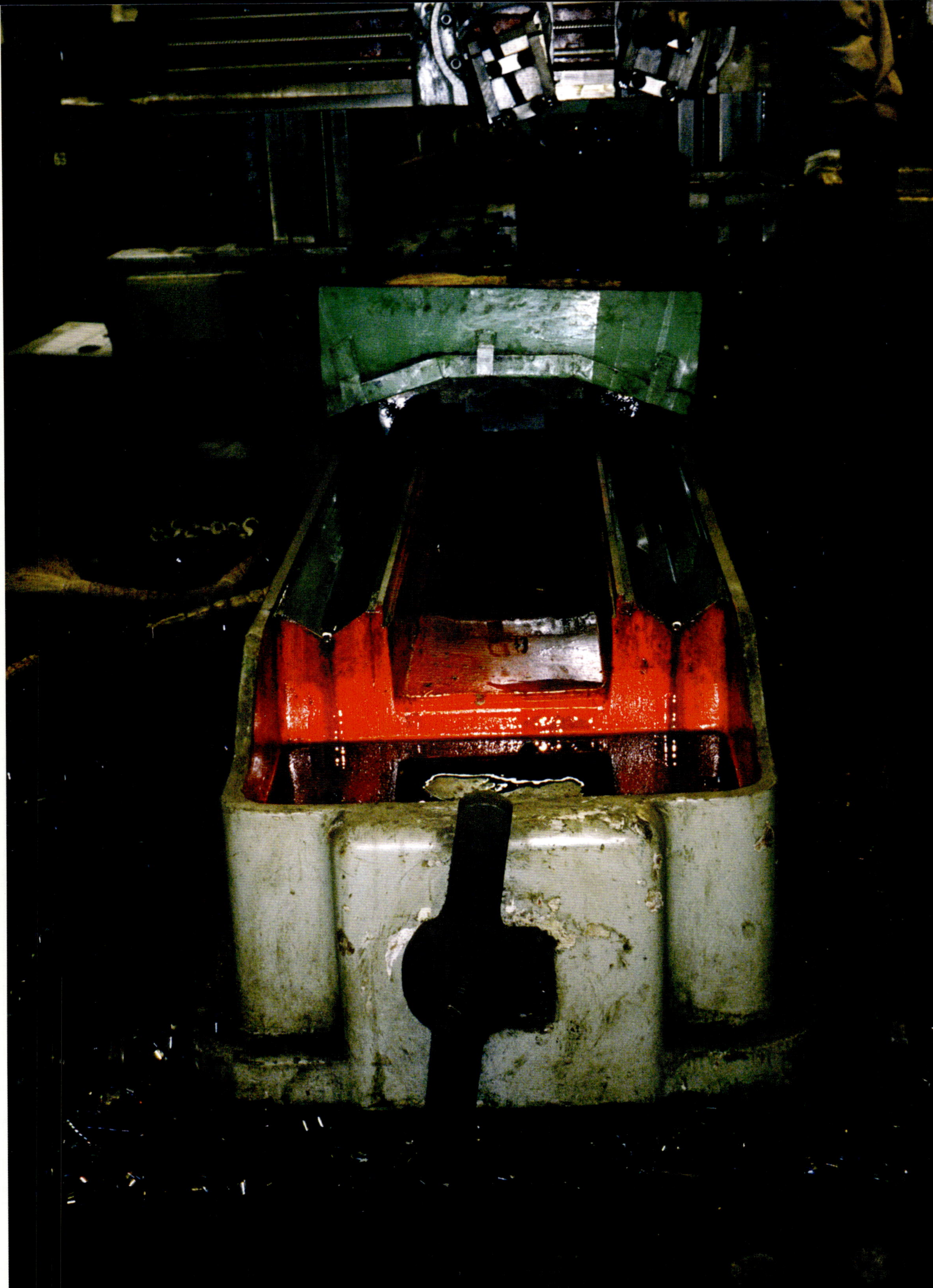

Workshop 车间

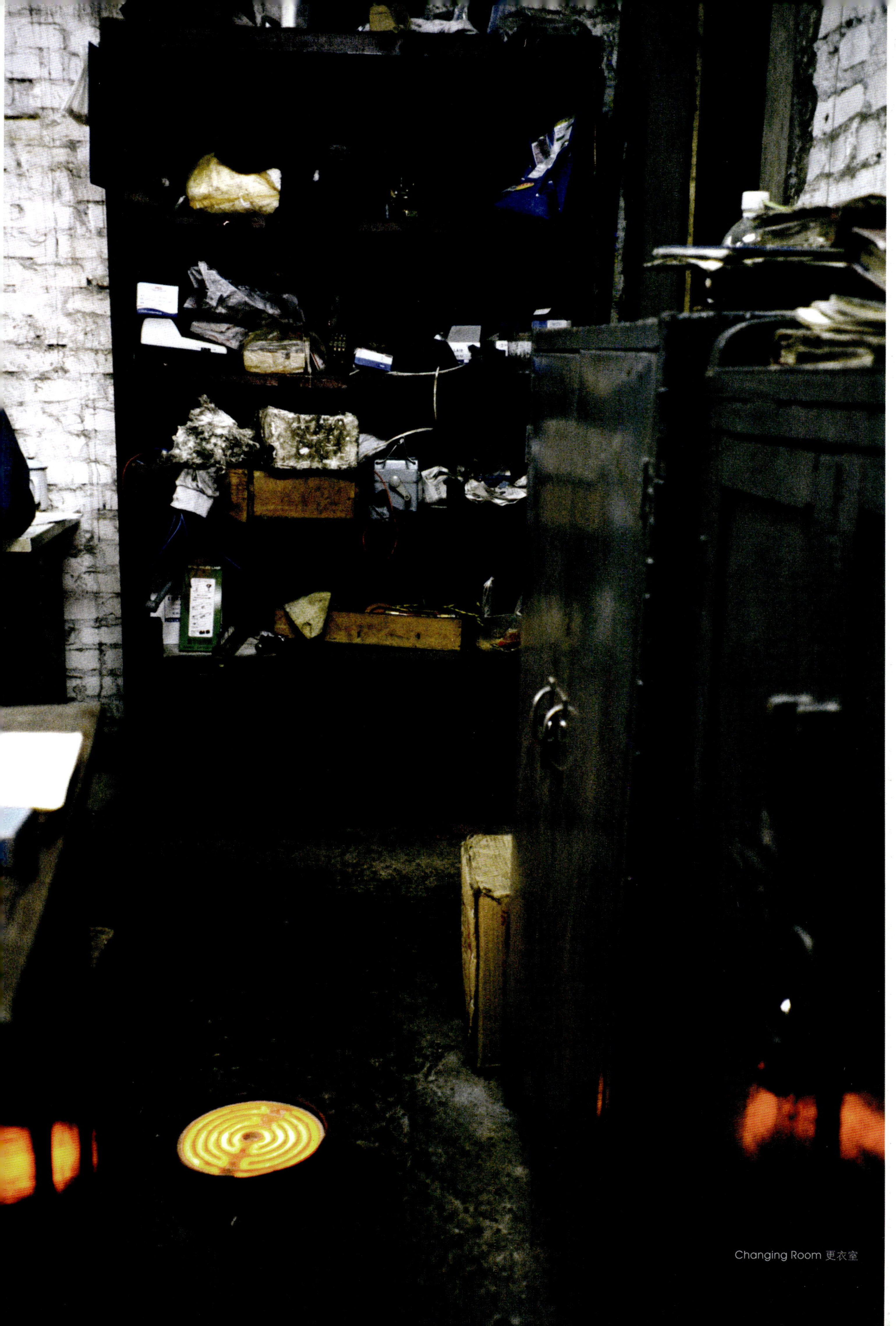

Changing Room 更衣室

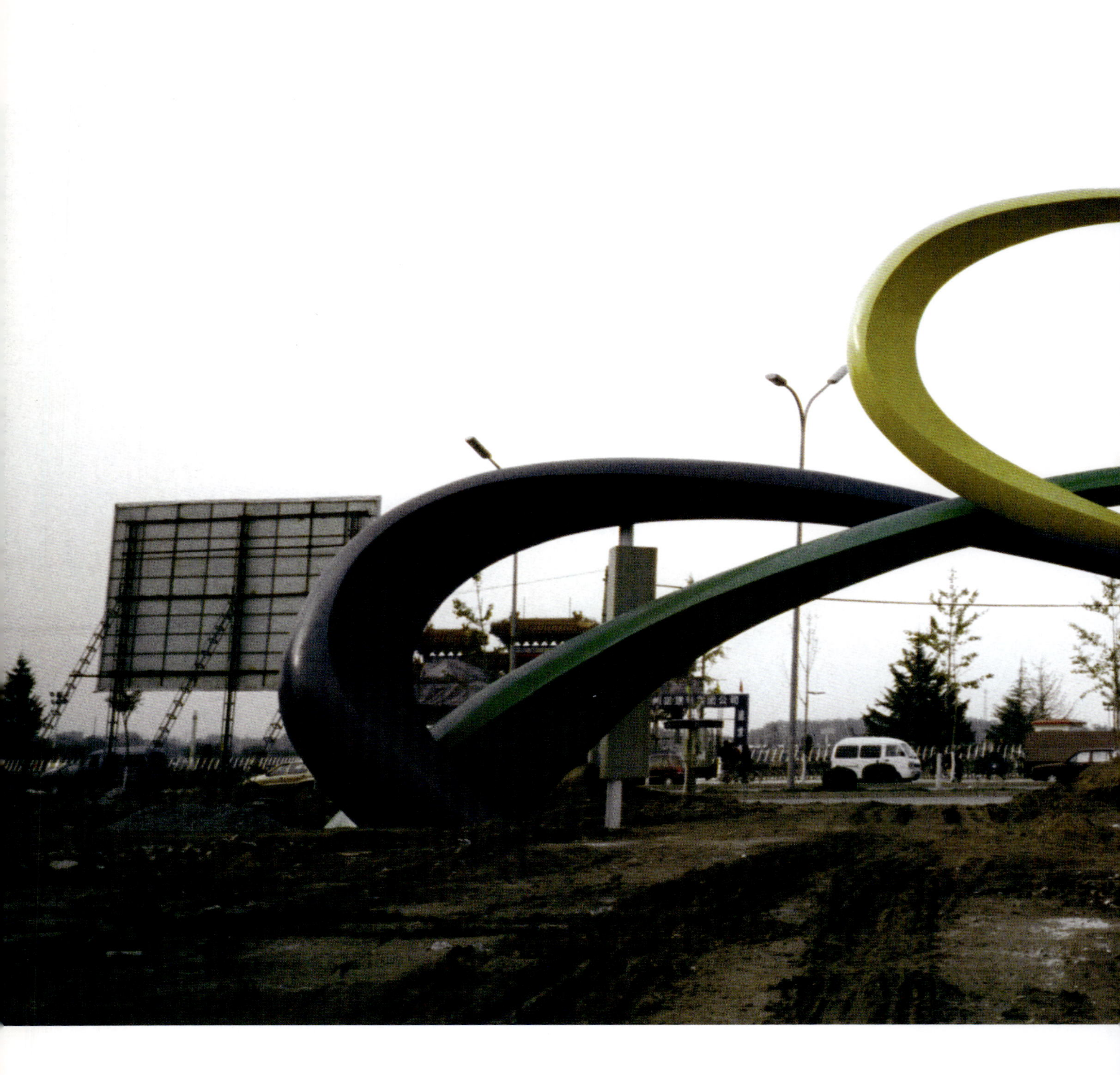

Olympic Park 奥体公园

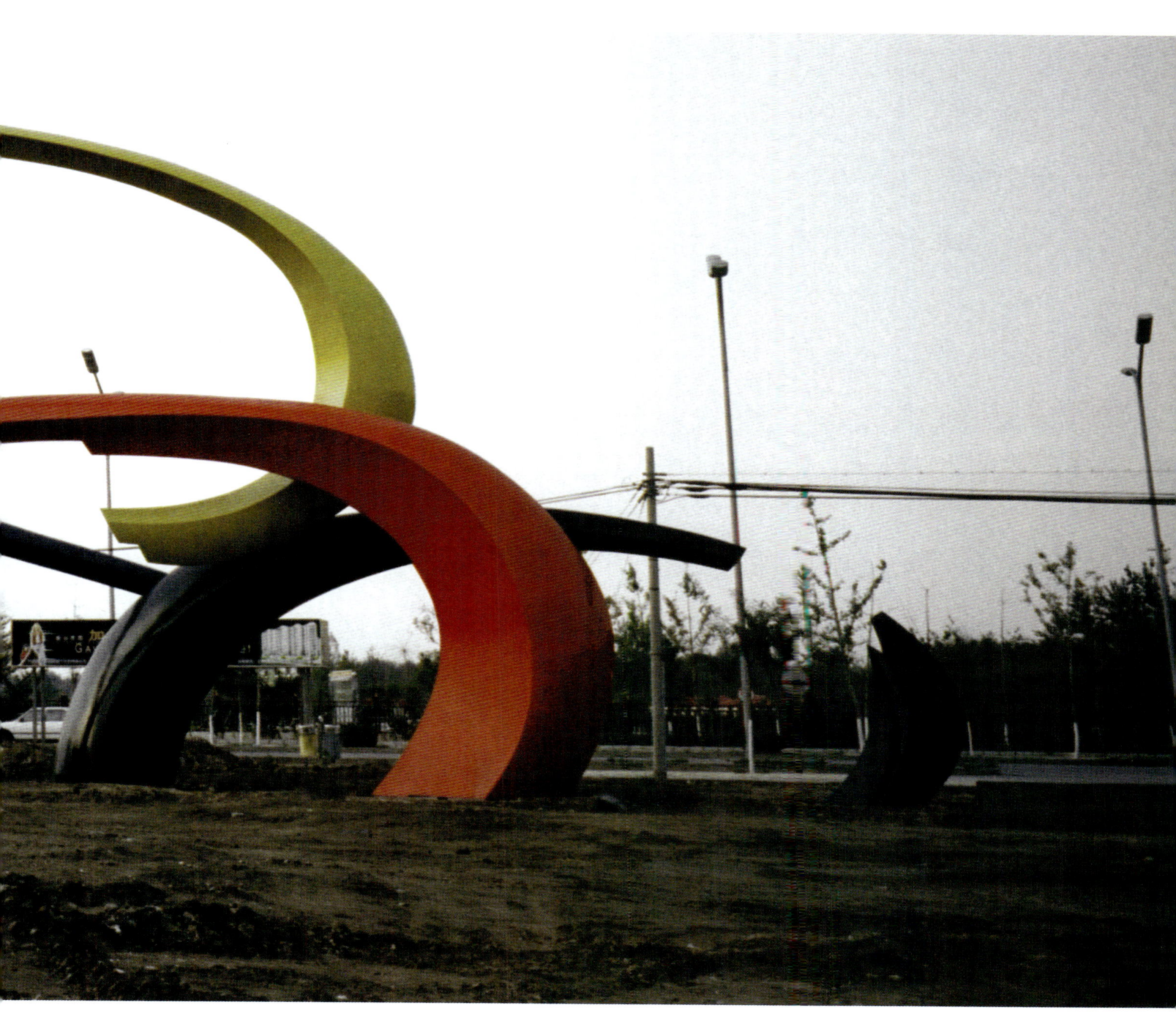

Born: 1963   Yumen, Gansu Province, China

Current: Independent artist living and working in Beijing, China

Solo Exhibitions

1988   Oil Paintings by Zhuang Hui, Luoyang Workers Cultural Palace, Luoyang, Henan Province, China

1996   Visual Art Week, Hamburg Art Museum, Hamburg, Germany

1997   Contemporary Photography from the People's Republic of China, N.B.K. Art Museum, Berlin, Germany
Chinese Photography and Video, Max Protetch Gallery, New York, USA

1998   It's Me, Forbidden City, Beijing, China
International Foto-Triennial Esslingen, Galerie der Stadt Esslingen, Germany
Chinese Art, Gallery Urs Miele, Lucerne, Switzerland

1999   Revelation Series: Common Distance, CANVAS International Art Foundation, Amsterdam, Holland
Representing the People, touring exhibition, Laing Art Gallery, Newcastle, UK
The First Fukuoka Asian Art Triennial, Fukuoka Asian Art Museum, Fukuoka, Japan
Salt of the Earth, Courtyard Gallery, Beijing, China
The 48th Venice Biennale, Venice Italian Pavilion, Italy
Lost Links, Kunst Museum of Art, Berne, Switzerland
Love: Contemporary Photography and Video from China, Tachikawa International Art Festival, Tokyo, Japan
Modern Chinese Art Foundation Inaugural Exhibition, Coermeklooster, Gent, Belgium
Beijing in London, ICA Contemporary Art Center, London, UK
Chinese Essentials, OTSO Museum of Art, Finland

2000   Lost Identity, Contemporary Art and Cultural Center, Milan, Italy
Zhuang Hui and Hideshi Ide, The Agency Gallery, London, UK
The Good Earth, Leeuwarden Art Museum, Leeuwarden, Netherlands
Biennale de Lyon, Lyon, France

2001   Abstraction and Installation, Beyeler Museum of Art, Beyeer, Switzerland
Hot Pot: Contemporary Chinese Art, Kustnernes Hus, Oslo, Norway
In Contradiction, Finnish Museum of Photography, Helsinki, Finland
Echoes from an Unstable Era, Lyon Museum of Contemporary Art, Lyon, France

2002   Art & Economy, Deichtorhallen, Hamburg, Germany
Run, Jump, Crawl, Walk, East Modern Art Centre, Beijing, China
The First Guangzhou Triennial, Guangdong Museum of Art, Guangzhou, China
Ten Years, Courtyard Gallery, Beijing, China

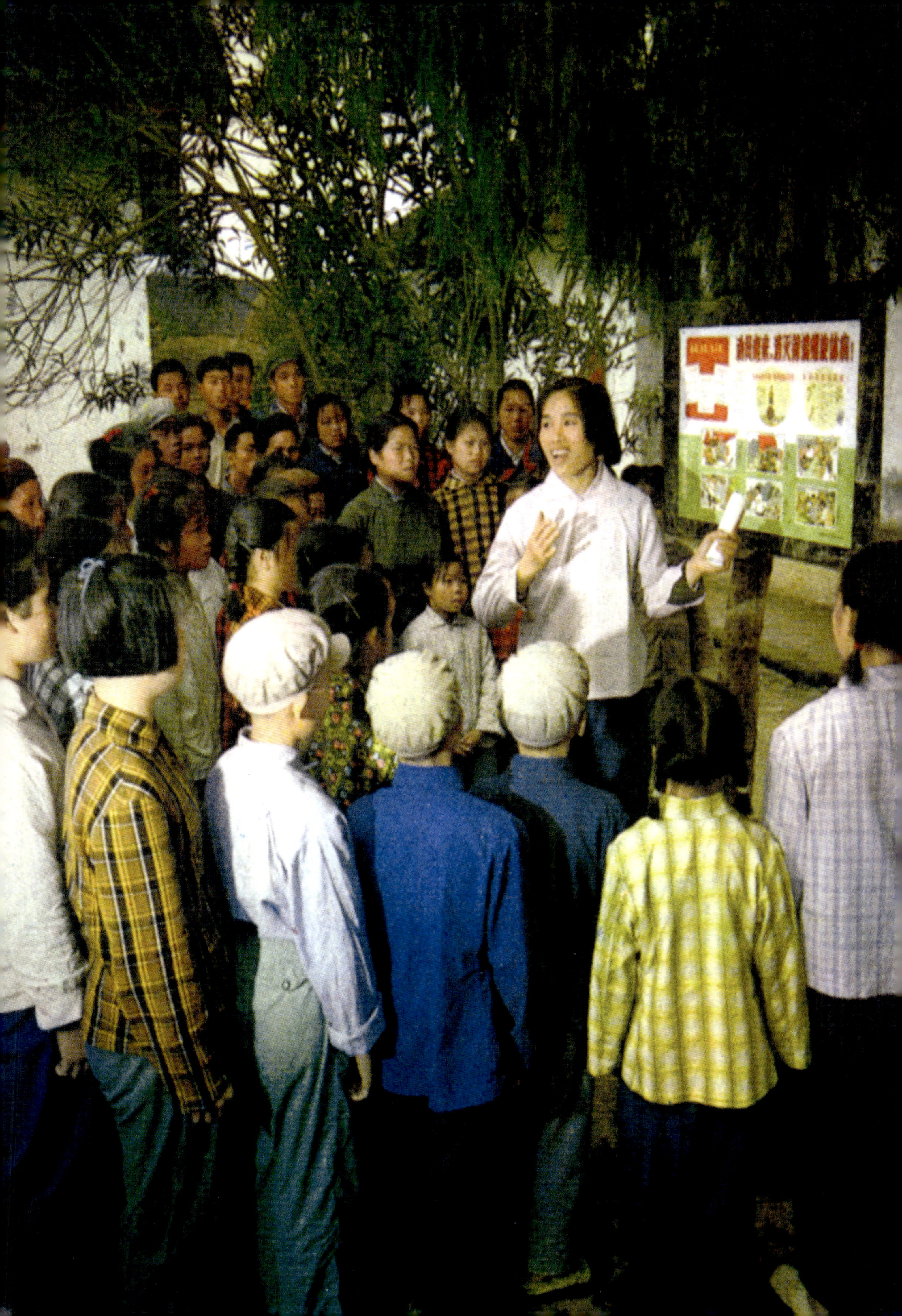

1963　　　　生于甘肃玉门，现居北京。

展　览

1988　　　　庄辉画展　　　　　　　　　　　洛阳·工人文化宫

1996　　　　视觉艺术周　　　　　　　　　　德国·汉堡美术馆
1997　　　　中国当代摄影展　　　　　　　　德国·柏林 NBK 艺术中心
　　　　　　中国摄影与录像　　　　　　　　美国·纽约　Max Proetch 画廊
1998　　　　是我!　　　　　　　　　　　　北京·太庙
　　　　　　第四届国际摄影三年展　　　　　德国·艾思林根博物馆
　　　　　　中国艺术　　　　　　　　　　　瑞士·卢塞恩　麦勒画廊
1999　　　　启示系列：共同的分离　　　　　荷兰·阿姆斯特丹 CANVAS 国际艺术基金会
　　　　　　人的再现　　　　　　　　　　　英国·纽卡斯尔　莱因艺术博物馆
　　　　　　第一届福冈亚洲美术三年展　　　日本·福冈　亚洲美术馆
　　　　　　沧海一粟　　　　　　　　　　　北京·四合苑画廊
　　　　　　第四十八届威尼斯双年展　　　　意大利·威尼斯
　　　　　　失去的锁链　　　　　　　　　　瑞士·伯尔尼　肯思特艺术博物馆
　　　　　　爱：中国当代摄影和录像　　　　日本·东京　立川国际艺术节
　　　　　　中国现代艺术　　　　　　　　　比利时·根特艺术中心
　　　　　　北京在伦敦　　　　　　　　　　英国·伦敦 ICA 当代艺术研究中心
　　　　　　中国概要　　　　　　　　　　　芬兰·埃斯塔 OTSO 美术馆
2000　　　　失去身份　　　　　　　　　　　意大利·米兰　当代文化艺术中心
　　　　　　里昂双年展　　　　　　　　　　法国·里昂
　　　　　　庄辉和Hideshi Ide　　　　　　英国·伦敦 Agency 画廊　包豪斯大学
　　　　　　友好的土地　　　　　　　　　　荷兰·利沃尔顿美术馆
2001　　　　抽象与装饰　　　　　　　　　　瑞士·巴塞尔 Beyeler 美术馆
　　　　　　火锅　　　　　　　　　　　　　挪威·奥斯陆
　　　　　　在矛盾中　　　　　　　　　　　芬兰·摄影美术馆
　　　　　　不稳定时代的回音－作品收藏展 法国·里昂　当代艺术馆
2002　　　　艺术与经济　　　　　　　　　　德国·汉堡 Deichterhaler Hamburg
　　　　　　跑、跳、爬、走　　　　　　　　北京·远洋艺术中心
　　　　　　广州三年展　　　　　　　　　　广州·广东美术馆
　　　　　　十年　　　　　　　　　　　　　北京·四合苑画廊

Curator 策划

Meg Maggio 马芝安

Catalogue Design 画册设计

Peng Donghui and He An 彭东会 何岸

Exhibition Design 展场设计

Antonio Ochoa 安东

Translation 翻译

Li Jianhua 李建华

English Proofreading 英文校对

Chin Chin Yap 叶晶晶

Chinese Proofreading 中文校对

Wu Penghui 兀鹏辉

Peng Wei 彭炜

Assistance 协助

Chin Chin Yap and Carole Lauvergne 叶晶晶 紫荷

Printing 画册印刷

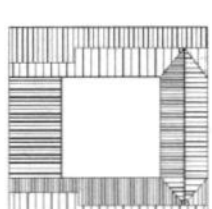

四合苑
CourtYard Gallery